A CRISIS WASTED

A CRISIS WASTED

Barack Obama's Defining Decisions

Reed Hundt

RosettaBooks®
NEW YORK 2019

First edition published 2019 by RosettaBooks

Cover design by Gerre Mae Barcebal
Interior design by Jay McNair
Cover photo: Charles Ommanney / Getty Images
President Barack Obama and ex-President George W. Bush
in the Capitol Building on Inauguration Day, January 20, 2009.

Library of Congress Control Number: 2018950743
ISBN-13 (print): 978-1-9481-2231-3

www.RosettaBooks.com
Printed in Canada

RosettaBooks®

This book is dedicated to my beloved wife and three dear children.
Elizabeth Ann Katz, Adam Elias Hundt,
Nathaniel Pullan Hundt, and Sara Jordan Hundt

Contents

Timeline of Events

2003

December: Reed Hundt meets Barack Obama

2004

March 16: Obama wins a landslide victory in the Democratic primary of the U.S. Senate election in Illinois

July 27: Obama gives the keynote address at the Democratic National Convention

November 2: Obama wins a seat in the U.S. Senate, George W. Bush wins reelection over John Kerry

December: Obama assembles Senate office with eye on presidency

2005

Early 2005: Obama dines with Bob Rubin

2006

November 7: The Democratic Party wins House and Senate

December: Obama meets Al Gore

Late 2006: Experts begin to predict that the housing bubble will pop

2007

February 10: Obama announces his candidacy for the presidency in Springfield, Illinois

March: Reed Hundt and wife Betsy Katz co-host Obama's first campaign fund-raiser on the East Coast

March 24: At first healthcare forum for presidential candidates in
Las Vegas, Obama embarrassed by his healthcare policy

April: Treasury Secretary Hank Paulson says that housing prices are
near bottom, will soon begin to rise

June: Obama outlines liberal agenda at Knox College

Late 2007: Larry Summers identifies middle class insecurity as
major theme

2008

January 16: Summers recommends "timely, targeted, temporary"
stimulus

February 13: President Bush signs $170 billion stimulus into law

March 7: Summers warns Secretary Paulson that Fannie Mae,
Freddie Mac are bankrupt

March 14: The Fed loans Bear Stearns $25 billion to arrange
JPMorgan purchase; Summers, Sheila Bair, and Obama criticize
the bailout

March 27: Obama outlines reform proposals at Cooper Union in
New York

June: Hillary Clinton concedes nomination to Barack Obama

June 26: Obama cements alliance with Clinton at the Mayflower
Hotel in D.C.

Summer 2008: Obama appoints John Podesta to head transition
team

July 30: Housing and Economic Recovery Act is signed into law by
President Bush

August 28: Obama accepts Democratic presidential nomination in
Mile-High Stadium, Denver, endorses "all of the above" energy
policy

Late summer 2008: Secretary Paulson tries unsuccessfully to convince banks to buy Lehman; Summers and other experts begin
to advise Obama on economy

September 7: U.S. government seizes Fannie Mae and Freddie Mac

September 15: Lehman files for bankruptcy

September 16: AIG insolvent; Fed loans it $85 billion

September 23: Ben Bernanke and Paulson testify in Congress about need for legislation to end financial crisis; the next day, President Bush appears on television to call for big bailout

September 25: Presidential candidates and President Bush meet in the Roosevelt Room to discuss the crisis; Sheila Bair's FDIC resolves Washington Mutual

September 29: House votes down Troubled Asset Relief Program; stock market plummets

October 3: House passes a revised TARP bill passed by the Senate two days earlier, including two tranches of $350 billion in bailout money

Early October: Obama's advisers suggest to him a stimulus of $175 billion

October 14: Bair announces FDIC's Temporary Liquidity Guarantee Program

October 17: Obama interviews Timothy Geithner for treasury secretary

October 28: Paulson uses $200 billion of allotted $350 billion from TARP to buy stock in nine big banks

November: China announces $600 billion stimulus program; Joseph Stiglitz writes in New York Times that U.S. stimulus should be more than $1 trillion spent over two years

November 2: Josh Steiner and Jack Lew stimulus proposal for $300 billion circulates in a 36-page memo on November 2nd, reduced to 11 pages and given to Obama by Jason Furman

November 4: Obama wins presidential election; Democrats hold Senate and House by big margins

November 7: President-elect Obama calls press conference in Chicago to outline his economic recovery plan

November 9: Obama announces Rahm Emanuel chief of staff

November 16: President-elect Obama interviews Geithner and Summers for treasury secretary

November 17: At Wall Street Journal conference Summers calls for a $500–$700 billion stimulus

November 22: President-elect Obama outlines the stimulus in a radio address dedicated to "saving or creating" 2.5 million jobs

November 23: Treasury Department guarantees $300 billion of Citigroup's debt

November 25: President-elect Obama announces Christy Romer as chair of Council of Economic Advisers, Summers director of National Economic Council, Geithner secretary of treasury

November 26: Obama announces Peter Orszag as head of OMB

November: Jon Favreau meets with Obama to begin work on inaugural address

December 2: At National Governors' Association meeting in Philadelphia, President-elect Obama announces an economic recovery plan that would help save or create 2.5 million jobs

December 5: Obama further explains economic recovery plan, creating or saving two to three million jobs

December 5: Blair Levin advises how to spend stimulus money on broadband

Early December: Reed Hundt brings his idea for Green Recovery Investment Plan to Obama economic team

December 5: Tom Daschle announces that President-elect Obama has made health reform one of his top priorities

December 6: Bureau of Labor Statistics announces unemployment 7.1 percent in November

December 6: Summers and Furman circulate four-page memo outlining the "American Economic Recovery Plan," which calls for $580 billion stimulus

December 7: Obama says stimulus is his top priority

December 9: Gore meets Obama in Chicago

December 11: Daschle is appointed both secretary of Health and Human Services and White House healthcare czar

December 12: Carol Browner announced as energy czar

December 15: Alice Rivlin, former head of CBO and OMB, predicts unemployment will continue to rise to at least 10 percent

December 16: President-elect Obama's economic advisers meet in Chicago, persuade him to adopt economic recovery plan

2009

January 8: President-elect Obama urges Congress to pass stimulus as soon as possible, warns unemployment otherwise will be in double digits

January 9: Christy Romer and Jared Bernstein report that unemployment will reach 9 percent but for stimulus, will be 7.3 percent if $800 billion stimulus passed

January 9: Bureau of Labor Statistics announces December unemployment 8 percent and climbing

January 10: Paul Krugman notes inconsistencies between the Romer-Bernstein report and the unemployment numbers from the Bureau of Labor Statistics, writes that stimulus is too small

January 11: Summers writes to congressional leaders that President-elect Obama wants authority to implement rest of the financial rescue plan (second half of TARP)

January 15: Herb Allison outlines his plan for housing market for Summers and Geithner in three-page memo

January 15: Summers writes to congressional leaders promising Obama administration will commit $50 billion to address foreclosure crisis

January 16: President-elect Obama says that stimulus would save or create 3–4 million jobs

January 20: Barack Obama is inaugurated 44th president of the United States

January 28: House passes stimulus bill of $820 billion

February 6: Bair meets with Summers and other advisers to express her concern about proposed policy of subsidizing mortgage modifications

February 10: Senate passes stimulus bill of $838 billion

February 16: Congress passes American Recovery and Reinvestment Act, $787 billion counting AMT postponement

February 17: President Obama signs ARRA

February 17: Obama sends budget to Hill

February 18: Treasury announces program to reduce foreclosures, called Making Home Affordable, which includes Home Affordable Modification Program; Bair supports

February 24: In speech to Congress, President Obama asks Congress to pass healthcare reform and cap-and-trade

April: Romer first suggests second stimulus to President Obama

April 30: Dick Durbin fails to pass cramdown legislation to mitigate foreclosures

November 2009: The president's economic advisers unable to agree on terms of second stimulus

December 4: President Obama endorses new jobs tax credit and $50 billion of infrastructure and state fiscal relief at speech at Brookings Institution

December 16: President attends UN Climate Change Conference in Copenhagen

2010

March 23: President Obama signs Affordable Care Act

July 21: President Obama signs Dodd-Frank Wall Street Reform and Consumer Protection Act

Summer 2010: Orszag leaves White House for Citigroup

September: Romer leaves CEA for Berkeley; Rahm Emanuel leaves Chief of Staff post to run for mayor of Chicago

October: Treasury announces that HAMP will be reduced to $29.9 billion in subsidy payments (rather than $50 billion)

November 2: Democratic Party loses House in midterm election

December 15: Summers leaves White House

December 17: Second stimulus of $900 billion (Tax Relief, Unemployment Insurance Reauthorization, and Job Creation Act of 2010) passes by bipartisan vote

2012

November 6: Barack Obama reelected president; Republican Party holds House; Democrats, Senate

2014

November 4: Republican Party wins Senate, House

2016

November 8: Donald Trump wins presidential election, Republicans control Senate, House

2017

January 20: Donald Trump is inaugurated as 45th president of the United States

Cast of Characters

Persons named in the narrative are identified by their position in the Obama administration, former notable positions (the president whom they served in former positions follow in parentheses), and/or current notable positions.

DARON ACEMOGLU, b. 1967, professor of economics at MIT

JOSEPH "JOE" ALDY, b. 1971, special assistant to the president for Energy and Environment, former Council of Economic Advisers staff (Bill Clinton), current associate professor of public policy at the Harvard Kennedy School

HERBERT "HERB" ALLISON, b. 1943, d. 2013, assistant secretary of the Treasury for Financial Stability, former president and CEO of Fannie Mae and president of Merrill Lynch

DAVID AXELROD, b. 1955, chief strategist for the Obama campaign and senior adviser to the president, former writer for the Chicago Tribune and political consultant, current director of the Institute of Politics at the University of Chicago and senior political commentator at CNN

SHEILA BAIR, b. 1954, Chair of the Federal Deposit Insurance Corporation, and former assistant secretary of the Treasury for Financial Institutions (George W. Bush), president of Washington College

BEN BERNANKE, b. 1953, chairman of the Federal Reserve, former chairman of the Council of Economic Advisers (George W. Bush) and professor of economics at Princeton University, current fellow at the Brookings Institutions and senior adviser at Citadel

JARED BERNSTEIN, b. 1955, chief economist and economic policy adviser for the vice president of the United States, former deputy chief economist at the Department of Labor (Bill Clinton), current senior fellow at the Center on Budget and Policy Priorities and member of the Congressional Budget Office's Advisory Committee

JOSEPH "JOE" BIDEN, b. 1942, vice president of the United States, former U.S. senator from Delaware

CAROL BROWNER, b. 1955, director of the Office of Energy and Climate Change Policy, former administrator of the Environmental Protection Agency (Bill Clinton), current senior counselor at Albright Stonebridge Group and senior fellow at the Center for American Progress

ANNA BURGER, b. 1950, member of the president's Economic Recovery Advisory Board

GEORGE W. BUSH, b. 1946, former president of the United States and governor of Texas

HILLARY CLINTON, b. 1947, secretary of state, former U.S. senator from New York

WILLIAM "BILL" CLINTON, b. 1946, former president of the United States, former governor and attorney general of Arkansas

WILLIAM "BILL" DALEY, b. 1948, Former White House chief of staff, former secretary of commerce (Bill Clinton) and executive at JPMorgan Chase & Co.

THOMAS "TOM" DASCHLE, b. 1947, adviser for the Obama campaign, former U.S. senator from South Dakota and Senate majority and minority leader, current lobbyist at Baker Donelson

PAUL DE SA, b. 1962, chief of the Office of Strategic Planning and Policy Analysis at the Federal Communications Commission, former partner at McKinsey & Company and analyst at Bernstein Research, current partner at Quadra Partners

SHAUN DONOVAN, b. 1966, secretary of Housing and Urban Development and director of the Office of Management and Budget, former commissioner of the New York City Department of Housing Preservation and Development

DOUGLAS "DOUG" ELMENDORF, b. 1962, director of the Congressional Budget Office, former senior fellow at the Brookings Institution, current dean of the Harvard Kennedy School

RAHM EMANUEL, b. 1959, White House chief of staff, former member of the U.S. House of Representatives from Illinois and senior adviser to the president (Bill Clinton), current mayor of Chicago

MICHAEL "MIKE" FROMAN, b. 1962, U.S. Trade representative, former chief of staff for Secretary of the Treasury Bob Rubin

JASON FURMAN, b. 1970, chair of the Council of Economic Advisers, current professor at the Harvard Kennedy School and senior fellow at the Peterson Institute for International Economics

MARK GALLOGLY, b. 1957, member of the president's Economic Recovery Advisory Board, former senior managing director of the Blackstone Group, current managing principal at Centerbridge Partners and member of the Advisory Council of the Hamilton Project

TIMOTHY "TIM" GEITHNER, b. 1961, secretary of treasury, former president of the Federal Reserve Bank of New York and undersecretary of the Treasury for International Affairs (Bill Clinton), current president of Warburg Pincus

JULIUS GENACHOWSKI, b. 1962, chairman of the Federal Communications Commission (FCC), former chief counsel at the FCC and chief of Business Operations at InterActiveCorp, current managing director at the Carlyle Group

AUSTAN GOOLSBEE, b. 1969, chair of the Council of Economic Advisers, current professor at the University of Chicago's Booth School of Business

ALBERT "AL" GORE, JR., b. 1948, former vice president of the United States and U.S. senator and member of the U.S. House of Representatives from Tennessee

VALERIE JARRETT, b. 1956, senior adviser to the president and director of the Office of Public Engagement and Intergovernmental Affairs

MATTHEW "MATT" KABAKER, b. 1972, senior adviser to Treasury Secretary Timothy Geithner, former managing director at the Blackstone Group, current senior managing director at Centerbridge Partners

BOB KOCHER, b. 1970, special assistant to the president for Healthcare and Economic Policy on the National Economic Council, former partner at McKinsey & Company, current partner at Venrock and consulting professor at Stanford University School of Medicine

BLAIR LEVIN, b. 1954, executive director for the effort that led to the National Broadband Plan, former chief of staff to FCC Chair Reed Hundt, current fellow at the Brookings Institution

JACOB "JACK" LEW, b. 1955, secretary of the Treasury and White House chief of staff and director of the Office of Management and Budget, former director of the Office of Management and Budget (Bill Clinton) and COO of Citigroup

JAMES B. LOCKHART III, b. 1946, director (CEO) and chairman of the Oversight Board of the Federal Housing Finance Agency, vice chairman of W.L. Ross & Co.

CHESTER "TRENT" LOTT, b. 1941, former member of the U.S. House of Representatives from Mississippi and House minority whip and U.S. senator from Mississippi and Senate minority/majority whip/leader

THOMAS "TOM" MANN, b. 1944, current senior fellow at the Brookings Institution and member of the Council on Foreign Relations

EDWARD "ED" MARKEY, b. 1946, member of the U.S. House of Representatives from Massachusetts, current U.S. senator from Massachusetts

JIM MESSINA, b. 1969, White House deputy chief of staff for Operations, current CEO of the Messina Group

BARACK OBAMA, b. 1961, President of the United States, former U.S. senator from Illinois

NORMAN ORNSTEIN, b. 1948, resident scholar at the American Enterprise Institute and writer, former professor of political science at Catholic University

PETER ORSZAG, b. 1968, director of the Office of Management and Budget, former director of the Congressional Budget Office and chairman of the Financial Strategy and Solutions Group at Citigroup, current managing director at Lazard

HENRY "HANK" PAULSON, b. 1946, former secretary of the Treasury (George W. Bush), former chairman and CEO of Goldman Sachs, current fellow at the Harris School of Public Policy and chairman of the Paulson Institute at the University of Chicago

JOHN PODESTA, b. 1949, chairman of the Obama-Biden transition project and counselor to the president, former White House chief of staff (Bill Clinton) and chairman of the 2016 Hillary Clinton presidential campaign, current chair and counselor of the Center for American Progress

ROBERT REICH, b. 1946, political commentator and professor of public policy at the Goldman School of Public Policy at the University of California, Berkeley, former secretary of labor (Bill Clinton)

ALICE RIVLIN, b. 1931, member of the National Commission on Fiscal Responsibility and Reform, former director of the Congressional Budget Office and director of the Office of Management and Budget and vice chair of the Federal Reserve System (Bill Clinton)

CHRISTINA ROMER, b. 1958, chairwoman of the Council of Economic Advisers, current professor of economics at the University of California, Berkeley

WILLARD MITT ROMNEY, b. 1947, former governor of Massachusetts

PETE ROUSE, b. 1946, counselor to the president and acting White House chief of staff, former chief of staff to Senate Democratic Leader Tom Daschle, current senior policy adviser at Perkins Coie

ROBERT "BOB" RUBIN, b. 1938, chairman of Citigroup, former secretary of the Treasury and director of the National Economic Council (Bill Clinton)

LEWIS "LEE" SACHS, b. 1947, counselor to Treasury Secretary Tim Geithner, former assistant secretary of the Treasury for Financial Markets (Bill Clinton), current managing director of Gallatin Point Capital

PHIL SCHILIRO, b. 1956, White House director of legislative affairs, former chief of staff to Representative Henry Waxman

JOSHUA "JOSH" STEINER, b. 1965, adviser to the Obama transition team, former chief of staff to the Treasury Department (Bill Clinton)

JOSEPH "JOE" STIGLITZ, b. 1943, professor at Columbia University, Nobel Prize in Economics winner, former chief economist at the World Bank and chair of the Council of Economic Advisers (Bill Clinton)

LAWRENCE "LARRY" SUMMERS, b. 1954, director of the National Economic Council, former secretary of the Treasury (Bill Clinton), president of Harvard University, chief economist of the World Bank, current university professor at Harvard

DONALD TRUMP, b. 1946, current president of the United States, proprietor of the Trump Organization, former TV show host

CHRISTOPHER "CHRIS" VAN HOLLEN, b. 1959, member of the U.S. House of Representatives from Maryland, current U.S. senator from Maryland

PAUL VOLCKER, b. 1927, chair of the president's Economic Recovery Advisory Board, former chairman of the Federal Reserve (Jimmy Carter and Ronald Reagan), president of the Federal Reserve Bank of New York and undersecretary of the Treasury for International Affairs (Richard Nixon)

GERARD "GERRY" WALDRON, b. 1960, former senior counsel to the House Subcommittee on Telecommunications, current partner at Covington & Burling

DAVID WARSH, b. 1944, proprietor of Economic Principals, former writer for the Boston Globe

HENRY WAXMAN, b. 1939, former member of the U.S. House of Representatives from California and chairman of the House Oversight Committee and chairman of the House Energy Committee

MARK WINER, b. 1954, former senior vice president at Fannie Mae

Preface

This book was prompted by a desire to find out how Barack Obama handled the economic calamity of 2008. The title comes from an observation made by one of Obama's most trusted advisers: "You never want a serious crisis to go to waste."

What does that mean?

If more than a wisecrack, the remark means that by its nature a crisis provides both an opportunity and a demand for leaders to think differently from their predecessors. No one expressed this idea more eloquently than Abraham Lincoln in his message to Congress on December 1, 1862: "We must disenthrall ourselves, and then we shall save our country."

The thesis of this book is that Obama and team did not do well by Lincoln's standard. Faced with the most severe economic crisis since the Great Depression, they declined to adopt broad measures benefitting the middle class far into the future. Instead they chose to expand the market for healthcare insurance by a mix of fiat and subsidies, and futilely sought to license the use of carbon-based power sources. Taking office at one of the most dramatic moments in American history, Obama declined to seek the profound change that he promised during his long, brilliant campaign for the presidency.

I have reached this conclusion reluctantly. I was an early Obama supporter. My whole family campaigned for his election. After years of research and extensive interviews with dozens of the key players in the great drama that unfolded after September 2008, the facts have led me to this melancholy judgment. In *The Sportswriter*, Richard Ford writes that "for your life to be worth anything you must sooner or later face the possibility of terrible, searing regret" and somehow "manage to avoid it." When the next crisis creates again the necessity and chance to change history, this book is supposed to help the country and its leaders follow that guidance.

Introduction

The job of managing the economy's recovery from the Great Recession fell to Barack Obama. Everyone in boardrooms and living rooms across the country knew that the government had to fix what businesses had broken: the capability of Americans to have a high and rising standard of living. During the six weeks before the November 2008 election and the 10 weeks of transition to the inauguration on January 20, 2009, Obama made the decisions about recovery and legislation that defined his two-term presidency. He chose an economic recovery plan that benefitted educated, well-off people much more than the middle class. It helped the finance and technology sectors more than construction, manufacturing or retail. Residents of coastal states did much better than those in the flyover country.

The disappointingly protracted economic recovery and Obama's unpopular legislative initiatives cost the Democrats control of the House in 2010 and the Senate in 2014. In many other elections too, voters passed judgment against Democratic policies. By 2017 Obama's party held only 19 of 50 governorships and controlled only 12 state legislatures. Although Obama's personal appeal and his ability to obtain high turnout from a coalition of identity groups enabled him to win reelection in 2012, Republican opposition frustrated his ability to achieve transformational change. The fulfillment of his hopes for the country depended on Hillary Clinton winning in 2016.

In that election, Donald Trump had little difficulty winning 230 electoral votes from reliably red states. To become president, he needed to win 40 electors from the 89 available in the six states where the plurality turned out to be less than 2 percent: Florida, Michigan, Minnesota, New Hampshire, Pennsylvania, and Wisconsin. Obama's economic recovery plan, his legislative accomplishments, and his regulatory measures disappointed most people in these battleground states. Much has been made of Clinton's uninspiring campaign and other events that might have swayed voters. However, if Obama had delivered well before 2016 to everyone in these six states, or indeed the whole country, a robust economy and popular legislative solutions to common problems, then the opportunity presented to Trump would have been much diminished. Trump won in four of the six battlegrounds, easily prevailing in the Electoral College.

Nor was Trump merely the lucky beneficiary of the antiquated, anti-democratic method used to pick American presidents. He said he would have won the popular vote if the election system had required him to do so, and he might have been right. Indeed, subtracting all votes cast in the populous, prosperous states of New York and California where Trump did not compete, 48.6 percent of the remaining voters chose Trump and 45.7 percent voted for Clinton. The Republicans held control of both chambers of Congress. Democrats needed to understand that the election demonstrated widespread disaffection with the policies espoused by Obama and Clinton.

In January 2017 Obama was obliged to turn over the presidency to someone who challenged his birthplace, vowed to repudiate his accomplishments, and tried to reverse the direction of the ethical compass of the country. Ironically, the outgoing president bequeathed to his astonishing successor an economy at last on the verge of providing jobs for everyone. Timing is never unimportant.

All Decided Beforehand

Men at some time are masters of their fates;
The fault, dear Brutus, is not in our stars,
But in ourselves, that we are underlings.
— *Julius Caesar*, act 1, scene 2

The political failure and objective shortcomings of the Obama economic recovery plan can be traced back to the summer of 2008, when Obama recruited a team of ex-rivals, adopting Hillary Clinton's advisers as his own. Because people are policy, he therefore became a Clinton-style neoliberal. He no longer pursued his own tentatively progressive agenda.

In collaboration with the former Clinton advisers, in the fall of 2008 the Bush administration persuaded Obama to restore the profitability and power of a handful of Wall Street banks that had contributed mightily to hurting almost everyone in the country. The Obama team's advice restored Wall Street's stability, produced an anemic economic recovery, and cast a long shadow over his tenure. These advisers underestimated the severity of the recession all through 2008, causing Obama to underplay the necessary government action during the campaign and in the transition. When in January 2009 new economic statistics caused them to realize that their predictions would not come true, they did not change their advice or inform the public and Congress of the facts.

Although another depression did not ensue, the recession proved deep and long. As Obama's chief of communications David Axelrod acknowledged, the consolation that things could have been worse was "tough to message."[1]

In December 2008 and January 2009 the economic advisers also told Obama that there was nothing he could or should do to curtail the fall in housing prices or the evaporation of home equity that accounted for virtually all the savings of two-thirds of Americans—almost all those who had any savings at all. They rejected the policies he had promulgated during and after the second debate with John McCain in October. They

---

1. David Axelrod, interview with author.

insisted that he try to reduce mortgage foreclosures by not more than 1.5 million homes. Ultimately about 10 million homeowners lost their homes through foreclosure or a similar process. The Obama administration reduced that level by a negligible amount, if any.

In January 2009 Obama launched a healthcare reform initiative that required everyone to buy insurance. It raised costs for most Americans and ultimately extended insurance to only about 7 to 8 percent more Americans —less than half of the previously uninsured and also about half the number of people in homes lost to foreclosure or similar processes. Given the relatively small number of beneficiaries, one should not have been surprised that about half the country was unsatisfied with the Affordable Care Act. That opposition fueled Trump's campaign.

In that same January, Obama chose to seek legislation that limited greenhouse gas emissions in every sector of the economy but he did not make this initiative his top priority. The House passed the cap-and-trade bill, but the measure made little progress in the Senate during 2009. Obama chose not to push an alternative initiative that had bipartisan support in the Senate. As a result, nothing was passed.

The Republican Party's obduracy, the social media's fractionation of community, racism, the Supreme Court's sanction of unlimited campaign spending, and the balky structure of America's 18th-century government all contributed to the disappointment that followed Obama's brilliant victory in November 2008. These explanations, however, rationalize the economic and political outcomes of Obama's fateful early decisions. The gap between what should have been and what happened, ironically, came from what he called in his first inaugural address the "worn-out dogmas, that for far too long have strangled our politics."

That dogma was neoliberalism. A teenager growing up like me in a Democratic household during the Kennedy and Johnson administrations could hardly resist adopting the liberal perspective on politics. After the Vietnam War shattered my generation's international idealism, Jimmy Carter turned the Democratic domestic agenda toward neoliberalism. He entered the presidency with a filibuster-busting 61 Democratic votes in the Senate and a huge House majority swollen by the reaction to the Watergate scandal. Congress was poised to pass laws guaranteeing a government job for anyone if unemployment exceeded 3 percent, assuring a minimum income, granting universal day care and a national health insurance plan. Carter rejected that liberal agenda. Ted Kennedy's failed effort to take the party's nomination away from the incumbent in 1980 marked the end of New Deal liberalism.

The succeeding Reagan administration buried what Carter had killed. In 1992 Bill Clinton responded to Reaganism by mixing fiscal prudence with social liberalism to concoct a politically successful stew of ideas. This was an updated version of Carter's neoliberal agenda. The New Democratic thinking represented a political alliance between Wall Street's financial firms and the identity groups growing out of the rights revolution of the 1960s and 1970s. It echoed what the 19th century called liberalism: this dogma favored free trade, free labor, and robust capitalism, and disfavored state management of the economy, tariffs, and unions.

By one account classical liberalism argued that the state leave people alone: laissez-nous faire. Neoliberalism added the principles that the state must support the free market, and that government policies could never distort "the natural actions of the marketplace."[2] An intentional government with agency to act for the people was inferior to the price system. Clinton made the message sound appealing in his campaign, but in practice the policies lacked popular approval. In 1993 the new administration raised taxes and failed to reform healthcare. In 1994 Republicans took control of the House for the first time in 40 years. Impeachment and a quarter-century of increasing divisiveness followed.

One author has said correctly that neoliberalism is "used as a catchall for anything that smacks of deregulation, liberalization, privatization, or fiscal austerity."[3] Obama's advisers favored ideas that had exactly that sort of smack. By 2016 at least some academics concluded that in its long hegemony over policy, neoliberalism had not clearly produced

2. Stephen Metcalf, "Neoliberalism: The Idea That Swallowed the World," *The Guardian*, August 18, 2017, https://www.theguardian.com/news/2017/aug/18/neoliberalism-the-idea-that-changed-the-world.

3. Dani Rodrik, "Rescuing Economics from Neoliberalism," *Boston Review*, April 26, 2018, http://bostonreview.net/class-inequality/dani-rodrik-rescuing-economics-neoliberalism.

increased growth, and definitely had caused increased inequality that probably reduced growth.[4] But at the nadir of the Great Recession this "worn-out" thinking guided the economic recovery plan foisted on a willing Obama.

When Obama adopted Hillary Clinton's advisers, they brought with them their thinking from the 1990s. In both the Obama and Clinton transitions, the advisers conditioned their advice to the president-elects on a firm belief in the beneficial effects of limited government spending and limited regulation. They did not believe that government should guarantee a rising standard of living for everyone. In both 1992 and 2008 they thought government should stimulate growth, but only to a minimum level necessary for ensuring that the private sector would allocate capital according to the dictates of profit maximization. In 2008 they were loath to provide public funds sufficient to (1) replace the carbon-based power platform with cheaper, cleaner, and more efficiently consumed renewable power, (2) renovate transportation systems to provide cheaper, more efficient mechanisms for moving people and goods, (3) replace deteriorating and poisonous water systems, (4) extend high-speed broadband connectivity to everyone at affordable prices, and (5) replace deteriorating sewage systems. Instead of using government to build these platforms, the principal imperative was to maintain a well-functioning private financing system—in 1993 not crowded out by public debt and in 2008–2009 bolstered temporarily by government bailouts and stimulus.

Not only neoliberalism, but also Barack Obama's conception of presidential leadership limited his achievements. Lyndon Johnson turned the crisis of Kennedy's assassination into the impetus for sweeping extensions of welfare and civil rights. Franklin Roosevelt used the banking crisis of March 1933 and the Great Depression that had started in 1929 as a springboard for progressivism's political triumph over 19th-century liberalism. Ronald Reagan used the stagnation of the 1970s and

---

4. Jonathan D. Ostry, Prakash Loungani, and Davide Furceri, "Neoliberalism: Oversold?" *Finance & Development* 3, no. 2 (June 2016): 38-41, International Monetary Fund, http://www.imf.org/external/pubs/ft/fandd/2016/06/ostry.htm.

the double-dip recessions of the early 1980s as the basis for reversing the policies of Roosevelt and Johnson.[5] Perhaps aware of these lessons from history, in November 2008 Obama's designated chief of staff Rahm Emanuel warned against letting the "crisis go to waste."[6] But Obama aligned himself with the Bush administration, made his most important decisions too early, and mistakenly chose calmness instead of drama as the attribute of leadership revealed in his inaugural address. He did not use the crisis he faced—as serious as any since Lincoln's election—to make historic changes. How that happened is the story of this book.

I was part of the Clinton and Obama transition teams from the summer of their election years to their Inauguration Days. In 1993 President Clinton and Vice President Gore agreed to nominate me as chairman of the Federal Communications Commission, where I served from 1993 to 1997.[7] I joined Barack Obama's transition team in the summer of 2008. I knew almost all the people central to the pre-inauguration decision-making for both Clinton and Obama. For this book I interviewed more than 50 people involved in the Obama decisions. The interviewees approved the quotations from their interviews in this book.

What Do I Know?

I met Obama in 2003, when he was 42. A decade earlier, when my high school classmate Al Gore and I were 45, and my law school friend Bill Clinton was 47, the newly elected president and vice president agreed that I could be appointed chairman of the Federal Communications Commission. My tenure, from 1993 to 1997, covered the salad days of

---

5. "[D]uring the Reagan years…American liberals" failed "to develop a fresh political vision of the country's shared vision…Instead they threw themselves into the movement politics of identity, losing a sense of what we share as citizens…" Mark Lilla, *The Once and Future Liberal: After Identity Politics* (New York: Harper, 2017), 8-9.

6. Rahm Emanuel, interview with the *Wall Street Journal*, November 19, 2008, https://www.youtube.com/watch?v=_mzcbXi1Tkk.

7. It was reported in November 2015 that I was one of 146 donors who supported all six of the Clintons' federal races. Dan Keating, "Here Are the 146 Donors Who Have Supported All Six of the Clintons' Federal Races," *Washington Post*, November 19, 2015, https://www.washingtonpost.com/news/post-politics/wp/2015/11/19/here-are-the-146-donors-who-have-supported-all-six-of-the-clintons-federal-races/?noredirect=on&utm_term=.50752f74a08e.

both digital mobile communications and the Internet, when technology stimulated the economic boom that became Clinton's principal achievement. For a time I was reasonably well known in Washington, Silicon Valley, and on Wall Street. Some praised me for helping to jump-start the information revolution. Others pilloried me for causing the so-called dot-com bubble that led to the short recession used skillfully by George W. Bush to defeat Gore in 2000. I might not have deserved the approbation or contumely, but as Clint Eastwood's character in *Unforgiven* says, "It ain't about deserving."[8] In 2003 Obama saw me as an older, inside-the-Beltway type who could help fund his campaign for the Democratic Party nomination for the Illinois Senate seat open in 2004.

Obama's law school classmate Julius Genachowski was my senior legal adviser at the FCC. He told me to take the meeting because Obama "could go all the way." That meant not only could he become senator, but also that he would run for president. Most senators at least consider that prospect, so what stood out was Julius's estimation that Obama might be the first African-American elected to the presidency. Any Democrat would want to be part of that accomplishment. It could be rivaled only by helping to elect the first woman president.

We met in a windowless conference room at McKinsey & Company, where I was working as a consultant. Big-eared, big-toothed Obama radiated presumption and destiny. The electricity of potential presidents creates personal magnetism—the Maxwell's Law of Politics. I had observed this effect with Clinton in 1991 and Gore in 1987. Like them, Obama knew he had prospects, so it followed that he could get the money. The question was whether I wanted to be an early donor, or miss the ride.

I said, "If you had been in the Senate already, would you have voted for the Iraq invasion?" Not knowing the answer I expected, he commenced a balanced explanation of "on the one hand and the other."

I interrupted between hands. "There aren't going to be many Democratic voters who want to hear a yes to that question."

He said, "I would have voted against the war."

8. Clint Eastwood, *Unforgiven*. United States: Malpaso Productions/Warner Bros., 1992.

On that fulcrum rested the lever that would pry the nomination out of the grip of Hillary Clinton in the presidential primaries of 2008.

Then I said, "What about your name? Don't you think it would be better to go with Barry? Didn't you use that name in high school?"

He answered, with a smile that was only a cocky step short of a smirk, "They will get used to Barack."

I was one for two in the advice business. Anti-Iraq war, good! Suggested name change, bad! For Washington, that's a good average.[9]

Luck helps in every success story. In the primary contest for the Senate nomination, Obama's most formidable opponent was revealed to have hit his wife. In the general, his Republican rival had to drop out when the news broke that he had taken his then-wife to sex clubs. The replacement, Alan Keyes, was out of his depth, out of his mind, and from out of the state. Obama won the Senate seat in 2004 by a landslide.

In the galvanizing speech he made at the July 2004 Democratic National Convention, Obama effectively began his campaign for the presidency before his election to the Senate. Obama evoked a vision of unity among red states and blue states. He presented himself as a post-partisan unifier of a divided nation. During the Trump presidency, when this book was finished, the notion of a politics based on consensus and compromise seemed quaint, perhaps jejune. Yet Obama in a single speech built the rhetorical framework for the remarkable "hope and change" campaign for the presidency that he began less than three years later.

Because John Kerry lost to George W. Bush in 2004, the 2008 election would feature no incumbent in either party. Hillary Clinton had waited for this moment for many years. Her decision to run for the Senate from New York in the 2000 election validated her as an elected official. It also linked her to the Wall Street fund-raising base that the Clintons' neoliberalism had enabled them to cultivate since the 1980s. If Gore had won the 2000 election, and then gotten reelected, she would not have been a plausible candidate to succeed him. Sixteen years of

---

9. David Garrow reported in his 2017 biography that Obama had polled both these questions many months earlier. Barry was more acceptable, but Obama wanted to project an authentic image. His Iraq stance was very popular. David J. Garrow, *Rising Star: The Making of Barack Obama* (New York: HarperCollins, 2017).

Clinton-Gore would have satiated the nation. But she was the odds-on favorite to win the nomination in 2008: she had the name recognition, the funding, and the qualifications. Hillary Clinton also carried extraordinarily high negative approval numbers.

On January 26, 1992, on CBS's *60 Minutes*, she introduced herself to the country as a defender of her husband against Gennifer Flowers's charge of infidelity by saying, "You know, I'm not sitting here, some little woman standing by my man like Tammy Wynette." Two months later she explained her decision to practice law this way: "I suppose I could have stayed home and baked cookies and had teas."[10] The image created by these two remarks, like the apocryphal claim that Gore said he had "invented the Internet," proved indelible. Most men and many women did not like her dismissal of stay-at-home mothers. The Right stigmatized her for apparently rejecting the conventional, media-manufactured postwar ideal of a family led by a working husband and homemaker wife.

In addition, Clinton voted to invade Iraq.

Unlike his principal rival and her spouse, if he ran in the 2008 campaign, Barack Obama and his wife, Michelle, could paint their own images on a nearly blank canvas. With beautiful brush strokes they depicted themselves as luminous examples of the American Dream, rising from extremely modest circumstances to extraordinary success. Their stories promised the beginning of an era of tolerance, compassion for others, and unification. In addition, if he could win the Iowa caucus, a person of color had a huge advantage in the Democratic primaries in the South that followed.

In the winter of 2004–2005, a number of my former FCC colleagues urged Obama to organize his Senate office in a way that could support a presidential campaign, pressing what we considered to be a progressive agenda. Karen Kornbluh, one of the leadership team at the FCC, became Obama's domestic policy adviser. She had been writing about the impact

---

10. Hillary Clinton, "Making Hillary Clinton an Issue," interview by Ted Koppel, *Nightline*, ABC, March 26, 1992. Frontline, https://www.pbs.org/wgbh/pages/frontline/shows/clinton/etc/03261992.html.

of the changing economy on families and the need for new policies to address economic insecurity. In that role she argued, and inserted in drafts of his speeches, the case for a fundamental transformation of the platforms on which the American economy was based.

Only in the '90s, of all the decades since the '60s, did every quintile on the income ladder enjoy growth. In our FCC group's view, the "golden decade" of the '90s found its root cause in the stupendous investment in information technology. That and the consequent stock market run-up led to surprising new tax revenues and a budget surplus. New business creation boomed. Education, expression, and community formation gained new dimensions. Global competition and economic upheaval seemed compatible with rising income and declining poverty.

We learned that government should use regulation to open closed markets and create new markets, while occasionally spending public funds to draw the private sector into paying for new platforms. That had been the FCC policy for the information and communications sector. Obviously we had not created the technological underpinnings of digital cellular or Internet access, but our policies had encouraged investment in these platforms. Constantly falling prices and increased services from the new technologies would drive adoption by all Americans. To us, the progressive prescription should be platform creation for power, transportation, broadband, water, and sewage, as well as using government to extend the benefits of these platforms to everyone.[11]

The Clinton camp interpreted the boom differently. They thought the new technologies had just happened to come out of laboratories in about 1993 and the government had gotten out of the way. They thought investors spent prodigiously on the new networks because they could borrow at low interest rates. Thanks for that in their view was due to the 1993 Omnibus Budget Reconciliation Act that had raised taxes,

---

11. As many as 20 million Americans are affected by unsafe drinking water in a given year. Brad Plumer and Nadja Popovich, "Here Are the Places That Struggle to Meet the Rules on Safe Drinking Water," *New York Times*, February 12, 2018, https://www.nytimes.com/2018/02/12/climate/drinking-water-safety.html.

reduced federal expenditures, and thus vanquished the risk of federal borrowing crowding out private lending.[12]

Our FCC group believed we had played a helpful, perhaps pivotal, role in catalyzing investment in the new information platform. The Clinton camp thought our regulations almost, but fortunately not quite, got in the way of private-sector decision-making. This difference in opinion was a subterranean conflict with the Clintonites. They attributed Gore's defeat to his populist campaign strategy and the Supreme Court. We blamed the unwillingness of the Clinton administration to spend the surprising surplus on new benefits for the middle class.

After Kerry's defeat in 2004, the Clinton group began planning for the restoration of their ideology in a second Clinton administration. Again they would press for a reduction in the size, capacity, and purpose of the public sector. By shrinking government's aspirations, the budget could be balanced. By contrast, Obama began articulating in speeches, and in his book *The Audacity of Hope*, an ambitious, if vague, vision of government as an active agent for the people.

In October 2006 Obama asked me to introduce him to Al Gore.

I said, "You've never met?"

"Nope," he said, "but if he runs again I'd like to be considered for his vice president."

By the time I could coordinate their schedules it was December. The Democrats had won the House and Senate in the November election. The next election looked good for Democrats. By then Obama was interested not in the vice presidency, but in whether Gore and Clinton would both be running for president.

Michelle and Barack Obama flew to Nashville for lunch with Al and Tipper Gore. Obama presented himself as a worthy champion of progressive causes, especially including the battle against burning coal to make electricity. The Obamas left with the impression that they could

---

12. For a polite debunking of the success claims for the budget plan, and an implicit, perhaps unconscious endorsement of our FCC explanation, see Alan Binder and Janet Yellen, *The Fabulous Decade: Macroeconomic Lessons from the 1990s* (New York: Century Foundation, 2001).

go forward, and Gore would not be a rival. Obama announced his presidential candidacy in January 2007.

In March my wife and I hosted the first Obama presidential campaign fund-raiser on the East Coast. We hit $600,000. The *Wall Street Journal*, a chronicler of Democratic troubles real and speculative, reported my apostasy from the Clintons.

In June, my wife and second son, who had just graduated from college, drove to Iowa and set up the Obama office in Algona, a town of 6,000 in a sea of corn. Hard work, charm, and a great golf swing helped Nathaniel Hundt persuade the majority of delegates from his counties to vote for Obama in the January 2008 caucus. Natty went on to Colorado (victory), Ohio (defeat), and North Carolina (victory) during Obama's long fight for the nomination, and then back to Colorado for the general election (carried the state). Meanwhile, in the summer, I joined the transition team that was in charge of preparing Barack Obama for a successful presidency if he won the election.

Podesta Began Transition Planning in Summer

In 2003 John Podesta, a veteran of Bill Clinton's White House, founded what became the leading Democratic think tank, the Center for American Progress. Podesta wrote a book about being a progressive, but for the most part CAP generated mainstream neoliberal policies. It functioned as a shadow government for the Clintons from then until the summer of 2008.

After Hillary conceded the nomination, Obama asked John Podesta to organize the Obama presidential transition team. Combining the rival teams is typically part of the nominee's move to the general election. Reagan, for instance, invited Jim Baker from the defeated George H. W. Bush campaign on to his team in 1980. Still it was remarkable that Obama, the avatar of change, chose the organizer of Democratic consensus and longtime Clinton aide as his transition chief.

The two opposing parties' transition teams plan in the summer how the candidate's new administration will take over from the old one. They study all the pending matters in the departments and agencies, all the activities of a federal government that accounts for about one-quarter of spending in the economy. In the late summer and early fall, they outline what they will change and what they will continue. After the election, the winning candidate selects people for key posts. They receive the transition team's plans, then read or throw them away.

Podesta himself was surprised to be asked to run Obama's transition. In that capacity, he could give Clintonites a leg up in the contest of ideas and scramble for jobs. Demonstrating deference to his new boss, however, Podesta asked Obama which of his loyalists the nominee wanted on the team.

Coming back from that meeting with only a handful of names, Podesta said, "He travels light."[13]

The Clintons were like an ancient city: they had layers of friends, allies, and acquaintances, some from decades back, some created yesterday. Their transition team swelled from a dozen in early summer of 1992 to many hundreds by Christmas. The unofficial adviser list was even longer. Ideas abounded. Organization evaporated.

Obama had raced so rapidly up the political ladder that he owed far fewer people. He needed even less. Obama picked no more than a basketball team of friends to help him. He included David Axelrod and Valerie Jarrett from Chicago. Axelrod recruited Rahm Emanuel. A couple more veterans from the long campaign and classmates from law school completed Obama's list. For most of the top posts in the transition and later, his government, he let Podesta and the Clintonites do the picking.

Trying to avoid the burgeoning chaos of the Clinton transition in 1992–1993, Podesta limited the planning role of the Obama pre-election transition team. Podesta intended to persuade the president-elect to pick his top people very quickly if he won the election. Podesta would hand to the anointed outlines of the major policy issues in the ambit of their

---

13. You will find herein many quotations from interviews I did in 2011 and 2012. In 2018 I gave the interviewees the opportunity to edit their quotes. Some did so, although a few changed nothing. Only one, a lieutenant to Treasury Secretary Tim Geithner, did not want any quotes to be used, and I complied. In addition, in some places I report words said outside the context of an interview: I either heard these words or sources convinced me they were said. Podesta's comments here fall in this category.

posts. The selectees would make recommendations to the president-elect in December. Podesta would not let Obama repeat Bill Clinton's stumbling start in 1993.

The End Came from the Beginning

The only correct objective of economic policy for the President of the United States, taught Harvard professor Michael Porter, is to create a high and rising standard of living for American citizens.[14] Cicero used different words to make the same point: *Salus populi suprema lex esto* ("The welfare of the people shall be the supreme law").

Obama said it this way in August 2008 in his speech accepting the Democratic presidential nomination:

"We measure progress by how many people can find a job that pays the mortgage; whether you can put a little extra money away at the end of each month so you can someday watch your child receive her college diploma. We measure progress in the 23 million new jobs that were created when Bill Clinton was president—when the average American family saw its income go up $7,500 instead of down $2,000 like it has under George Bush."

No one believes that everyone in society will ever have exactly the same standard of living. Cervantes in the first novel said it: "There are only two families in the world, my old grandmother used to say, the Haves and the Have-Nots." In 2012 Mitt Romney, Obama's reelection opponent, described the separation less sympathetically: "There are 47 percent of the people…who are dependent on government, who believe that they are victims…who pay no income tax."[15] Politics revolves around reactions to the division. Progressives want government to provide more and better jobs, security, and education to the have-nots. They believe public spending and regulation are useful tactics. Neoliberals believe a growing economy is the primary means to this end, and while some

---

14. Michael E. Porter, *The Competitive Advantage of Nations* (London: Macmillan, 1990), 1.
15. Mitt Romney, in a secretly recorded speech at a private fund-raising event, May 17, 2012, https://www.motherjones.com/politics/2012/09/full-transcript-mitt-romney-secret-video/.

modest income transfers are acceptable, they distrust deviations from allocative efficiency. Conservatives assert that taxing to transfer income from the haves to the have-nots and regulating capitalism are unfair, ineffective and counter-productive uses of government, which in any case is an untrustworthy institution with a dangerous monopoly over law-making and police power. Clinton's treasury secretary, Robert Rubin, contended that a rapidly growing economy was the best welfare policy because unemployment would fall and wages would rise for everyone. This optimistic view justified reduction in government benefits and opposition to new ideas for spending public money.

While this economic policy debate evolved, the individualism of the 1960s rights revolution ossified into identity politics. Groups defined by race, ethnicity, gender, and sexual orientation sought justice and opportunity. The backlash of groups outside the Democratic Party's coalition increased the Democrats' difficulty in obtaining electoral and legislative success, but in the 1990s gains in every income class compensated for conflicts driven by identity politics and the parsimony of Bill Clinton's neoliberalism.[16]

Obama was not so fortunate. As he accepted the nomination in Denver that August, he knew that deepening recession would define the general election campaign, and that race might stir resentments deepened by economic plight. Then, if he won he would have to decide how and who the government should help, while addressing the claims for justice by the groups in his coalition. He would have to figure out how to pursue a transformational agenda while most people worried about losing their jobs or the savings in their homes' equity, or even their homes.

16. "Some time during the 1960s, the Western left abandoned the politics of solidarity to embrace one of person liberation." Edward Luce, *The Retreat of Western Liberalism* (London: Little, Brown, 2017), 188.

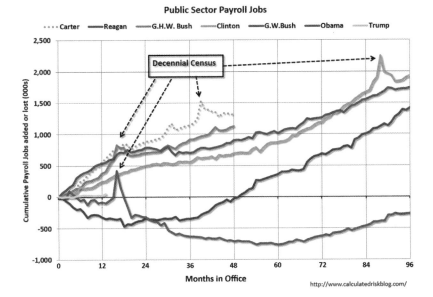

Graph 1 from Bill McBride, "Public and Private Sector Payroll Jobs: Carter, Reagan, Bush, Clinton, Bush, Obama, Trump," Calculated Risk, August 4, 2017, http://www.calculatedriskblog.com/2017/08/ public-and-private-sector-payroll-jobs.html#4LiKpIzsz4pvChhS.99. Used with permission.

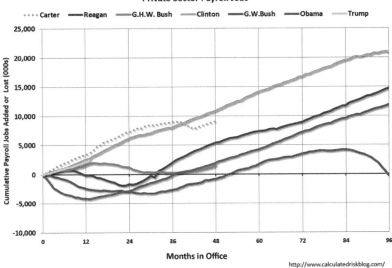

Graph 2 from Bill McBride, "Public and Private Sector Payroll Jobs: Carter, Reagan, Bush, Clinton, Bush, Obama, Trump," Calculated Risk, August 4, 2017, http://www.calculatedriskblog.com/2017/08/ public-and-private-sector-payroll-jobs.html#4LiKpIzsz4pvChhS.99. Used with permission.

Average Hourly Earning of all Employees, Year-over-year Change

Graph 1 from Bill McBride, "Question #6 for 2018: How Much Will Wages Increase in 2018?," Calculated Risk, December 31, 2017, http://www.calculatedriskblog.com/2017/12/question-6-for-2018-how-much-will-wages.html#mXvO2lLKhmD6p7g7.99. Used with permission.

In deciding on an economic recovery plan, Obama also was choosing the fate of the Democratic Party. Neoliberalism had subtly elevated global concerns over national interests. (Indeed, energy reform plainly rested on the premise that Americans should pay more for clean power in order to benefit primarily people in other countries.) Neoliberal economists plainly preferred non-democratic governance, such as by the Fed or the World Trade Organization, rather than by Congress, much less state legislatures.[17] Would executive or legislative authority be Obama's principal method of acting? Would he align himself with democracy, and then aim to help directly the great preponderance of Americans in their time of obvious need? If his plan failed, the triumphalist American narrative might peter out, after more than two centuries of turning dreams into reality.[18]

17. Alan Blinder, "Is Government Too Political?,," Foreign Affairs, no. 76 (November 1997): 115-26.
18. "[T]he failure of parties might indeed imply the failure of democracy." Peter Mair, Ruling the Void: The Hollowing of Western Democracy (London: Verso, 2013), 15.

Berkeley Professor Wendy Brown notes three "salient features" of "neoliberal political rationality."[19] It proposes to use law and policy to create markets, requires the state to see itself in market terms, and turns "governance criteria" into business measurement. As a result it undermines "an already weak investment in an active citizenry and an already thin concept of a public good."[20] Obama's campaign, indeed his own self-image, ran directly against neoliberal tenets. His rhetoric promised collective action that solved common problems and created shared benefits. However, in the throes of the financial crisis, his advisers were unable to translate the moral grounding of his candidacy and personal life into policy recommendations. Instead, they led him to adopt policies that tragically met Brown's description.

The financial crisis of September caused both private- and public-sector employment to plummet. State governments cut employment in response as their tax revenue evaporated. In either nominal or real terms, average hourly earnings disappointed. A huge gap opened between private savings and business investment. It explains why the economy grew so slowly during the Obama administration.[21]

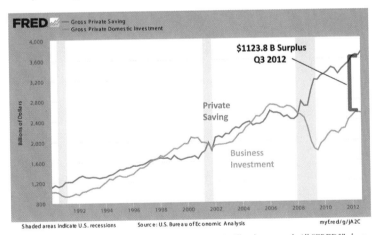

"FRED®" charts ©Federal Reserve Bank of St. Louis. 2015. All rights reserved. All "FRED®" charts appear courtesy of Federal Reserve Bank of St. Louis. http://research.stlouisfed.org/fred2/.

19. Wendy Brown, "American Nightmare: Neoliberalism, Neoconservatism, and De-Democratization," *Political Theory*, no. 34 (December 2006): 1, doi:10.7312/blau17412-078.
20. Ibid.
21. Academics tended to attribute poor wage growth to poor productivity growth, but that stemmed from weak investment growth. "During the recovery from the great recession, growth in capital

Economic woes and unpopular legislative initiatives rapidly drove Obama's approval rating down after his inauguration on January 20, 2009.[22] Only at the end of his two terms did a healthy economy and the contrast between him and his successor give him an approval rating that approached the support he had when he became president.

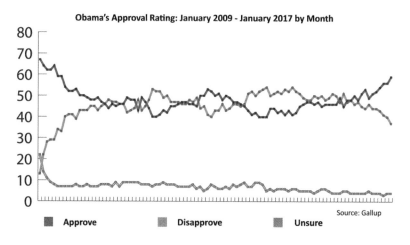

Original graph created by Deborah Nicholls. Data source: Gallup, http://news.gallup.com.

Obama ran for president to solve problems that no one in the Oval Office before him was able to solve. He would meld immigrants with the descendants of immigrants from long before, give everyone confidence in a better tomorrow, guarantee affordable healthcare to all, and stop global warming. The structure and function of the economy would be changed to produce rising productivity and an increasing standard of living for all. As incomes grew and inequality of wealth and opportunity diminished, Americans would renew their vows of tolerance and optimism. Only if the Trump tenure leads to a counter reaction, and a progressive president

intensity (the ratio of capital services to labor hours) has fallen far short of historical norms, even contracting in 2011 and 2012." "Labor Productivity Growth Has Slowed, Restraining Wage Growth," The Hamilton Project, September 26, 2017, http://www.hamiltonproject.org/charts/labor_productivity_growth_has_slowed_restraining_wage_growth.

22. "A sicker, more unequal, more racially divided country: This is the legacy of the Great Recession." Annie Lowrey, "The Great Recession Is Still With Us," *The Atlantic*, December 1, 2017, https://www.theatlantic.com/business/archive/2017/12/great-recession-still-with-us/547268/.

chooses the same goals but different policies than did Obama, will these hopes come true.

Now let us stop thinking about tomorrow. Instead, we begin with a crucial day in Chicago: December 16, 2008.

1

To Chicago in the Snow

History is valuable, to begin with, because it is true...
— Bertrand Russell, "On History," 1904

The Chicago winter sun clocks short, ineffectual hours, counting on electricity to do the inside jobs, abandoning the outside to whatever Canada exports. The 16th of December in 2008 welcomes the Obama advisers coming in from Washington to O'Hare with miserable weather that is a metaphor for the awful economy. The thermometer will do no more than squeak barely above 20 degrees Fahrenheit. Rising wind will push out dawn's polluted fog and fill the air with the third big snowfall of the season.

The advisers take the train from the airport to the campaign's downtown office. Not yet recognizable even for a C-SPAN watcher, they draw no attention as they head for the meeting that will establish their personal role in history. They are to explain to the president-elect what he must do, and cannot do, to help America recover from the worst economic crisis in 60 years.

The advisers cannot believe how shaky is the ground under the finance industry. Based on their studies over three decades during which they got their advanced degrees, gained prestigious appointments, and became prominent in their circles, they believe that what is happening in the economy cannot be happening. Markets are supposed to have so much information that they can never be paralyzed by uncertainty. Businesses do not lay off workers only because of perturbations in the price of obscure securities. Depositors and creditors cannot doubt that the most prestigious banks could pay their debts. The transparent economy does not have shockingly opaque and frightful depths. Nevertheless these experts have to explain to Obama what had happened, was happening, and was to come.

They all believe that the great accomplishments, the transformations of society, that Obama had run for the highest office in order to achieve, lie on the other side of stabilizing the financial sector and ending the recession. However, each speaker has a different agenda. No two have the same priority in mind.

Famously brilliant Larry Summers has not persuaded the president-elect to give him a second tour as treasury secretary. Chagrined, he nevertheless has accepted Obama's offer to run the National Economic Council. This White House staff job puts him in charge of coordinating the economic recovery plan. He has a deist's conviction in a clockwork economy that runs efficiently without government intervention. In the event of a recession, the standard Keynesian remedy of federal spending will get the machinery of capitalism ticking again.

The extra dimension of the present situation is a cascade of bank runs, the worst culminating in the bankruptcy of Lehman Brothers in September. The resulting crisis still threatens the survival of the biggest banks on Wall Street. The night before, Summers sent to Obama a long memorandum recommending decisions intended to save Wall Street, stimulate the economy, prevent inflation, and address foreclosures. It described a more dramatic, multidimensional economic problem than any president-elect in modern history had seen since Franklin Roosevelt was elected in 1932. It aimed at delivering as a solution an unemployment rate that is about the same as the level that enabled Bill Clinton to throw George H. W. Bush out of office.

Presumably, in the wee hours, the smart young law professor, a night owl, read the executive summary and skimmed the rest. In the meeting he probably will engage in a disquisition. He will show leadership, confidence in his new team, and calm in a time of trouble.

Summers is ready for the colloquy. He has orchestrated the long meeting, coached the soloists, and arranged the different movements so that the president-elect would approve the whole plan. As critical as are the problems, he will present to Obama a narrow range of policy options. Obama will choose what Summers wants. After the meeting, Summers will dictate the details of implementation to the few aides who constitute the White House-in-formation. While the staff dots the *i*'s, crosses the *t*'s, Obama will go on a much-deserved vacation. When the new Congress assembles on January 3, the president-elect's team will deliver the package to the leadership and ask for rapid approval.

Berkeley economist Christy Romer, utterly new to every aspect of this strange process, will make the opening presentation. She is starting in government at the top for academics in her field—Obama wants her to head the Council of Economic Advisers, the White House's mini–think tank. She is a recognized expert on the macroeconomics of the Great Depression. She faces the final examination for which she has studied her whole life. She favors reducing unemployment as the principal objective for Obama.

The previous summer, Harvard insulted Romer when university president Drew Gilpin Faust, Summers's successor, vetoed a prestigious tenure offer made by the economics department. Some said that New Classicists on the Harvard faculty who disapproved of Romer's New Keynesian thinking had persuaded Faust, a historian, that Romer's economic models were defective. Now there is more need of Keynesian policy than ever before in the lifetimes of anyone teaching at Harvard or anywhere else. Romer will have the last laugh, if she can persuade Obama to go as high in the range of government stimulus spending as Summers has let her advocate.

Bushy-haired, boyish Tim Geithner, the head of the New York Federal Reserve bank in the Bush administration and Obama's treasury secretary-designate, will explain in the meeting that the financial crisis has not ended. Geithner considers the meeting to be less important than the others do. In his memoir written years later, he called the gathering "mythic," meaning that he made important decisions before and after the meeting, and less happened on December 16 than reported.

In the previous 18 months, about half of the biggest Wall Street firms had gone bankrupt or merged to prevent collapse. In September, Geithner had not stopped the Bush administration from letting Lehman go bankrupt, precipitating the biggest financial crisis in the history of capitalism. In the wake of that event, he helped persuade Obama and the Democratic Congress to pass the bank bailout law called the Troubled Asset Relief Program (TARP). In October Geithner and others convinced Sheila Bair, who ran the Federal Deposit Insurance Corporation (FDIC), to guarantee the debts of the Wall Street banks. That same month, Treasury invested $200 billion in big banks. Geithner believes the government's principal objective is to stop runs on important banks. His intent in Chicago is to quash debate over this strategic decision.

To that end, when it comes his turn to talk, Geithner intends to scare everyone. He will warn of the prospect of a continuing financial crisis that causes a repeat of the Great Depression. He thinks Romer will help him make his case. Then he will persuade Obama to get the half of the $700 billion in TARP money that Congress had withheld from Treasury. That is not a crowd-pleaser, from a political point of view, but Geithner does not care about the ramifications for Democratic politicians. He is committed to reestablishing the *status quo ante* on Wall Street. He warned Obama that this conviction will be unpopular, except among bankers and business people. Obama picked him anyhow.

Gimlet-eyed Peter Orszag has to outline the president's budget. The shrinking economy will reduce revenue by a huge amount, and the stimulus will increase spending by a record amount. Named to be director of the Office of Management on Budget, Orszag's first task is to present Congress with a record-breaking peacetime deficit. He sees the gap between government revenue and spending as the major problem for the Obama administration.

Orszag was one of the more promising noviitiates in the deficit-loathing School of Rubin, where Summers was the moral equivalent of dean and cofounder. Adhering to its axioms, Orszag wants the stimulus to be only just big enough to end the recession. As soon as the economy stops shrinking, Orszag thinks the government should constrain spending, making the budget deficit decline. He adheres to the neoliberal postulate that the percentage of the annual federal deficit should be equal to or lower than GDP growth, so that as a percentage of the size of the economy, the aggregate federal debt stays the same or falls.

In Orszag's view, if Obama runs the total debt too high in the early years of his first term, inflation will ensue and interest rates will climb, possibly creating a second, double-dip recession. Obama then will be running for a second term just as a second downturn occurs: awful for the country, disastrous for Obama. Therefore, the stimulus spending in 2009 and 2010 cannot be big enough to guarantee full employment. The "stimulated" private sector will have to spend what is necessary to reach that level in the fullness of time, even though wages will not rise until, more or less, everyone who can work can find a job.[1]

Rahm Emanuel is designated chief of staff. He was a Clinton White House staffer, and then as a Chicago congressman was Speaker Nancy Pelosi's chief strategist for winning the majority in the House in 2006 and increasing the margin in 2008. Emanuel is that guy who begins every discussion with his conclusion. He hates discourse. He likes to say that the Obama team must "put points on the board." That means persuading Congress to pass as many bills as possible.

Emanuel needs the meeting to end without discord or unresolved issues. He already knows how big the stimulus should be. The economists say a little less than $800 billion will push unemployment below 8 percent by the midterms in 2010. That is good enough given the need to pass the other bills that constitute Obama's transformational agenda. The economists also say speed matters more than anything. Therefore, the bill cannot contain new ideas. Innovative ideas trouble legislatures. In addition, Obama wants to be a bipartisan leader, and needs Republican votes to avoid filibusters of his healthcare and energy reforms. So Emanuel and Tom Daschle, former Senate majority leader and a de facto co-chief of staff, will not resort to the reconciliation technique that requires only 51 votes in the Senate on a budgetary matter. They will

---

1. Ten years later, economists would be puzzled about why what they thought was full employment did not produce rising wages. See Paul Krugman, "Monopsony, Rigidity, and the Wage Puzzle (Wonkish)," *New York Times*, May 20, 2018, https://www.nytimes.com/2018/05/20/opinion/monopsony-rigidity-and-the-wage-puzzle-wonkish.html.

seek 60, the number that precludes filibuster. That requires at least two Republican votes. To get those, the stimulus bill needs to be not much larger than the TARP bank bailout, around $700 billion.

Moreover, Daschle wants to start the healthcare push after the inauguration. That underscores the need to get the stimulus done quickly. The details will be worked out later, after the boss heads to Hawaii. Emanuel will have final say over the package. The December 16 meeting is a formality. It will show the advisers how Emanuel, with Obama's authority, runs the circus.

Phil Schiliro, a longtime aide to Congressman Henry Waxman, will manage Obama's negotiations with Congress. He also wants speed. The faster Obama signs laws, the more he increases his political capital. This president plays basketball. Using that sport as a metaphor, the plan is run-and-gun. Shoot quickly, score a lot. The crowd (voters) will cheer. The opposition (Republicans in Congress) will get tired and play less hard. Obama will wear them out.

Emanuel and Schiliro intend to begin talking to the congressional leadership about the economic recovery plan right after the meeting.

Amusing, smart, collegial Austan Goolsbee might carry a grudge into the meeting. Two years earlier, Obama recruited him from the University of Chicago to be chief economic adviser to the campaign. Then, two weeks after the election, Goolsbee suffered the sort of disappointment that princes mete out to courtiers. The president-elect chose Christy Romer, a stranger who had done nothing on the campaign, had probably even supported Hillary Clinton, to run the Council of Economic Advisers. Obama promised Goolsbee that if he would wait his turn he could run CEA in a couple of years, and that the University of Chicago would surely not deny his return to a tenure position after serving in the Obama White House. All that would come true. But now Goolsbee has the less prestigious assignment of dealing with housing issues. The economists on the team believe that housing and unemployment are effects. The meeting is about changing the causes—the financial crisis and falling demand—of economic trouble. Still, Goolsbee has a speaking role on the topic of the housing market.

For two long years Obama's message strategist, David Axelrod, has advised the candidate hourly, daily, night after night, about how to appeal to voters. Now, after the great victory, he thinks making the American people like the bank bailout and the stimulus is impossible. He worries that explaining truthfully the severity of the economic problem will deepen despair, undercut Obama's message of "hope and change." Axelrod wants Obama to show steadiness at the helm in the face of the economic storm. To that end, the president-elect has already publicly guaranteed creating or saving several million jobs. That target may be short of what the situation requires. The economists will give their prediction in a pre-meeting with Axelrod.

For passing legislation on the Hill, Axelrod depends on Emanuel. He held the huppah at Emanuel's wedding. He trusts the chief of staff to look out for Obama's best interests vis-à-vis Congress.

Not present, except in the memory and beliefs of the ex-Clinton people, is Robert Rubin. His exquisite touch with prickly egotists enabled him to create loyalists in two of the most byzantine and back-stabbing palaces in the world: Goldman Sachs and the Clinton White House. In both those environments, a growing economy made his job a little easier. Now the converse prevails: a shrinking economy creates poor choices. It is the worst of all welfare policies. It hurts the poor very badly, shrinks the size and security of the middle class, frightens the rich. Public money has to be spent to stop the recession. But the central commandment of Rubinomics is that federal borrowing competes with corporate borrowing, and therefore raises interest rates and reduces economic growth.

Baptist preacher William Miller predicted the Second Coming of Christ would occur on March 21, 1844, and though nothing like that happened then or later, the Seventh-Day Adventist Church still holds that the Second Coming is on its way. Similarly, the members of the School of Rubin in the Chicago meeting see no evidence of inflation, but they continue to believe it is coming. Therefore, they will tell Obama that the deficit-increasing stimulus cannot be too big or last too long.

Others in the Chicago meeting are transition chair John Podesta and Carol Browner, the recently named energy czar. As EPA administrator in the Clinton administration, Browner disputed the neoliberal view that her regulatory agenda innately conflicted with capitalism, and retarded economic growth. Now she is heading back into the White House with the vastly broader mission of reducing all carbon combustion in order to save the world. She knows cap-and-trade legislation will impose a higher cost for power on all business and consumer users. She anticipates that the prioritization of financial stability and job creation will cause the economists again to question the importance of her agenda.

Besides, Browner is a czar in name only. She lacks empire or serfs, an agency or staff. Before the meeting she agreed with Summers to discourage Obama from asking for a plan to build a national transmission network connecting Great Plains clean power to mid-western utility distribution grids. She hopes that in return he will stay quiet while she collaborates with House Speaker Nancy Pelosi and Senate Majority Leader Harry Reid to make come true the environmental dream of curtailing greenhouse-gas emissions. Summers wants to save the global economy. She wants to save the planet.

Other advisers in attendance include Jason Furman, with the print on his economics PhD still drying, and Jared Bernstein, who has a doctorate in social welfare. Furman wants to resolve all debates, and create a workable recovery plan. Bernstein is supposed to speak for labor.

The members of the newly assembled team understand that Obama will be assessing them, and they, him. Most of them scarcely know Obama, and as Clintonites they have their doubts. They considered his nomination strategy to be more cunning than fair. Obama won more delegates than Clinton by beating her in states that as the nominee he could not hope to win in November: five southern states (South Carolina, Georgia, Alabama, Mississippi, and Louisiana) and seven Great Plains and northwestern strongholds of the Republican Party (Idaho, Montana, Wyoming, Utah, North Dakota, Kansas, and Nebraska). Clinton won the primaries in the Democratic heartland—every state between New York and Indiana, plus California. In the nomination contests, Clinton and Obama effectively tied in total votes, each obtaining about 18 million, but her votes came more from the states that under the Electoral College system a Democrat had to win. Many of Obama's primary voters would not matter in the general. Besides, the Clintonites did not consider Obama as well prepared for the job as Mrs. Clinton, and they smarted from his criticisms of her and her husband.

Perhaps eager to subdue this last sentiment, Obama turned most of his transition planning to Clinton's people, picked many of them for powerful posts, and named her Secretary of State. He could not do more to bond with the Clintons. Her advisers had the inside track on persuading Obama to do what they would have told Hillary Clinton to do: restore Wall Street to profitability and end the recession without spending too much money. After that, Congress can pass laws that create efficient markets in which private-sector supply and demand would optimize outcomes in healthcare and power consumption. Neoliberalism will reign again in America.

2

As Obama Entered Congress, The Economy Began to Crack

Capt. Benjamin Willard:
Every man gets everything he wants. I wanted a mission. And for my sins they gave me one. Brought it up to me like room service.
— *Apocalypse Now*

Not long after Barack Obama took his Senate seat in 2005, Bob Rubin met him for dinner at the Jefferson Hotel, Rubin's residence when he was in the Clinton administration. The French décor and indifferent cuisine characterized Washington's mélange of aristocratic power and bourgeois sensibility. (As 2017 would show, that ridiculous town made an easy mark for a huckster president.) Obama understood that dinner with the most successful treasury secretary in modern times constituted still another entrance examination for his admission into the acceptance world.

Rubin quizzed the young lawyer's beliefs. Obama convinced Rubin of his socially liberal, fiscally conservative beliefs. The steward of neoliberalism could not have envisioned the new senator as Hillary Clinton's rival less than two years later, but he must have noted the intelligence, the ability to please while staying aloof. Afterward, Obama told one of his staffers that the conversation convinced him that it was time for new ideas.

Speaking at Knox College in June 2005, Obama began the process of articulating a new approach. He suggested making "college affordable for everyone, job retraining and lifelong education, healthcare, and a pension that stayed with you always so that each of us have the flexibility to move to a better job or start a new business."[1] Each of these four new or expanded benefits would require federal funding. He omitted that part.

In 2005 neither Rubin nor Obama recognized that the foundation of the economy was cracking. Democratic and Republican policy thinking lagged behind reality. Mortgage lending against precarious housing values and massive securities trading linked to those prices threatened to cause a recession.

As Bill McBride, an astute blogger, noted in 2005, "It wouldn't take a RE bust to impact the general economy. Just a slowdown in both volume (to impact employment) and in prices (to slow down borrowing) might push the general economy into recession. An actual bust, especially with all of the extensive sub-prime lending, might cause a serious problem."[2]

By 2006 *Fortune*, *Barron's*, Nouriel Roubini, and Joe Stiglitz all predicted that soon the housing bubble would pop, prices would drop, wealth would disappear, consumers would stop buying, and the economy would begin to shrink. Larry Lindsey, the head of the National Economic Council in the first Bush term, said the big tax cut he helped craft, coupled with government tax breaks for housing, had caused real estate prices to rise above their natural level.

Al Hubbard, the cheerful business school graduate who then headed the Council of Economic Advisers, dismissed the dire predictions. President Bush, who had a lifelong inability to heed warnings, liked that optimism. Treasury Secretary Hank Paulson offered his own happy talk, saying in April 2007, "the housing market is at or near the bottom" and prices will soon begin to rise.[3]

---

1. Barack Obama, "Knox College Commencement Speech," June 4, 2005, Galesburg, IL.

2. Bill McBride, "Mortgage Debt and the 'Recovery,'" Calculated Risk, February 24, 2005, http://www.calculatedriskblog.com/2005/02/mortgage-debt-and-recovery.html.

3. Greg Robb, "Paulson Says U.S. Housing Sector 'At or Near Bottom,'" MarketWatch, April 20, 2007, https://www.marketwatch.com/story/paulson-says-us-housing-sector-at-or-near-bottom.

In his memoir, Paulson explained that he thought then that subprime mortgage problems—meaning loans to people who might not be able to pay—were "largely contained."[4] In retrospect, Paulson admitted he was "just plain wrong." Prices would fall much farther, and would not return to the level of 2007 until 2017. He also misdiagnosed the causation. Subprime loans accounted for only about 20 percent of mortgages. As the continued price decline pushed more homeowners into ever deeper negative equity over the years, many more prime borrowers lost their homes than subprime borrowers, even if they did not start out with high loan-to-value ratios.[5] In the moment, however, blaming the subprime market sounded like a criticism of low-income and imprudent house-holds. If marginal homeowners left the market, values for the middle

Graph 1 from Bill McBride, "New Home Sales Increased Sharply to 619,000 Annual Rate in April," Calculated Risk, May 24, 2016), http://www.calculatedriskblog.com/2016/05/new-home-sales-increased-sharply-to.html. Used with permission.

4. Henry M. Paulson, *On the Brink: Inside the Race to Stop the Collapse of the Global Financial System* (New York: Business Plus, 2010), 66.

5. Over the long run of the slump, twice as many prime borrowers lost their homes as subprime borrowers. Fernando Ferreira and Joseph Gyourko, "A New Look at the U.S. Foreclosure Crisis: Panel Data Evidence of Prime and Subprime Borrowers from 1997 to 2012," *National Bureau of Economic Research Working Paper Series*, June 2015, doi:10.3386/w21261.

and upper income families' households would not be affected. Everyone could breathe easily.

As the Iraq war soured and the housing market slumped, Democrats won big in the November 2006 elections. Democrats controlled both chambers of Congress and held a 28–22 advantage in governorships. Nancy Pelosi became the first female Speaker of the House. Addressing the Democratic Congress, in November 2007 Larry Summers suggested a stimulus spending bill to forestall a recession. He wrote that "the odds now favor a U.S. recession that slows growth significantly on a global basis. Without stronger policy responses than have been observed to date, moreover, there is the risk that the adverse impacts will be felt for the rest of the decade and beyond."[6] This stimulus proposal became a feature of Obama's economic recovery plan a year later, but the recession's impact did indeed stretch far beyond the decade.

On December 19, 2007, speaking at Brookings (the neoliberal venue of choice in D.C.), Summers pronounced middle class insecurity as "the defining issue of our time." This ambiguous observation implied policy responses that Obama's transformation agenda might have provided. But the country's immediate economic trouble would overwhelm chronic issues like slowing productivity gains and increasing income inequality. The fear of losing a job or a home leeched confidence and drained hope from the middle class. In response to the looming downturn, Summers recommended a stimulus of "two digits, not three," meaning less than $100 billion. He reasoned that the Fed could lower interest rates to complement federal deficit spending.[7]

Testifying before the congressional joint economic committee on January 16, 2008, Summers urged that the stimulus be timely, targeted, and temporary.[8] "Timely" argued against new programs. "Targeted"

---

6. Lawrence Summers, "Wake up to the Dangers of a Deepening Crisis," *Financial Times*, November 25, 2007, https://www.ft.com/content/b56079a8-9b71-11dc-8aad-0000779fd2ac.

7. "2007 Brookings Blum Roundtable: Development's Changing Face—New Players, Old Challenges, Fresh Opportunities," August 1, 2007, https://www.brookings.edu/events/2007-brookings-blum-roundtable-developments-changing-face-new-players-old-challenges-fresh-opportunities/1219/.

8. Lawrence Summers, testimony at Joint Economic Committee Hearing on "What Should the Federal Government Do to Avoid a Recession?" January 16, 2008.

meant spending or giving money to those who would spend, rather than cutting taxes for those who might save instead. "Temporary" required ending the stimulus a year from enactment, in order to avoid raising "long-term interest rates" and increasing "capital costs." At the end of the year, Summers applied the same mantra to the stimulus plan.

In that testimony, Summers continued to underestimate the downturn. He suggested that Congress should appropriate $50 to $75 billion to stimulate economic growth. Doug Elmendorf and Jason Furman, neoliberal bench strength for Rubin and Summers in the Clinton administration, supported Summers in a primer they published on January 10.[9] In January 2008 Fed chair Ben Bernanke also testified that "fiscal action could be helpful in principle."[10]

The prime working-age population reached its highest level in 2007, fell until the end of 2012, began climbing again, but in 2017 was still below the 2007 level. This decade-long structural demographic problem meant that the stimulus would be less effective than in a time when more people were joining the prime working-age group. It argued for increasing the size of the stimulus. This point had no discernible impact on economists' thinking in 2008.

On February 11, 2008, President Bush signed a bipartisan stimulus bill adding up to $170 billion, mostly comprising tax cuts. It was a digit more than Summers had mentioned a month earlier. This bill anticipated the story of the Obama stimulus in three ways. It exemplified the Republican preference for tax cuts. It was too small for the situation. It misled the Obama advisers into thinking that Republicans in Congress might support a stimulus sought by Democrats.

With this spending lined up, the new head of the White House Council of Economic Advisers, Edward Lazear, confidently asserted on the pages of the *Wall Street Journal* in May 2008 that "the data are pretty

9. Douglas W. Elmendorf and Jason Furman, "If, When, How: A Primer on Fiscal Stimulus," Brookings, January 10, 2008, https://www.brookings.edu/research/if-when-how-a-primer-on-fiscal-stimulus/.

10. Paul R. La Monica, "Bernanke: Juice the Economy 'Quickly,'" CNN Money, January 17, 2008, http://money.cnn.com/2008/01/17/news/economy/fed_bernanke/index.htm.

clear that we are not in a recession."[11] Later a board of academics concluded that the recession started in December 2007.[12]

Tim Geithner confessed in his memoir that early in 2008 the Federal Reserve "did analyze scenarios where house prices fell sharply across the country. Unfortunately, we concluded that the impact on the financial system and the broader economy would be relatively modest...we didn't examine the possibility that the initial fears associated with subprime mortgages and the general fall in house prices could trigger a classic financial crisis, followed by a crash in household wealth and a collapse of the broader economy."[13]

Geithner excused the Bush team and himself: "At the start of any crisis, there's an inevitable fog of diagnosis."[14] However, in the moment Summers saw the situation clearly. On March 7, 2008, at a Stanford conference involving many notables of economic policy making, Summers said, "I believe that we are facing the most serious combination of macroeconomic and financial stresses that the United States has faced in at least a generation—and, possibly, much longer than that."[15] He identified the housing market as the immediate cause of the problem. He said the "priority" has to be "to stimulate and push the economy forward." The Bush stimulus was bigger than he had recommended, but the housing market's continuing troubles convinced Summers it was too small.

In Summers's view, home prices would drop by a total of 25 percent, and a third of mortgages would be underwater—the owners of the homes would owe more than the value of the home. Under these circumstances, Fannie Mae and Freddie Mac, the primary financiers of

11. Henry J. Pulizzi and John D. McKinnon, "Lazear Sees No Recession for U.S. Economy," *Wall Street Journal*, May 8, 2008, https://www.wsj.com/articles/SB121019473822674751.

12. Emily Kaiser, "Recession Started in December 2007: Panel," *Reuters*, December 1, 2008, https://www.reuters.com/article/us-usa-economy-recession/recession-started-in-december-2007-panel-idUSTRE4B05YX20081201.

13. Timothy F. Geithner, *Stress Test: Reflections on Financial Crises* (New York: Crown Publishers, 2014), 13.

14. Ibid.

15. Lawrence Summers, "SIEPR Economic Summit Opening Remarks," March 7, 2008, Stanford, CA, http://delong.typepad.com/larry-summers-stanford-march-7-2008.pdf.

residential housing, would not have enough money to pay the debts they incurred and the guarantees they had made on mortgage payments.

During the Stanford conference, Summers took Treasury Secretary Paulson "aside and told him that Fannie and Freddie were going to fail." At about the same time, Summers went to the regulator for these government-sponsored enterprises (GSEs), James Lockhart, and "basically told him that the things he was saying weren't right. Basically, I was saying I hoped he didn't believe the things he was saying." Summers concluded from his conversations with Paulson and Lockhart that they were "deer in the headlights, and that "they couldn't really conceive that these institutions were just belly up, which was my confident assessment."[16]

Paulson had a different recollection. He wrote in his memoir that Summers told him that the GSEs needed a lot of capital. Paulson disagreed. He thought the bond insurers "presented a more immediate problem."[17] They were both right.

The Bear Bailout Foretold the Future

A run on Bear Stearns drove the GSEs' problems off Paulson's desk. On March 14 the Federal Reserve Bank of New York sweetened Bear Stearns' balance sheet with a loan of $25 billion in cheap money. Following the playbook of the Clinton Treasury Department, Paulson and Geithner arranged a bailout by persuading JP Morgan to buy Bear, using that extra cash.

The Clinton and George W. Bush Treasury Departments believed that government had to keep big financial firms out of bankruptcy. The FDIC could "resolve" commercial banks, through a form of structured bankruptcy that reduced the value of stock and creditors' loans. It drew money from all commercial banks to do these restructurings. The big Wall Street firms, on the other hand, saved each other informally. When one of their kind suffered a run, the others would buy the bank or loan it money. To facilitate these private-sector-led bailouts, the government

16. Lawrence Summers, interview with author.
17. Paulson, *On the Brink*, 88.

typically provided a low-cost loan or some other incentive to close the deal.

The half-dozen biggest firms accounted for more than half the borrowing and lending in the financial sector. If they went out of business, business would be halted. For government to keep them solvent and liquid, it was cronyism, but necessary to keep capitalism going.

However, Larry Summers, one of the principal authors of this playbook in the 1990s, by email blasted Bernanke for doing the Bear deal.[18] Some banks were perhaps too big to be allowed to fail, but Bear was not one of them. The government should have let Bear's collapse teach Wall Street a lesson: Avoid risky lending, especially in the housing sector. If the government jollied Wall Street firms into mergers that saved imprudent firms, others would be encouraged to take even greater risks. Saving Bear would, in the jargon, create the "hazard" of "moral" misconduct: namely, imprudent borrowing and lending. This concept of right and wrong caused no end of trouble for Obama later in the year.

Although Sheila Bair, the head of the FDIC, had no regulatory responsibility for saving Bear, she shared Summers's opinion about that bailout. She believed Bear "was one of the weaker firms that had fed on the subprime mortgage craze in the extreme. Why didn't the NY Fed just let it go down?"[19]

Bair thought "the Bear Stearns bailout was dealing with a symptom, not the cause, and it exacerbated the problem by setting up the expectation of further government intervention. Banks then decided, if the government is going to help me if I'm overleveraged, why do I need to worry about this? So the banks didn't raise new capital or pursue strategic partnerships when they could."[20]

18. Ben Bernanke, *The Courage to Act: A Memoir of a Crisis and Its Aftermath* (New York: W.W. Norton & Company, 2015).

19. Sheila Bair, *Bull by the Horns: Fighting to Save Main Street from Wall Street and Wall Street from Itself* (New York: Simon & Schuster, 2012), 74–75.

20. Sheila Bair, interview with author. Banks do not like to raise new capital because that means selling their stock. That selling makes their stock prices go down. Existing shareholders and management with equity compensation prefer their stock price to rise.

Obama and other prominent politicians also criticized the bailout. No one seemed to like it.

In his memoir Ben Bernanke asserted that the "intervention with Bear gave the financial system and the economy a nearly six-month respite," which sadly was not "enough to…prevent panic from breaking out again in the fall."[21] The alleged "respite" healed nothing. By condemning the Bear bailout, Summers and Obama contributed to the Bush Administration's failure to forestall the financial crisis by discouraging Bernanke and Paulson from acting when Lehman presented a far more compelling case for bailout. The result would be that in September Summers and Obama felt compelled to join with the people they had criticized when it came to supporting the bailout of all the big banks on Wall Street.

The Government Prepared to Save the GSEs

By the end of the second quarter of the year, the Fed at last concluded that Fannie and Freddie were "functionally insolvent."[22] As Summers had warned, the GSEs could not survive the housing slump. Paulson pushed Congress to give him authority to save the GSEs. In July Congress passed the Housing and Economic Recovery Act (HERA). This remarkable legislation guaranteed that the GSEs' debts and other obligations would be paid by the taxpayer if necessary. Treasury could spend whatever was required to meet any shortfall. That provision later gave Obama almost unlimited authority to restructure the housing market.

In illustration of the potential magnitude of HERA authority, Paulson suggested to President Bush that Fannie and Freddie should help the banking sector get out of the bad loans that stemmed from the housing slump. Backed by government guarantees, the GSEs would buy at face value the mortgage-backed securities that had traded down during the housing price slump.[23] In this way, they would boost the banks' balance

---

21. Bernanke, *The Courage to Act*, 225.

22. Paulson, *On the Brink*, 171.

23. Alice Rivlin had a number of other ideas: "The government could channel federal money through local community groups that could buy properties in the foreclosure process and resell or lease them. Another was to create a new government corporation [with this mission]. Or Fannie

sheets while leaving homeowners with the same principal and interest to pay. Paulson despised the quasi-public nature of Fannie and Freddie, but he was willing to use them for this purpose.

This fantastical idea depended on a public explanation of the problem that needed solving. In the absence of that, his proposal petered out. It might have prevented the financial crisis. However, as Paulson explained in an interview[24] in 2018, during the summer of 2008 he decided not to inform Congress about the precarious condition of the big banks' assets and their excessive liabilities.

Under HERA, a new regulator would be responsible for scrutinizing the practices of the GSEs. The head of the Office of Federal Housing Enterprise Oversight (OFHEO) could authorize Treasury to seize Fannie and Freddie. To run OFHEO President Bush elevated James Lockhart from running a smaller agency that had played in this space. Lockhart and Bush were friends at Andover and Yale, and in Delta Kappa Epsilon. Both went on to Harvard Business School. I suspect in college I heard George W. Bush describe him as a "good man." I recall the characterization from lunchtime conversations. I thought that meant a booster, a Babbit. Upbeat Lockhart stayed true to this type. He echoed Paulson's general optimism about the direction of the housing market, assuring television audiences that the GSEs were well managed.

Pursuant to HERA, the Treasury launched a program to help homeowners who were underwater on their mortgages. It would spend up to $300 billion to guarantee 30-year fixed-rate mortgages, provided that lenders wrote down the mortgages to 90 percent of the appraised value of the house in question. In other words, the lenders had to take a haircut. They would lose some of the value of their loans in order to get the government to guarantee payment on any defaulted mortgage up to 90 percent of the appraised value.

---

and Freddie could carry out that mission, or give investors government bonds in exchange for whole mortgage pools." Alice Rivlin, interview with author.

24. Timothy Geithner, Ben Bernanke, and Henry Paulson. "Panic, Fear, and Regret," interview by Kai Ryssdal, *Marketplace*, APM, March 13, 2018, https://features.marketplace.org/bernanke-paulson-geithner/.

By the middle of 2008, appraised values were often far below the face amount of their mortgages. If lenders did appraisals, observers would recognize that the lenders' overall portfolio of assets was worth much less than widely thought. That could lead to collapse in the equity value of the mortgage holders, or even runs on the firms. Treasury's proposal was not generous enough to entice mortgage lenders into taking the risk of participation. It had little impact.[25]

A different, far bigger problem emerged. In a few months it would define Obama's legacy. During the long rise in housing prices, big Wall Street firms invented strange new securities based on housing values. They divided mortgages into different pieces, bundled these "tranches," and sold them to investors. In addition, they sold securities that constituted bets on the ability of borrowers to pay on their mortgages. As the housing-based recession deepened, these lines of business evaporated, leaving sellers with bad inventory and buyers with regrettable purchases. Fear that a bank deep into exotic housing-based trading might lack money to pay debts (illiquidity), or have more liabilities than assets (insolvency), could spark a run. The really big banks and the investment banks had no HERA or FDIC to save them, but the Fed and the Treasury might choose to help them as they had done with Bear. Or they might not, for fear of the backlash to the Bear deal or out of adherence to the Bair philosophy of punishing bad judgment. (History creates uncanny homonyms.)

Lehman Became Central Concern

In the summer of 2008, Paulson knew "Lehman was in a precarious position."[26] He told a colleague, "If they fail, we are all in deep trouble." He meant that a run on that bank could lead to runs on the other big banks outside the FDIC system. A cascade of such runs would freeze all finance. Businesses could not borrow. They would stop spending,

---

25. As a lagniappe for some borrowers, in August the administration launched a program called F.H.A. Secure. It aimed at helping less than 100,000 homeowners refinance in order to avoid foreclosure. It also had no measurable effect.
26. Paulson, *On the Brink*, 130.

fire employees, close factories. Many would go bankrupt. The economy would shrivel. Then only the government could restart the capitalist engine. It can buy and loan, like an active agent in the economy. Or it can resuscitate the finance sector so that it will loan again. To do that, government must buy stock in banks, guarantee payment of their debts, loan them money, or take all three of these measures.

The Fed and Treasury officials in the Bush Administration believed that risk-taking lenders should suffer the consequences of their bad judgment. This principle applied to businesses and homeowners. Big banks were different. In their well-paid way, they resembled government itself. For the benefit of everyone, they must always survive. They could never go out of business. They could not even be punished for imprudence because limiting their pursuit of profit in any way meant curtailing economic growth.

Neither Republicans nor Democrats liked bailouts. To the right, government intervention in the economy was tantamount to socialism. To the left, government bailouts of big banks was socialism for the rich. The two sides agreed, however, on disliking the alternative chosen by Herbert Hoover's Treasury secretary, Andrew Mellon—let the economy shrink, and watch millions go hungry. To avoid taking responsibility for the hard choice that would result from Lehman's collapse, all summer Paulson worked the phones, looking for a bank that would buy Lehman.

Paulson would not have needed to contrive that acquisition if the government had "the ability to wind down a failing nonbank"—like Lehman—"outside of bankruptcy." That required new legislation—a HERA for banks. Although he did not explain fully his fears that government might need to save Wall Street, he "raised the issue publicly for the first time at a speech in Washington in June." Former Fed chair Alan Greenspan was more forthright: he urged the administration to "get authority to wind Lehman down, in case of failure."[27] Paulson said that leading Democratic congressman Barney Frank was "supportive but cautioned us against trying to push legislation that was so complex substantively and politically."

---

27. Ibid., 144.

Frank, chair of the relevant House committee and member of the Democratic leadership in Congress, wanted Paulson to preserve Wall Street from bank runs even by acting without clear legal authority if necessary. Paulson admitted that Frank "encouraged the Fed and Treasury to interpret our existing powers broadly to protect the system." Frank added, "If you do so, I'm not going to raise legal issues."[28] Frank meant that the Treasury and Fed should loan as needed to "troubled" firms whose collapse would precipitate a financial crisis without seeking new legislation.

Everyone in government should understand that the leaders of the majority party in Congress and the president usually want the heads of departments and agencies to do what's necessary to keep their segments of the system from crashing. In a crisis, the executive branch officers are supposed to adopt an elastic interpretation of their legal authority. This hard, fast, and unwritten rule applied to issues like Katrina, the BP oil rig explosion, and the looming collapse of Lehman.

The explanation may lie in Paulson's failure to attract congressional support for his preferred bailout. In a memo called "Break the Glass," Neel Kashkari and Phillip Swagel, key staffers to Treasury Secretary Paulson, discussed "the use of asset auctions to remove mortgage-related assets from bank balance sheets."[29] In other words, Paulson would use public money to buy assets of dubious value in an auction. Some of Treasury's hired experts cut their teeth on the spectrum auctions I conducted as FCC chairman in the 1990s. I could have told Paulson that auctions can be designed well or poorly, but never simply or easily. Buying troubled assets in auction, for example, required a decision about purpose. The buyer could aim to pay a lot for the most dubious securities held by the shakiest firms, or pay as little as possible for the best assets sold by the strongest firms. These two nearly opposite goals required a strategic choice about auction design. Paulson proved unable to respond to congressional questions about his purpose. His auction plan went nowhere.

28. Ibid., 139.
29. Philip Mirowski, *Never Let a Serious Crisis Go to Waste: How Neoliberalism Survived the Financial Meltdown* (London: Verso, 2014), 190.

By pushing his asset purchase plan because of its use of markets, rather than government, to set prices, Paulson delayed and jeopardized a far more sensible plan, namely, equity purchase. He used up time that should have been devoted to striking a bargain in which the Wall Street beneficiaries would have had to give up something for the common good. They might have shared with the public some of the value from their expected stock price increase, agreed to tax financial transactions, limited their future compensation, or at least loaned into public infrastructure platforms at favorable terms. Paulson did not seek any way in which Wall Street might help the economy or the public, other than by making more profits. Instead, he buffaloed the Democrats into capitulating to the needs of the big banks.[30]

Paulson decided that "with the congressional recess on the way and presidential elections in November" he could not "get what we needed passed." He also decided that "aggressively making the case for new authorities might itself precipitate Lehman's failure."[31] His lack of "aggression" on the topic inevitably led him to depend on, and pass the buck to, Barack Obama. That was probably his intent from the summer on.

In his memoir, Bernanke conceded that Congress gave the Fed broad 13(3) authority in 1932 so that the central bank could compensate for the "evaporation of credit that followed the collapse of thousands of banks in the early 1930s."[32] Using that would have followed Frank's advice to do what was necessary, even if in a gray area of legal authority. But for six decades the Fed and others had persuaded itself not to make such loans, because they would protect "nonbank firms from the consequences of the risks they took." The other reason was that Fed chairmen doubted they would preserve the independence of their agency from congressional interference if they bailed out too many banks with too much money. Bernanke too was counting on the next president to bear the responsibility for action.

As July turned into August and August into September, Paulson continued to phone the CEOs of big banks in the United States and Europe

---

30. See ibid., 302–313.
31. Paulson, *On the Brink*, 139.
32. Bernanke, *The Courage to Act*, 205.

in search of buyers for Lehman. Despite Frank's encouragement, he offered no public money to the buyers or the seller. He "repeatedly told" the Lehman CEO that the "government had no legal authority to inject capital in an investment bank."[33] Without a government incentive, no buyer emerged. For its part, Lehman did not want to engage in a fire sale.

As Labor Day approached, Paulson "put a team together to deal with" a Lehman bankruptcy. He claimed later that he knew it would be "disastrous" and would "trigger a global shock."[34] Like a kaiser, king, or czar in August 1914, he marched toward an inevitable disaster, unwilling to choose an alternative.

33. Paulson, *On the Brink*, 173.
34. Ibid., 178.

3

As 2008 Unfolded,
Obama Changed His Team and Themes

There's battle lines being drawn
Nobody's right if everybody's wrong
— Buffalo Springfield, "For What It's Worth,"
lyrics by Stephen A. Stills

In his campaign, Obama adopted the economic analysis expounded by University of Chicago economist Austan Goolsbee: "The expansion of the 2000s was way heavy on consumer spending and way heavy on residential construction, but way light on export growth, way light on business investment." This "unbalanced growth was not sustainable." In the Bush administration, Goolsbee observed, the United States experienced the "first boom we've ever had when median family income fell $2,000 during expansion. The canonical experience in most previous decades had been growth with substantially rising inequality. That took the form of the top going way up, the bottom going way down, and the middle two-thirds of the country doing about as well as the economy is doing. The 2000s then became the first expansion when the broad middle, like the bottom, was also not doing well."[1]

---

1. Austan Goolsbee, interview with author.

To Goolsbee, the problem lay in the structure of the economy: too many people could find only dead-end jobs providing stagnant or faltering wages. Many lacked the skills for the well-paid jobs of the present and future. As president, Obama should change the prospects of the middle class. To that end, government needed new strategic objectives. Government should reform what and how teachers taught. People should save in the stock market, not through equity in their homes. Healthcare should be affordable and adequate, so that workers could move to the best jobs without losing coverage.

Major structural problems also included zero savings, growth fueled by debt, a housing bubble, and skimpy financial regulation. If elected, Obama would reform the tax code, government spending, and regulation to change the underpinning of the economy. Examples included longer unemployment payments,[2] payroll tax cuts, investments in science, technology, and education, and the reregulation of financial markets.

Events overtook Obama's explication of this strategic vision. On March 27, 2008, at the Cooper Union in New York, Obama said the recession had already started. He decried imminent foreclosures, students' inability to get loans for tuition, and states' lack of capability to borrow for infrastructure projects. He said, "Most urgently, we have to confront the housing crisis." He proposed to help homeowners refinance loans, and change bankruptcy law to permit "cram down," a term describing mortgage reduction. Forecasting new spending, Obama called for government to "put Americans to work" in green jobs and in "rebuilding our nation's infrastructure." He said that government should spend money on schools, teachers, lowering college tuition, broadband, and scientific research.

Obama here reached what proved to be his high-water mark of articulating a liberal plan for stimulus. In December 2008 his neoliberal

---

2. Research later showed that extending unemployment insurance did not cause meaningful increases in unemployment. Christopher Boon, Arindrajit Dube, Lucas Goodman, and Ethan Kaplan, "Unemployment Insurance and Employment during the Great Recession," *Vox*, January 8, 2017, https://voxeu.org/article/unemployment-insurance-and-employment-during-great-recession.

advisers proposed spending on only some of these objectives, and not enough on any to change the structure or function of the economy.

By June Obama won the nomination. On June 26, 2008, he stood with Clinton at the Mayflower Hotel in Washington, D.C., and appealed to hundreds of her fund-raisers for reconciliation. To cement the alliance with Clinton, Obama turned the transition planning over to John Podesta, Bill Clinton's chief of staff in the latter part of that presidency.

On the way to Logan airport with Podesta, after a meeting with Al Gore at the Kennedy School to prepare the post-election Democratic plan to stop climate change, I suggested that Hillary should be Obama's secretary of state. Podesta often speaks in clipped phrases, as if reading bullet points from a memorandum on the back of his forehead. In that taxi he simply said, "Obama only needs to ask." I sent that message to Obama. Presumably others also assured him that she was wiling. Presidents, like young men with engagement rings in hand, do not like to propose unless they can count on a positive reception. Eventually Obama offered, and she accepted.

By selecting Joe Biden as vice president, Obama gave Hillary still another gift: she would succeed him as the next Democratic presidential nominee. Typically the vice president is the presumptive successor. But Biden was older than Hillary Clinton, and far less famous. In 2008 Obama signaled that in 2016 she could combine Obama's multiethnic coalition with the establishment wing of the Democratic Party and be the Democratic nominee. It would be her turn at last. By contrast, if Obama had selected as vice president another female, or a Hispanic, or anyone young, that person would have been Hillary's natural opponent. As Obama arranged matters, any opponent for her could come only from outside the mainstream—like socialist Bernie Sanders.

The incoming Clinton advisers denied the existing campaign advisers leadership roles in the transition team. Clintonites also infiltrated the campaign, importing their neoliberal axioms. When Obama added Clinton adviser Jason Furman to his campaign team on June 27, Reuters reported: "'One of the important lessons he's drawn from Bob Rubin is the importance of fiscal discipline,' Furman said, adding that Obama agrees with 'a key pillar of "Rubinomics"—the idea that lower deficits can help bring down long-term interest rates, which in turn is favorable to economic growth.'"[3] People are policy. By adopting the Clinton advisers, Obama found himself expressing at their urging the same views that he found wanting in that dinner in the Jefferson Hotel two and a half years earlier. However, in that time he had not fleshed out a sufficiently robust alternative approach to economic policy. Facing the intensity of the general election campaign, he needed unity within the Democratic Party. Between the convention and the election, no one had the leisure to ponder the inadequacies of neoliberalism's policy prescriptions as applied to the rapidly changing economic and political situation.

Summer 2008: Summers Began to Advise Obama

Summers first met Obama standing in line outside Boston's Fleet Center during the 2004 Democratic Convention. Obama was smoking a cigarette, gathering himself just then for the great, hopeful, and inaccurate speech that launched his rocket ship ride to political glory: "There's not a liberal America and a conservative America, there's the United States of America." Summers did not connect with Obama again until the summer of 2008, when Jason Furman included him in weekly conference calls advising the candidate about the rapidly deteriorating economic situation. Other participants included former Fed Chairman Paul Volcker, the "sage of Omaha" Warren Buffett, and New York investors Robert Wolf and Mark Gallogly.

Gallogly said, "Starting in July, a small group of us would get on the phone with Senator Obama and talk about what was going on in the economy and why. We'd speak every couple of weeks or a little less frequently. The calls lasted 30 to 45 minutes. Over time, Larry Summers became the most important outside adviser's voice on the phone call."[4]

---

3. Caren Bohan, "Obama Seeks to Counter Anti-business Image," *Reuters*, June 27, 2008, https://www.reuters.com/article/us-usa-politics-obama-economy/obama-seeks-to-counter-anti-business-image-idUSN2732916620080627.
4. Mark Gallogly, interview with author.

As Summers put it, "It became a little bit of a habit of having me frame the issues at the beginning of the call."[5] As the economy grew more parlous, the prospect of returning to power must have become increasingly irresistible to Summers. Every expert in every domain relishes the president's adoption of their opinions.

Summers had unmatched ability to expound on the machinery of the macroeconomy. Explaining is power, especially when time is short. Didactic Summers's authoritative baritone and robust vocabulary commanded attention. He seemed to understand money. His oracular statements had the ring of truth. He also showed deference to the candidate. All successful advisers—those who are invited back—know how to make the advisee feel good.

Obama too impressed in these calls. Summers saw that a very bright student had enrolled in his course. Gallogly observed, "Obama listened carefully. He could quickly prioritize and summarize complex ideas and provide them back to us as succinct points. People on the call were taken by that. Professionals who had been in finance for over 30 years didn't know what was going on in the economy. Obama was listening, probing, asking questions, and getting very specific. I think we all had a sense, 'this guy is on his game.'"[6]

Advisers ruthlessly judge the candidate they advise. They want to know if they have picked a winner. In my experience, Al Gore and Bill Clinton were Obama's equals in learning quickly, although they interrupted more often. In his briefings Gore introduced topics to the group drawn from his own late-night reading. Clinton liked to try out different messages. Obama specialized in restating what he had been told, crisply and sonorously. He kept his own views in reserve.

Distance came naturally to Obama. He was an outsider by birth and upbringing. He chose his persona quite consciously. He became who he thought he should be. Like Gore, he learned to keep his vulnerable self backstage. Like George W. Bush and unlike Bill Clinton, he expected to be treated with respect. More than any politician I have known, he kept

---

5. Summers, interview with author.
6. Gallogly, interview with author.

his cool. He was cocky, but many liked that touch of edginess. Obama showed that he had a destiny.

September: Stimulus Took Shape

The worsening performance of the general economy caused advisers to contemplate bigger measures than had been previously discussed. John Podesta organized a group to prepare a substantial stimulus spending plan. In September he sent Josh Steiner, a New York investor and friend of Tim Geithner, to Chicago to meet with Bill Daley, brother and son of famous Chicago mayors. They added quiet, brilliant Jack Lew, who would become one of Obama's treasury secretaries, to compose the nucleus of a small economic policy planning team. All had served in the Clinton administration.

Mike Froman loosely tied the Clinton and Obama camps together in the transition team. He had been Rubin's chief of staff in Treasury and was Obama's law school classmate. Everyone regarded Summers as first among equals in the group. Jared Bernstein agreed. "If you think about high-prestige Democratic economists who've been through global economic crises, there's Summers and maybe a couple of others and I'm not even sure who else would fit in that circle."[7]

None of these advisers were "freshwater economists" who believed a stimulus would only borrow growth from the future, and would not produce a bigger economy in the long run. None held the Austrian school view that government could not and should not battle the inevitable cycles of investment, housing values, and growth. In this crisis they sided with Keynes: spend money.

However, they had more experience with the theory of stimulus than with its practice. They had spent years arguing against spending public money. Many a creative policy died in the meeting rooms of the Clinton administration on the grounds that it would increase the deficit or belonged in the private sector. In 1993, for example, the administration's

---

7. Jared Bernstein, interview with author.

economic advisers had mildly favored a modest stimulus, but let a Democratic Congress kill it, while they demanded and got a big tax increase later in the year.

In his 2003 memoir Rubin conceded the political imperfections of this policy: "The economic benefits were not felt on a sustained basis by the time of the 1994 midterm election, and had we listened more to the concerns of the political advisers, we might have focused better on framing our deficit reduction message in a more politically effective way."[8] The same pattern presented an even bigger risk for Obama in 2009 and 2010. A "politically effective" recovery meant much lower unemployment before the mid-term elections in November 2010.

Summers and his profession had a model to explain when to spend and when to stop spending, when to cut taxes and when to tax. It was IS-LM, also known as Hicks-Hansen. This showed two intersecting lines on a graph drawn by the variables of interest rates and savings, liquidity and money. It shows the interaction of the market for goods

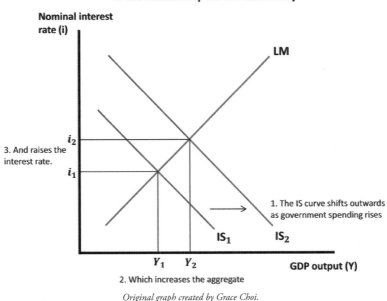

IS-LM Model: Impact of Fiscal Policy

Original graph created by Grace Choi.

8. Robert Edward Rubin and Jacob Weisberg, *In an Uncertain World: Tough Choices from Wall Street to Washington* (New York: Random House Trade Paperbacks, 2004), 123.

(IS or "investment savings") with the market for money (LM or "liquidity-preference, money supply"). Like all economic models, it represented mathematically certain assumptions about behavior.

The IS line on the IS-LM model graph assumes that when people save more, they buy less. Firms produce less, the economy shrinks. As a result, people then have less money. Unless something changes they save still more and the economy shrinks faster. Doubt and fear about the future cause this worsening cycle to spin across the entire economy. *I may be fired, I might not be able to make the payments on my house, so I'd better put my money under the floorboards instead of buying things, even though if everyone does this the odds that I will be fired go way up.*

The LM line on the graph reflects the assumption that a low interest rate will lead to increased borrowing. The borrowers will invest. The economy will grow.

The IS and LM lines cross on a chart at a point that reveals simultaneously the interest rate and the GDP. In bad times, they cross down low and to the left. Down there, even low interest rates—also known as "easy money"—can correlate with a disappointingly small GDP. The lines also can cross up toward the right, where even at higher interest rates the GDP is bigger.

The stimulus was supposed to move the intersection from $i1$ to $i2$, toward a bigger GDP and therefore to full employment. For political and humanitarian reasons, the direction of movement had to be clear by early 2010.

In 2011 Paul Krugman explained that the IS-LM model had predicted correctly in 2008 and '09 that interest rates would stay low and that even if the monetary base tripled inflation would not spike. That meant Obama's advisers could and should install a huge stimulus without worrying that deficit spending would cause inflation. In 2012 Berkeley economist Brad DeLong and Larry Summers proved mathematically that the more the government spent in 2009 the more tax revenues would increase.[9] Summers did not apprehend or trust these conclusions

9. J. Bradford DeLong and Lawrence H. Summers. "Fiscal Policy in a Depressed Economy." Brookings Papers on Economic Activity, Spring 2012, https://www.brookings.edu/bpea-articles/

in 2008. Neither he nor the other economists used this thinking in calculating the size of the stimulus.

Most of Obama's advisers believed that the recession resembled the experience of 1991 and '92. The recovery would probably be V-shaped. That meant the GDP would drop sharply, then rise rapidly. To them, the big risk was that excessive deficit spending might cause the private sector to demand higher interest rates out of fear of inflation. Therefore, the new administration should quickly inject a stimulus, but then cut back spending. In fact, from 2008 until 2016, the GDP drew more of an L than a V—the recovery was protracted and lackluster. The Clintonites proceeded on the wrong assumption.

Framing policy principally as a macroeconomic problem was itself a dubious choice. By asking for and following the views of the neoliberal economists, Obama adopted not only their assumptions about the economy's behavior, but also their moral code. All advice—whether from lawyers, consultants, economists, or doctors—comes from a world view. The advisers' code of right or wrong limits the range of options they can present. Their behavioral assumptions constrain their vision of the relationship between the leader and the followers, the president and the people. The IS-LM model does not contain a variable for inspiration, hope, or change.

Advisers from other disciplines would have suggested a different staging ground for Obama. If Michael Oakeshott had been on the conference calls with Obama, that philosopher might have said that the practical questions around resuscitating the economy had no correct answers.[10] He would have labeled as "rationalism" the fallacious belief that formulas would tell Obama what policies to adopt.[11] That caution might have led Obama to bolder action, and to describe the economic crisis as a time for resetting the country's priorities. The changes in the economy outlined

fiscal-policy-in-a-depressed-economy/.

10. In this connection, note "matters of the spirit are widely and instantly grasped. Except of course by people who are in heavily fortified positions, mental opponents trained to resist what everyone is born knowing." Saul Bellow, *Humboldt's Gift* (New York: Viking Press, 1975), 91.

11. The blank slate of the stimulus created in theological and political terms an opportunity to immanentize the eschaton. You can look it up.

at Knox College could have shaped the economic recovery program. The new president could have given his tax and spending policies a moral grounding.

The hyper-rationalists on Obama's advisory team interpreted the country's situation as their career-long thinking conditioned them. Through their IS-LM glasses they saw line graphs, the runes of our age, that guaranteed outcomes. These advisers thought a thousand CEOs and investors needed confidence that recovery was just around the corner. The economists would speak from authority, imparting to business the elusive, essential belief that they could spend money to make money. To this end, the advisers persuaded Obama to make the largest political commitment to rationalism in the history of the United States.

For the economists, the task of inspiring collective action toward a common goal belonged to others. Obama's "Yes We Can" was derived from the United Farm Workers' "Si se puede." It had a distinguished legacy in building a different sort of confidence—a working-class conviction in the American Dream. That political philosophy lacked expression in the policies chosen in the December 16 meeting.

4

Lehman Changed Everything

Capt. Benjamin Willard:
Part of me was afraid of what I would find and what I would do
when I got there. I knew the risks, or imagined I knew.

— *Apocalypse Now*

On September 4, 2008, Treasury Secretary Paulson told President Bush that the Treasury should "seize control" of Fannie Mae and Freddie Mac, "fire their bosses," and fund each company with $100 billion in cash to stop an earthquake in the housing market from destroying the financial sector and bringing economic activity to a halt.[1] With Bush's consent, on September 7, less than six weeks after Treasury had obtained the authority from Congress to act, Paulson asked regulator James Lockhart to seize Fannie and Freddie.

Bush told Paulson that "we have to make it clear that what we are doing now is transitory, because otherwise it looks like nationalization."[2] That transition never happened. Paulson had no desire to change the business models of the GSEs or the big banks. He would just tell "everybody" that the government guaranteed the GSEs debts "to make sure

---

1. Paulson, *On the Brink*, 3.
2. Ibid., 5.

there's mortgage finance available in this country"[3] and to make sure that doubt about the GSEs did not spark a run on the big banks.[4]

In July 2017, Jerome Powell, made the Fed chairman in 2018, said, "the great unfinished business of post-financial crisis reform" was "fundamental reform of our system of housing finance." Initially unwilling, then unable, to change that "system," the Obama administration never found a way to use finance to improve housing conditions in general, such as by installing rooftop solar panels or more efficient heating and cooling.[5] Moreover, even when controlling the GSEs, the government did not stop them from disproportionally favoring upper income households in the purchase of ever larger houses on more expensive plots of land, rather than helping middle and low income families to buy their own homes. Notwithstanding the government support of home finance, in the 21st century the percentage of families owning a home has oscillated between 63 percent and 69 percent, lower than it was in the late 1960s and much lower than in many European countries.

Paulson persuaded Herb Allison to become Fannie Mae's new CEO. Of his first day at Fannie May on September 8, Allison said, "When I arrived Monday morning, I found the organization in disarray because the employees, including the senior management, had only found out about this change in their legal status the previous Friday night. They had lost all of their savings in Fannie Mae stock. Some were facing negative net worth because they had to pay taxes on the receipt of stock that was valued at the time of the grant and the stock was now next to worthless. So they were in pretty desperate financial straits. They felt betrayed by James Lockhart who had indicated six weeks earlier that their financial situation was acceptable.

"We had to orient the organization toward being conservatively managed, and secondly, toward keeping people in their homes, trying to maintain stable markets in mortgage-backed securities. Then we had to

---

3. Ibid.
4. Ibid., 169.
5. Jerome H. Powell, "The Case for Housing Finance Reform," speech at American Enterprise Institute, Washington, D.C., July 6, 2017.

explore ways of trying to modify mortgages if possible [by reducing the amount owed and lowering the interest rates] so that people could stay in their houses."[6] Allison quickly put Fannie in reasonable operating shape. Freddie too stayed in business. If the government took over an institution, it could keep it operating. The government was not completely incapable with the right people in charge.

The next question was whether Wall Street would suffer the bank runs that had caused the government to nationalize the GSEs. At the beginning of 2008, five firms ruled the American investment banking business: Goldman, Morgan, Merrill, Lehman, and Bear. All had loans and mortgage-backed securities on their balance sheets that vastly exceeded the value of their shares at ratios ranging as high as 30 times.

But Paulson had done all the "nationalization" he could bring himself to do.

On September 11, Paulson reiterated that he would provide no public money for Lehman. Bernanke did not object.

Paulson claimed later that he and Geithner were bluffing. He said, "We both knew that if a Bear Stearns–style rescue was the only option, we would take it."[7] The bluff worked so well that the potential buyers left the poker table, leaving Lehman alone, certain to lose when its bet was called.

Paulson had put himself, and the entire economy, in a corner. He had not sought legal authority in the summer to buy some or all of Lehman, or to guarantee its debts. He had effectively forbidden Bernanke to save Lehman. Although Frank had told him to obtain and act on a broad "interpretation" of his authority, he had not sought the necessarily expansive legal advice from his own department.[8]

Tim Geithner greatly feared the aftermath of Lehman's collapse. The three-month LIBOR-OIS interest rate spread, which measures "the combination of a liquidity premium and compensation for counterparty

---

6. Herb Allison, interview with author.

7. Paulson, *On the Brink*, 181.

8. Practicing lawyers know that clients generally can get the legal advice they want, and sometimes the advice they need.

risk," is a barometer of nervousness in the financial industry.[9] It spiked in July 2007 and stayed high until September 2009, at which point it multiplied by a factor of seven, reaching levels no one had ever seen. By January 2009 it was down to the July 2007 level but did not return to normal until January 2010. This marked the three-year period of anxiety for Tim Geithner.

Bernanke too claimed later that he understood "forcing" Lehman into bankruptcy "could unleash financial chaos."[10] Lehman was 50 percent bigger than Bear. Its failure would bring "horrific consequences." Nevertheless, Bernanke did not "press" Paulson on the purposely leaked statements that he had "ruled out putting government money into Lehman."[11]

Geithner believed "there was no chance a crisis this huge would be solved without putting more public money at risk."[12] In Geithner's view, Paulson was making a monumental miscalculation: "Whatever the merits of no-public-money as a bargaining position, I didn't think it made sense as actual public policy."[13] Geithner hoped Paulson would abandon the bluff, but, "by Thursday night, when Hank forcefully repeated his no-public-money stance…I began to worry that he actually meant it. He declared that he didn't want to be known as 'Mr. Bailout.'"[14]

Geithner, who was not a lawyer, did not help the situation by concluding that the Fed lacked "legal authority to guarantee Lehman's trading liabilities…even…under 13(3)."[15] Perhaps more germane, Geithner "did not believe we could have rescued Lehman…without damaging our ability to deal credibly and effectively with the terrible challenges still ahead of us."[16]

9. Stephen G. Cecchetti and Kermit L. Schoenholtz, "Looking Back: The Financial Crisis Began 10 Years Ago This Week," Money, Banking and Financial Markets, August 7, 2017, https://www.moneyandbanking.com/commentary/2017/8/6/looking-back-the-financial-crisis-began-10-years-ago-this-week.

10. Bernanke, *The Courage to Act*, 252.

11. Ibid.

12. Geithner, *Stress Test*, 175.

13. Ibid., 178.

14. Ibid., 179.

15. Ibid., 186.

16. Ibid., 207.

Geithner meant that if Treasury and the Fed saved Lehman, Congress would not appropriate the bailout money that he wanted to invest in banks and forestall runs. He also wanted Congress to pass a law making something like the FDIC's resolution authority apply to the biggest firms. Lehman had to go under so that Treasury could get the "legislative authority to try to repair the entire system."[17]

Commanding federal economic policy in the absence of an engaged president, Paulson was the most powerful actor in the economy. As such he focused on restoring the financial sector rather than recovery of the real economy. He did not conceive of his job as ending the recession, or even keeping it from deepening. He successfully transmitted to Obama's advisers this focus on Wall Street rather than Main Street.

Paulson's primacy in setting policy was not set in statutory stone. Indeed, Bernanke conceded that the Fed, not the Treasury, had the responsibility to decide whether to provide public money to facilitate some sort of bailout of Lehman. Bernanke admitted that the Fed "was created to do what must be done—what others cannot or will not do," especially when the decisions were "politically unpopular" but were "for the long-run benefit of the country."[18] Obviously, Bernanke did not act on that principle in letting Lehman go into bankruptcy. Later he insisted that he lacked legal authority to save Lehman.

Laurence Ball of Johns Hopkins University has studied the record evidence in detail and concluded that Bernanke was wrong: "Lehman only needed the kind of well-secured liquidity support that the Fed provided liberally to other financial institutions" and "a perceived lack of authority was not the reason for the Fed's inaction." Instead, the Fed did not rescue Lehman because "the primary decision maker was Treasury Secretary Henry Paulson, even though he had no legal authority over the Fed's lending decisions." Paulson was not only "influenced by the strong political opposition to financial rescuers" but also he and Bernanke "did

17. Ibid., 208.
18. Bernanke, *The Courage to Act*, xiii.

not fully anticipate the severe damage to the financial system that Lehman's collapse" would cause.[19]

If it deemed a firm solvent, the Fed could loan unlimited amounts. No one could have challenged a Fed decision that Lehman was solvent (although a bailout loan would have drawn loud, bipartisan criticism, especially in the heat of the election campaign). Similarly, under HERA Treasury could provide unlimited funds to the GSEs which in turn could have guaranteed any housing-related debt. With respect to almost all commercial banks, the FDIC had ample money to handle imminent bankruptcies while keeping the financial system in operation.

Rather than using these authorities to forestall the crisis, Paulson wanted the congressional imprimatur on bailouts. He worried that the commercial markets would gain confidence in the big banks only if Congress appropriated hundreds of billions of dollars for public investment in these banks. He feared that full, truthful disclosure of the perilous condition of the big banks' assets would precipitate a financial crisis, and he believed a crisis would lead to the congressional action he wanted.

For Bernanke, the explanation for precipitating the crisis probably lay in the independence of the Fed. That fundamentally secretive, non-democratic agency had a century of experience in negotiating compromises with pressuring presidents, yammering legislators, and refractory banks.[20] In the summer of 2008, however, Bernanke could not find a way to align all the stakeholders behind a Fed-driven recapitalization of Wall Street. Paulson and Geithner wanted a legislative bailout. Bernanke concluded that "even if it had somehow been possible for the Fed on its own to save Lehman...we would not have had either the capacity or the political support to undertake any future financial rescues."[21] Treasury cared most about preserving Wall Street, the Fed about independence, Geithner about getting billions for future bailouts. Toward their separate ends, they collaborated on letting the Lehman bankruptcy cause the

---

19. Laurence M. Ball, *The Fed and Lehman Brothers: Setting the Record Straight on a Financial Disaster*, (Cambridge, UK: Cambridge University Press, 2018), 13, 225.
20. Bernanke, *The Courage to Act*, 290.
21. Ibid.

crisis that they used to arm-twist Congress into passing the legislation they wanted.

For Republicans Paulson and Bernanke, this move had the added advantage of putting the responsibility for coping with the crisis in the hands of politicians in the Democratic party.[22] A crisis would produce bipartisan action. Over the last weekend Paulson called his wife and said Lehman would go bankrupt. He asked her, "What if the system collapses? Everybody is looking to me, and I don't have the answer. I am really scared." She told him his job was to "reflect God, Infinite Mind, and [he] can rely on Him."[23] This comfort obscured the fact that Paulson actually relied on Barack Obama.

22. Geithner, *Stress Test*, 175.
23. Paulson, *On the Brink*, 215.

5

Paulson Snared Obama

"Will you walk into my parlour?" said the Spider to the Fly.
— Mary Howitt, "The Spider and the Fly"

On Sunday night, September 14, Hank Paulson instructed SEC Chairman Chris Cox to call Lehman's board of directors and tell them to file for bankruptcy. On Monday, September 15, Lehman declared bankruptcy. Stock markets dropped more than 4 percent on the day.

On Tuesday AIG, the huge insurance company, could not pay its debts.[1] Fed Chairman Bernanke did not then repeat his Lehman inaction. Perhaps he had done enough to build the case for congressional action. Or perhaps the scale of the market reaction to Lehman's collapse outstripped his expectation. In either case, the Fed immediately loaned AIG $85 billion in return for nearly 80 percent of its stock, thus out-and-out "nationalizing" it. That did not stop other bank runs from commencing.

Geithner said, "By Thursday morning, September 18, panic was engulfing the system."[2] To him, "it looked like the system was going to collapse, taking down the strong firms along with the weak. We had just suffered a financial shock worse than the one that had led to the Great

1. Kimberly Amadeo, "AIG Bailout, Cost, Timeline, Bonuses, Causes Effects," *The Balance*, updated May 9, 2018, https://www.thebalance.com/aig-bailout-cost-timeline-bonuses-causes-effects-3305693.
2. Geithner, *Stress Test*, 198.

Depression."[3] He thought "we were looking at another global depression that would hurt billions of people."[4] Perhaps he underestimated the scale of the business chaos he had chosen not to prevent.

Bernanke and Paulson explained to Bush that they had not been able to save Lehman but lawfully could bail out AIG. Bernanke told Bush that "the Fed could lend to AIG to keep it afloat [because] the company had enough value to serve as collateral for the loan."[5] Bush did not question this hair-splitting legalism from two non-lawyers. Instead he told his appointees, "Someday you guys are going to have to tell me how we ended up with a system like this and what we need to do to fix it."[6] The right day for that explanation had come and gone many months earlier. Now the "fix" depended on whether Barack Obama would get Democrats to vote for the Wall Street bail-out.

Bernanke "had been telling Hank [Paulson] for months that ultimately, there would have to be a comprehensive legislative solution to the crisis, authorizing the government to take a lot more risk." After the Lehman bankruptcy "Hank now agreed it was time to seek emergency legislation…we couldn't keep doing late-night repairs with duct tape and comfort letters." [7]

Paulson Produced Three Pages

Paulson's staff pulled an all-nighter on Wednesday, September 17, in order to present something to Bush at 3:30 p.m. on Thursday, September 18, and to the congressional leadership at seven p.m. the same day. More all-nighters would have helped. Paulson's team generated only three pages. This was the Troubled Asset Relief Program (TARP). Paulson later admitted he made a "three-page political mistake." He confessed that he "ought to have sent up the three pages as bullet points, rather than as

3. Ibid., 199.
4. Ibid.
5. Bernanke, *The Courage to Act*, xi.
6. Paulson, *On the Brink*, 237.
7. Bernanke, *The Courage to Act*, 189.

draft legislation," and that he should have sent it up sooner than mid-night, while also explaining "the language more clearly."[8]

Short as it was, the bill empowered Paulson to restructure Wall Street firms as he might wish. Because the Democrats controlled both chambers, the treasury secretary was making their presidential nominee, Barack Obama, the champion of Wall Street. Paulson asked Congress to let him buy "at least $500 billion of bad assets" from troubled banks—the same amount of money as the annual government spending on defense.[9] Consistent with their collaboration, Bernanke affirmed to the congressional leadership that Paulson really needed the money to prop up all Wall Street, because "it is a matter of days before there is a meltdown in the global financial system."[10]

However, Bernanke thought the number—$500 billion—"was fairly arbitrary" and was "small" in comparison to the $11 trillion of residential mortgages.[11] On Friday, September 19, Paulson upped the number to $700 billion. He said that "wasn't just a political judgment." He believed that he would "need to buy only a small amount" of bad mortgages to "energize the markets," and that $700 billion was "enough to make a difference,"[12] probably by buying assets from big banks as he planned in the summer. However, the number itself, according to a Treasury spokes-woman, was "not based on any particular data point. We just wanted to choose a really large number."[13]

8. Paulson, *On the Brink*, 267–78.

9. The federal budget in a nutshell in the Obama years: Defense about $500 to $700 billion a year. Non-defense about the same. (In the Reagan years, defense was half again higher, but Clinton and then Obama increased non-defense toward rough parity.) Social Security, Medicaid, and Medicare run about four times defense, or almost two-thirds of the total federal spending. These so-called entitlements represent redistribution, taking from one group of Americans and paying to some of them but mostly to those who pay little in federal income tax. Interest on public debt is at a little more than $200 billion a year. TARP and the stimulus added together nearly doubled the total of non-defense and defense in fiscal year 2009, attributable politically to Obama, not Bush.

10. Paulson, *On the Brink*, 259.

11. Bernanke, *The Courage to Act*, 312.

12. Paulson, *On the Brink*, 266.

13. Brian Wingfield and Josh Zumbrun, "Bad News For The Bailout," *Forbes*, September 23, 2008, https://www.forbes.com/2008/09/23/bailout-paulson-congress-biz-beltway-cx_jz_bw_0923bailout.html.

Democrats assumed the banks needed the shocking amount because Paulson and Bernanke said they did. It was, however, such a pure guess that Paulson said he might need it all for the banks, and so could not add other laudable uses—such as keeping homeowners from foreclosure—to the authorizing language. As a further limitation on the government's flexibility in alleviating the aftermath of the financial crisis, in accordance with the political version of Newton's third law of motion (colloquially known as "you got yours, now I get mine"), many in Congress later decided that the government's Keynesian response to soaring unemployment should be the same size as the amount for recapitalizing banks.

Geithner "liked" the "sweeping grant of authority"[14] but did not think "it granted Treasury broad enough powers."[15] Paulson only wanted to buy assets, including loans that might not be paid back. Geithner wanted legislation authorizing Treasury to "inject capital directly into banks." In the opinion of Bernanke and Geithner, "That's how banking crises get solved."[16] However, Paulson believed that "putting public capital [directly] into financial institutions" was a "political nonstarter."[17] because it looked "socialistic." He thought "direct capital investment…rais[ed] the specter of nationalization…sounded un-American, and aid to the institutions that caused the crisis sounded corrupt."[18] Similar concerns would constrain the imagination of Obama's advisers concerning both TARP and the stimulus.

Paulson's post-Bear reluctance to mix government and private-sector money revealed his cultural conviction that government should not tell businessmen how to conduct their affairs. A big equity investor might have a board seat. At the minimum, it would have shares to vote. But if the government acted in that way, it could control the big banks. That was tantamount to socialism, perhaps even communism.

Paulson did not want government to make money on its investments in the banks. If the government bought stock in a firm, and other

14. Geithner, *Stress Test*, 209.
15. Ibid., 199.
16. Ibid., 209.
17. Paulson, *On the Brink*, 302.
18. Ibid., 224.

investors regained confidence in the firm, then the stock price would rise. The government could sell its stock at a profit. For Paulson that was bad (although when the GSEs generated profits for the next decade, Treasury contentedly accepted the revenue). Government should not take advantage of the temporary troubles of capitalists. If profits were to be made by investing in banks, then other capitalists should make them. An example was Warren Buffett's investment in Goldman Sachs at about the same time. He hit a three-bagger—he roughly tripled his money.[19] That was good capitalism. If government did the same thing, that was bad socialism.

Driven more by fear of bank runs, Geithner had moved past such "political" or "moral hazard" concerns.[20] He did the math: injecting capital would produce 20 times the stabilizing effect, because for every dollar of additional equity capital a bank could make 20 dollars in loans. Good loans were good assets on the balance sheet. That was the essence of fractional banking. By comparison, "asset purchases seemed like a way to burn through our cash without solving the problem."[21]

Chris Van Hollen, elected senator from Maryland in 2016 but a representative on Speaker Pelosi's leadership team in 2008, said the Democratic leadership's reaction to Paulson's three-page proposal was "you've got to be kidding." There was "no provision for trying to allow taxpayers to recoup their money." However, he admitted that "there was no big Democratic political strategy at that time. There was really a desire to just do what was right for the country. Knowing it was a hard vote, we also recognized that if we did not take that action, the economy would go down the tubes."[22]

Speaker Pelosi told Paulson there had to be money for Main Street as well as Wall Street. He responded, "This isn't the time for stimulus."[23]

19. See Patrick Morris, "Why Goldman Sachs Is One of the Biggest Warren Buffett Stocks," Motley Fool, November 18, 2014, https://www.fool.com/investing/general/2014/11/18/why-goldman-sachs-is-one-of-the-biggest-warren-buf.aspx.

20. Geithner, *Stress Test*, 212.

21. Ibid., 225.

22. Chris Van Hollen, interview with author.

23. Paulson, *On the Brink*, 255.

Perhaps he meant he personally did not have the time to develop a stimulus proposal. In any case, Pelosi did not insist on a reciprocal measure as part of the desperately hurried TARP process. Maybe she did not have her proposal ready at the time, although the recession had been growing in plain sight for at least a year. She might have wanted to wait for Obama to be elected. It could be that she thought the Democrats would design an ideal package after the voters gave them control of both ends of Pennsylvania Avenue in a few weeks.

Every elected official knew that the American people would be outraged by their government giving 5 percent of the GDP of the country to bankers. Paulson did not expect to stay in his post after the election. Bernanke's term had two more years to run. The November voting would probably reinstall a Democratic Congress and Obama might beat McCain. Under these circumstances, the Bush appointees chose to pin the tail of responsibility on the Democratic donkey.

Paulson had trapped the Democratic presidential candidate. If Obama did not go along and more bank runs occurred, he would be blamed for the resulting impact on both the financial and the real economy. Obama and his party could not take that chance. By supporting Paulson, if elected Obama would be President Bailout.

McCain Blew His Chance

On September 23 Paulson and Bernanke testified in Congress about the necessity of legislative action.[24] On September 24 President Bush went on national television to plead for a bipartisan vote. That same day John McCain said he would suspend his campaign the next day, and might not participate in the first presidential debate, set for September 26. At McCain's insistence, President Bush held a meeting of both candidates and congressional leaders from both parties in the Roosevelt Room of the White House on September 25. President Bush began the

---

24. "The Fed did have good grip by the time of TARP on what was happening; but neither the Bush administration or candidates McCain and Obama had language, much less an analytic framework, with which to think and speak clearly about it." David Warsh, interview with author.

meeting with: "If [you folks don't do something], this sucker's going to go down."[25] Obama responded by offering a measured statement of the situation that focused on the need to stop bank runs. Obama thereby made the first and most significant decision of his presidency. He chose bank bailouts—euphemistically, stabilizing finance—as his top strategic goal. He let Paulson pick his presidential priority.

When McCain spoke, no one understood what he was proposing. Barney Frank baited him, demanding to hear the Republican plan. McCain had avoided the topic of banking since 1987. In that year he inserted himself into the deliberations of the Federal Home Loan Bank Board concerning Charles Keating and his Lincoln Savings and Loan Association. Keating had given McCain large campaign donations, taken him on plane trips, and otherwise created an opportunistic friendship. While the FHLBB discussed bailing out the company's risky portfolio (including huge loans to real estate developers), Lincoln went bankrupt. Its resolution alone cost the taxpayers $3 billion, as Congress spent more than $100 billion to protect depositors from losses in savings and loan bankruptcies.

McCain and four other senators (dubbed the "Keating Five") were accused of corruption because they had allegedly tried to influence FHLBB's bailout decision in Keating's favor. The Senate Ethics Committee ruled that McCain was guilty of "poor judgment." When the Republicans took control of Congress in 1995, following their election victories in November 1994, McCain called me, the FCC chair, and said he never again wanted to be charged with interfering with a regulator on behalf of a campaign contributor. I should make my own decisions.

Once burned, twice shy, and yet there he was 21 years later, again confronting a collapse in the banking industry, just as some polls showed his campaign closing on Obama. Now Paulson and Obama wanted him to endorse a banking bailout many times bigger than the amount taxpayers spent to resolve the failure of a third of the savings and loan associations. Moreover, by adopting a pro–Wall Street attitude, his Democratic

25. Henry Blodget, "Bush on Economy: 'This Sucker Could Go Down,'" *Business Insider*, September 26, 2008, http://www.businessinsider.com/2008/9/bush-on-economy-this-sucker-could-go-down-.

opponent had moved to the right on the political spectrum, occupying the Republican's space. Donald Trump might have chosen to be the populist warrior against the banks, but John McCain was not that guy. He temporized, deciding only that he would do the debate after all.

On Thursday, September 25, the same day as the Roosevelt Room meeting, Sheila Bair put to work her very different policy by having the FDIC resolve Washington Mutual, the sixth largest bank in the United States. She punished creditors by refusing to pay them in full the money they had loaned to WaMu. Geithner despaired. He thought "the U.S. government had sent a message that creditors of U.S. financial institutions were not safe, precisely the wrong message to send at a time of peril."[26]

A run on Wachovia, the fifth biggest bank, began, just as Geithner feared. Over the weekend Geithner insisted that Bair not impose a haircut on lenders to Wachovia. Bringing in Bernanke to support him, he wanted government to facilitate Citi's acquisition of Wachovia. Geithner was very worried about Citi's weak balance sheet. He thought that merger would help both firms. Bair preferred to put Citi into resolution, or some other version of a restructuring akin to bankruptcy. Geithner considered her to be vindictive, ignorant of how her push to punish could trigger unstoppable bank runs.

Then Wells Fargo stepped in to buy Wachovia. Geithner had not obtained the deal he favored. However, he called the transaction a win because he had "elevated no-haircuts-in-a-panic to the level of doctrine." He and Bernanke felt they had crushed Bair's opposition to bailouts. But they still needed the TARP money to make the "commitment fully credible,"[27] meaning that Treasury would be able to bail out big banks in trouble, while holding lenders and depositors harmless, and keep bank managers in place.

I wrote a memorandum to the economic adviser on the campaign, Jason Furman, saying Obama had to insist that Treasury buy stock in banks instead of acquiring assets of dubious value. Obama needed

---

26. Geithner, *Stress Test*, 216.
27. Ibid., 219.

to promise taxpayers that when the crisis passed they would get their money back, and then some. Austan Goolsbee had the same view: "In September and October we were saying to the Bush administration, you've got to use that TARP money to recapitalize the banks. They were saying, 'No, no, we've got to buy up the toxic assets.' They did not want to recapitalize the banks. The problem was that just buying toxic assets is not an efficient way to do it. You would give payments to lots of holders of these assets that weren't about to collapse and you would still have some undercapitalized banks that didn't hold lots of these assets."[28]

Neither congressional Democrats nor the Obama team offered a robust written alternative to Paulson's plan. They settled for directing some of the TARP money to help "homeowners facing foreclosure."[29]

The other big question for the elected officials was: Were management officials in the troubled banks going to suffer any loss of compensation? A board of a public company, or activist shareholders, might insist on linking pay to performance—in this case, the worst performance imaginable. Paulson opposed "tougher comp restrictions" and Geithner agreed "because reducing them seemed like a secondary objective in a crisis."[30] Geithner cared little about the apparent injustice of helping the rich stay rich. He was the ultimate plumber. All that mattered was cleaning up the big banks' balance sheets with government money. Then the big banks again would make loans to investors, ending the recession. Keeping this goal uppermost was Geithner's unrelenting focus.

Henry Waxman reported that the congressional Democratic leadership met in Speaker Pelosi's office to discuss this part of TARP: "Bob Rubin [then an adviser to Citi] was on a conference call with us. Paulson had said we couldn't limit the compensation of the CEOs because they would walk away from the bailout money. They wouldn't agree to participate in selling stock or assets. They didn't want to give up their salary and their bonuses. I suggested limiting bonuses to several million dollars. I asked Bob Rubin, 'Don't you think the CEOs could live with that?' And he

28. Goolsbee, interview.
29. Bernanke, *The Courage to Act*, 345.
30. Geithner, *Stress Test*, 220.

said, 'No, they can't.' They wouldn't take any limits on the millions that they were going to get. They refused to help their businesses survive if they couldn't continue to get the extraordinarily high compensation that they had been getting."[31]

In negotiating TARP with Paulson, the Democrats obtained only very mild restrictions on executive compensation, a toothless hint of a tax that would never be paid, a little money for housing, and the expansion of authority to buy equity (or warrants) instead of just bad assets. Even these mild terms, plus the anxiety and fatigue, got to Paulson. He had an attack of dry heaves.[32] This physical manifestation of psychic distress did not persuade the bulk of House Republicans to support the bill. Nevertheless, after midnight on Sunday night, Democratic congressional leaders and the Bush administration agreed to the plan Paulson wanted. President Bush said the bill would pass. On September 29, 2008, the House proved him wrong.

Democrats voted 140 to 95 in favor but Republicans voted 133 to 65 against. The bill failed. Waxman recalled, "In the cloakroom we had the television sets on and watched the stock market just drop. Like a lead balloon. It was a taste of instant consequences for the vote."[33]

The stock markets dropped about 8 percent in minutes. About $1.2 trillion in market value disappeared. Congressional leaders announced they would work on revisions to the plan. Optimism about that led to the stock markets recovering about two-thirds of the Monday loss the very next day. The congressional Democrats and Paulson divided the TARP funds into two pieces: $350 billion right away and $350 billion that could be requested in January 2009, unless the new Congress blocked it. "Paulson and his people were begging us not to attack the TARP and the rescue because the world will blow up if we don't do this," Goolsbee explained. The Bush administration's argument came down to "'We will spend the first $350 billion our way, and if you win, you will

31. Henry Waxman, interview with author.
32. Paulson, *On the Brink*, 313–14.
33. Waxman, interview.

have the second $350 billion to use your way.' But most of the money spent on the banks was already out by January 2009."[34]

This tactic may have won the necessary votes by seeming to empower a Democratic presidency and Congress to spend $350 billion "however" they wanted. However, it tightened Obama's commitment to the Paulson-Bernanke-Geithner prioritization of saving the big banks. Obama and the Democrats could have left the Bush appointees to manage bank runs as best they could without TARP money, or they could have agreed only to a onetime funding of $350 billion, while reserving further decision until after the election. Democratic leaders in Congress lacked the time, staff, and organizational capability to dispute the thesis that a depression loomed. Like a patient told by a surgeon that the operation must take place immediately, Congress lay down on the gurney and was sedated.

Paulson Got What He Wanted

On Wednesday night, October 1, the Senate passed the revised bailout bill 72 to 25, and on Friday, October 3, the House passed the Senate bill 263 to 171. Most Democrats and a few Republicans composed the majority. President Bush signed it within hours. The Treasury had $350 billion to invest in the big banks right away and could get the same amount in January by asking for it.

Geithner then persuaded Sheila Bair into committing the FDIC to guarantee the debts of financial institutions the same way that government had guaranteed the debts of Fannie Mae and Freddie Mac. On October 14, 2009, Bair announced that the FDIC had created the Temporary Liquidity Guarantee Program (TLGP). Her insurance agency, funded by most of the banks in the country, guaranteed the senior unsecured debt of the big banks issued on or before June 30, 2009—precisely the sort of debt that investors feared would not be paid. Now at least $1.5 trillion of distressed debt would certainly be paid. The FDIC also raised the deposit insurance limit from $100,000 to $250,000.

34. Goolsbee, interview.

Sheila Bair thought that was "the most distasteful thing" she did "in public life."[35] In retrospect she wondered "if we overreacted." She asked herself, "How many other smaller businesses and households could also have survived intact if the federal government had been willing to give them virtually unlimited amounts of capital investments, debt guarantees, and loans."[36] She was appalled that "within months of receiving such generous government assistance" the guaranteed firms "paid out big bonuses to their executives."[37]

Several days after she extended the guarantees, Bair told a *Wall Street Journal* reporter that the government was wrongly prioritizing banks over homeowners.[38] Treasury argued that the TARP legislation did not allow them to "promote loan modification." Bair said members of Congress were "incredulous."[39] She wanted to encourage loan modifications by promising that the government "would absorb half of the losses" from any "redefaults due to declining home prices." Bush Treasury and White House "free-market economists" killed her idea. She thought the "economists at the White House" and "Treasury" after the crisis "were still mired in the ideology of government laissez-faire and 'self-correcting' markets."[40] In her view the government "used up resources and political capital that could have been spent on other programs to help more Main Street Americans."[41]

Looking back at these events later Bair said, "If they had put all the mismanaged institutions into receivership and imposed accountability, fired the boards, fired the management—for instance, fired the yahoos who worked for AIG in London that put all those money-losing deals together to begin with—I think Obama would have been a hero. At last people would have seen some pain, some accountability. It just never happened."[42] She favored populist thinking. Sheila Bair was a Republican

35. Bair, *Bull by the Horns*, 118.
36. Ibid., 120.
37. Ibid., 119.
38. Ibid., 128.
39. Ibid., 131.
40. Ibid., 133–135.
41. Ibid., 7.
42. Bair, interview.

woman with a long-standing ties to Republican senators. She could have been a useful addition to Obama's adviser group.

Ultimately, Bair secured in Title 11 of Dodd-Frank the authority for FDIC to resolve an entire failing institution (not just the insured bank). Critically, it required the FDIC to give haircuts to creditors. Congress in this way repudiated the policy preference Geithner insisted upon in the winter of 2008–2009. The reversal came too late to change Obama's fateful link to the big banks.

Nearly four weeks later, on October 28, 2008, Paulson used a little more than $200 billion of the $350 billion in the first tranche of TARP money to buy securities from nine financial institutions. As Bair suspected, in November Citigroup needed another bailout. Even her FDIC guarantees had not sufficed to enable that firm to rebuild its balance sheet. On November 23 the government guaranteed payment on more than $300 billion of Citigroup's debt, and bought about $20 billion more in Citi equity. Apparently the crisis was not so urgent that all the TARP money had to be spent or that it needed to be invested immediately. This second bailout also came without making any change in management.

By going along with Paulson, Obama thought he was averting a repeat of the Great Depression. That is what his own economic advisers told him. It proved to be a repeated trope, used by his advisers to obtain rapid assent to their policy preferences. By this action, Obama passed on the opportunity to seek a mandate in the election to get the economy back to full employment, to end the housing slump, to keep people from losing their homes and savings and future prospects.

Even during the attention-deprived last weeks of the campaign, Obama must have realized that he was accepting the fundamental neoliberal idea that if the government stabilized the financial system, a healthy economy would soon emerge from the crisis. That was what Robert Rubin had persuaded Bill Clinton to believe in the less fraught circumstances of 1992. It was what the Rubin acolytes on the Obama team incorrectly believed in 2008. Other, more pessimistic voices had little access to the Obama circle. Doubters like Sheila Bair or Joe Stiglitz were treated as hysterics, populists, renegades.[43] The crisis was deemed too serious for their ideas to be entertained. Obama did not even meet with Bair until February 2009.

At the time, all involved praised Obama's rational, cool demeanor. His political advisers saw that lower-income households would mostly vote for Obama no matter what. Middle-income homeowners were inclined to vote against any Republican successor to Bush because under that administration they had lost home equity and now were losing their jobs too. For business to fall, at least temporarily, in love with Obama sealed the presidency for him. From the electoral perspective, the events of the week were fortunate.

Obama's advisers saw his decision, however, as apolitical. According to Goolsbee, "Obama did not condemn the TARP on the campaign trail when it clearly would have been politically advantageous to do so because he had been convinced early on that the economy was about to go through a horrible experience and he couldn't really afford to let the banks and the financial system disintegrate if he wanted to avert an economic collapse. But the lack of sufficient conditions on the banks that got the money was a decision made by the previous administration, and it was one that would come back to haunt us in the months and years to come. We could have forced more mortgage relief. We could have imposed tighter conditions on dividends or executive compensation."

Goolsbee went on, "You can see how things could be different if you looked at the one part of TARP where the new administration could make the conditions—autos. The Bush administration gave the automobile companies $18 billion with virtually no conditions in 2008. When that money ran out and they seek more from Obama in 2009, he provides money but only with a series of wrenching restructuring conditions. Half the management is fired. They go through bankruptcy. They restructure and end up succeeding. We could only impose those things because they needed more money. In the case of the banks, they

---

43. For a good description of Stiglitz's quite different, non-neoliberal ideas, see Michael Hirsh, *Capital Offense: How Washington's Wise Men Turned America's Future Over to Wall Street* (Hoboken, New Jersey: John Wiley & Sons, 2010).

were given the money in 2008. To get them to do something in 2009, they had to be induced. They already had their money."

On top of that, Goolsbee said, "After Lehman, Obama's desire to help transform the longer-run structure of the economy had to take a backseat to resolving the crisis. The new job one was making sure there wasn't going to be another Great Depression—meaning a big downturn in the real economy and a collapse of the financial system as per the 1930s. The risks of 2008 and 2009 in several ways were actually bigger than those in 1929. Finance was far more integrally involved in the economy than it was then and the financial shock to household wealth in the United States was far bigger in 2008 than it was in 1929. The housing prices going way down, stocks going way down produced impacts much more widespread than those that started the Great Depression."[44]

Financial writer Paul Blustein explained why the Obama alliance with Paulson mattered beyond Election Day: "Paulson was bullheaded. He was in way over his head."[45] Paulson's actions created urgency, but also limits on the stimulus. They left Obama with continuing concern about the economy, reflected in his decisions to bend the healthcare cost curve, de-emphasize energy reform, and shun housing fixes. TARP cast a long shadow of a miserable psychotherapeutic alliance between banks and the White House. The Democratic sense of doing the right thing perversely translated to helping the rich stay rich.

Notwithstanding the second round of TARP investment in Citi, Paulson opposed government investment in other industries. He said in a speech that, "we shouldn't use TARP money to bail out the automakers."[46] He would save banks, even if it made him sick to his stomach, but not other businesses, even if that threw millions out of work.

By the middle of December, however, Paulson again reversed course. He talked to Bush about the Detroit bailout over lunch.[47] Both understood that Obama wanted it to happen. They agreed to go along with the incoming president's wish.

44. Goolsbee, interview.
45. Paul Blustein, interview with author.
46. Paulson, *On the Brink*, 408.
47. Ibid., 424.

Still, as a matter of principle, Paulson did not want government to govern companies. The automobile companies and auto labor unions got the treatment Bair preferred for banks.

I accosted Gene Sperling, a National Economic Council chair in the Clinton administration who returned to government as Geithner's political adviser, on the street outside Treasury. I urged him to let Ken Feinberg decide how much had to be paid to the banks' employees. Feinberg, a famous dispute manager, had a reputation for parsimonious fairness, and he would bear the burden of decision. I said Obama should not take the heat for bonuses. For the American people, the government investment in the nine banks seemed to pay for billions of dollars in Christmas bonuses. Sperling listened impassively. He had discovered already that Geithner had no truck for what he considered a purely political issue like banker bonuses.

Just as Bair, Waxman, and others suspected would happen, Wall Street firms paid out $140 billion in compensation in 2009.[48]

If Obama had not joined up with a passive George W. Bush, and instead let the outgoing president cope with the economy until the inauguration on January 20, then the Democratic Congress and popular opinion could have supported far bolder policy moves than Obama chose. Obama could have "responsibly" stimulated full employment and rising wages. By not putting his decisions off until the magnitude and nature of the problem was known, Obama and his advisers caused millions more people to be out of work for a very long time.

48. Aaron Lucchetti and Stephen Grocer, "Wall Street on Track to Award Record Pay," *Wall Street Journal*, updated October 14, 2009, https://www.wsj.com/articles/SB125547830510183749.

6

Obama Picked His People and Thus His Policies

Intelligence alone is not nearly enough when it comes to acting wisely.

— Fyodor Dostoyevsky, *Crime and Punishment*

When Obama interviewed Geithner for treasury secretary on Friday, October 17, at the W Hotel in Midtown Manhattan, continuity was the theme. "This thing isn't over. It's still terrible, and it's going to be for a long time," Geithner told Obama. Hiring him would "look like an endorsement of all that he, Paulson, and Bernanke had done." He said he was "too much the face of the unpopular stuff." Besides, Geithner said, he was wedded to the prioritization of restoring Wall Street to profitability. He told Obama, "I'm proud of what we've done. I'm not going to renounce it or criticize it. And that would make it harder for you to chart a different course." He said that for these reasons, "Bob Rubin and Larry Summers would be better" choices for treasury secretary.[1] Suggesting Rubin showed either loyalty to a mentor or disingenuousness. Nothing could align Obama even more closely with Wall Street than selecting a Citi executive as treasury secretary. That was never going to happen.

---

1. Geithner, *Stress Test*, 243.

Obama responded by saying that "he was not concerned about political appearances."[2] Politicians make that statement when they endorse a business or factional interest against the preference of the populace. It is a claim of courage. Sometimes decisions are unpopular because they are wrong, and political intrepidity betrays the voters who put the person in power.

Earlier in October, Obama's advisers outlined to him a stimulus amounting to about $175 billion. He began talking about that in public. Romney had suggested a higher number at the beginning of the year when still a candidate for the Republican nomination.[3] On October 10, 2008, Paul Krugman warned on the pages of the *New York Times* that the stimulus had to be very large.

The same day Geithner and Obama met, Josh Steiner (who was then trying to persuade his friend Geithner to take the Treasury post if offered) and Jack Lew wrote a proposal for Obama sizing a stimulus at $300 billion, almost twice as large as what Obama was saying on the campaign trail. On November 2, 2008, two days before the election, Jack Lew circulated among the Obama advisers a 36-page outline of that stimulus.

Podesta had drawn "a very bright line" between the "transition efforts and the campaign efforts," according to Steiner. The campaign team should not be distracted by postelection planning. Podesta did think, however, that the transition planners needed a "firm understanding of the positions…articulated during the campaign," and for that, Steiner talked to Jason Furman about what might compose the stimulus.[4] Furman and Steiner agreed the stimulus spending should go to topics Obama had been talking about in the campaign, especially three of the four pillars—healthcare, energy, and education. The fourth, finance, had already gotten its spending package—the enormous TARP.

Bill Daley, who had served in the Clinton administration and was also part of the transition planning in Chicago, did not think the stimulus

---

2. Ibid., 244.
3. Michael Grunwald, *The New New Deal: The Hidden Story of Change in the Obama Era* (New York: Simon & Schuster Paperbacks, 2013), 75.
4. Josh Steiner, interview with author.

memo mattered much anyhow. According to Steiner, Daley thought that immediately after the election the nominees would do the real work of policy design. The October exercise was only "to accelerate the policy development of the nominees by a couple weeks."[5]

This small team also consulted a variety of experts including Tim Geithner to understand the scale and scope of the financial industry's problems. Collectively, the team decided that the stimulus should "minimize the impact" of the crisis on GDP by coming up with ways to "stimulate growth." They "didn't look at it as a jobs-creation agenda." Instead, they "looked at it as a series of silos that ultimately would benefit the economy as a whole," including "addressing the financial crisis, stimulus, trade, workforce training, and productivity growth." Steiner thought, "When you're in a very fluid and very damaging crisis, the fundamental objective has got to be to minimize the impact of that crisis, and if you can do that in a way that ultimately provides a series of long-term benefits as well, all the better. But tactical moves have to be about containment."

"Containment" expressed the goal of quickly addressing market failures. To that end, Daley and Steiner adopted as a framework for the stimulus design the three T's Summers had coined early in 2008: timely, targeted, and temporary. "Believe me, we used them a lot," said Steiner, who told the different transition policy teams, "We think we'll need a stimulus plan. So if you have ideas for us, they are very welcome, but the three T's have to be met."

What did the T's mean to Steiner?[6]

"Timely meant the money can be spent quickly. Temporary meant that it was not meant to be an extended entitlement program. Targeted, generally speaking, meant that you were trying to address a specific problem or a piece of society. The exception was tax policy that would have been less targeted, much broader." At the same time, the budget deficit "was something that was clearly on our minds." It was expected to rise, but not too much and not for long. If the stimulus "mitigated the contagion, then the economy would recover, and what you don't want to

5. Ibid.
6. Ibid.

have done in the process is permanently elevate the levels of government spending. Deficits do matter. There was an orthodoxy about this."[7]

The stimulus memorandum aimed to inform the individual nominees to cabinet jobs about spending programs in their departments. Existing programs were to be funded. New ideas were unwelcome. New programs would require new authorizing legislation. That process would slow down enactment of the stimulus bill and, if the ideas were popular, cost votes. The stimulus would pour new wine in old bottles.

Steiner said, "This wasn't an environment for broad strategies."

Sectoral reform of the sort that Obama contemplated in the Knox College or Cooper Union speeches would have to come later. The TARP, FDIC guarantees, stimulus, and Fed loose-money policies would stop the bank runs. Then the economy would begin to climb the back slope of a V-shaped recovery. The administration would dedicate the year to passing transformational legislation.

As the economy fell and rose, writing a V on the page of cyclical history, how many jobs would be lost? Steiner said they didn't do any modeling that might predict how many jobs would be created by the spending.[8] They did not have time or staff, and under the rules set by Podesta they could not ask others to help.

Because Daley, Steiner, and Lew knew unemployment certainly would rise, they proposed increases in unemployment benefits and food stamps.[9] They also allocated $70 billion for a one-year rebate of payroll taxes, reflecting Obama's campaign proposal called "Making Work Pay." Their memo linked Obama's pillars of change to the stimulus by labelling some spending as a "down payment on long-term goals," including health information technology ($20 billion), school renovation ($25 billion), and $60 billion for various energy projects, including renovating the electric grid, drawn from a "Green Stimulus" memo Carol Browner's policy team had prepared.[10]

7. Ibid.

8. Ibid.

9. Now called SNAP, this program is widely judged beneficial for low-income families. "SNAP Helps Low-Wage Workers," Center on Budget and Policy Priorities, May 10, 2017, http://www. cbpp.org/blog/snap-helps-low-wage-workers.

10. Grunwald, *The New New Deal*, 95–7.

The phrase "down payment" suggested that more federal spending would be added in the future to complete the task. However, no one on the transition team contemplated that step. According to neoliberal doctrine, private-sector investing, with a dollop of redistribution, would achieve most economic and social goals. If the stimulus contained down payments, private markets would make the installment payments.

On November 4, Obama won the election by a big popular vote margin, 53 percent to 46 percent. The victory buried the Republicans under a coalition of enthusiastic minorities, women, homeowners, and even business leaders. The Democrats had 58, maybe 59 Senate seats if the Minnesota recount confirmed Al Franken's win. They had a huge House majority, large enough to tolerate some "no" votes on liberal bills from Democrats in swing districts.

Obama took Podesta's advice and picked his top advisers quickly. A small in-group would come with him from Chicago. Most selections would come from the Clinton ranks. The newly named official advisers would gather in the D.C. transition headquarters.

The economy rapidly changed for the worse. The number of unemployed increased by 267,000 in August, 434,000 in September, and more than 600,000 in October, totaling more than 10 million unemployed. At the time of the election, the unemployment number was 6.5 percent—less than it was when Bill Clinton was elected, but rising rapidly. Obama's advisers had convinced him since the September meeting in the Roosevelt Room that he had a responsibility to convince business leaders to be confident about the future. Summers and Geithner believed that confidence would stymie bank runs.

Obama called a press conference in Chicago on November 7 to say he had met with his "Transition Economic Advisory Board," and decided, first, that a "fiscal stimulus plan that will jump-start economic growth is long overdue." Second, he would "address the spreading impact of the financial crisis" on business. Third, "we will review…this administration's financial program to ensure that the government's efforts are achieving their central goal of stabilizing financial markets." That included Treasury action to help "families avoid foreclosure." He said that if a "stimulus" does not "get done in the lame-duck session it will be the first thing I get done as president of the United States."[11]

In these remarks, Obama revealed three important decisions. He assigned top priority to ending bank runs and restoring the profitability of the big banks. He would decide the size and composition of the stimulus either in November, aiming to pass it in the lame-duck in December, or the new Congress in January. Getting it done quickly was more important than waiting to know the dimension of the need. Lastly, he would stem foreclosures, as opposed to curtailing the fall in house prices.

He concluded with a crack about Nancy Reagan doing séances. By ridiculing the sainted Reagan family, Obama gave his enemies an opening. At that moment, the right wing started a never-ending campaign of distortions and misrepresentations aimed at discrediting his fledgling presidency.

When I met Rupert Murdoch in 1993 after I became FCC chairman, he told me that the purpose of Fox News was to find and focus on a narrower audience. He would oppose the consensus fostered by the three networks and feed his viewers the content they wanted: what later was called alt-news. Within two decades he was hugely successful.

As he explained in the 2004 convention speech that launched him into national prominence, Obama wanted to be president not of blue or red states, but of a newly unified United States. As one-to-many content distribution methods, the old mediums of newspapers and the three big television networks intrinsically united people of differing race, age, and creed into a single audience. That community was unreal—its members did not really know each other. But all saw the same content, developed the same brand awareness, heard the same news. That suited Obama's theme of unity. But the decline of the old media hampered Obama's ability to bring Americans together, even to agree on incontrovertible facts.

---

11. David Greene and Robert Siegel, "Obama: Quick Action Needed on Economy," *All Things Considered*, NPR, November 07, 2008, https://www.npr.org/templates/story/story.php?storyId=96756663.

Obama became president in the early days of the mobile apps that brought social networks persistently, pervasively into the lives of nearly every American. These new media forms, principally Facebook and Twitter, became powerful platforms for fostering irrationality and recasting compromise as cowardice, consensus as betrayal.

On November 12, 2008, Jason Furman reduced the Steiner-Lew work to 11 pages that he gave the president-elect. It called for $335 billion in stimulus to be spent over two years. While Obama's advisers discussed how to calculate the right size of the stimulus, Henry Waxman already had a guideline in mind. "The TARP money at $700 billion was for their people, and next we needed to get a similar amount for our people."[12] He meant the lower-to-middle-income base of the Democratic Party.

Furman did not welcome that sort of thinking. He warned Obama that whatever he proposed, Congress would authorize much more—the new president would be "opening the floodgates."[13] Someone else might have advised that after this election and given the crisis, Congress will give you what you ask and what is needed to put Americans back to work. Instead, Furman maintained that the stimulus should be presented along with a "strategy to return to long-term fiscal discipline." That meant Obama had to plan for tax increases and spending cuts in the future.[14] That was in Rubin's 1993 playbook. Like a commandment from a failed religion, there was the balanced budget again in Furman's writing.

In thinking about growing out of the Great Recession, Obama's advisers did not look for ways to recreate the digital investing in the Clinton years. Those opportunities beckoned. Software-as-a-service, cloud computing, and the iPhone had been introduced in the previous two years. These innovations would revolutionize social and business networks, would call for hundreds of billions of dollars in network and data center investing. Breakthroughs in solar and wind power, as well as natural gas discoveries, called for hundreds of billions of dollars to scale out these

12. Waxman, interview.
13. Grunwald, *The New New Deal*, 96.
14. Ibid., 97.

sources of electricity generation. Stimulating economic growth along the lines of inevitable trends would have been easy. But Obama's Clintonite advisers thought if they injected just enough money in the economy to end the increase in unemployment, then for-profit investors (having regained their senses after the Lehman shock) would decide what the American people would want. Government should not develop or hold opinions about the sectors suitable for expansion. Picking a goal would lead to inefficient government-driven allocation of capital. Corruption or incompetence in the public sector would give birth to white elephants, build bridges to nowhere, encourage productivity-damaging investment. A crisis was no time to abandon neoliberalism's commitment to market fundamentalism.

Obama Selected His Court from a Short List

The Obama personnel team, centered around Froman, Jim Messina, and John Podesta, wanted people they knew. They were hiring for trustworthy adherence to neoliberal policy. They saw no benefit in bringing someone new, or even new ideas, into their ranks. For treasury secretary they focused on Geithner or Summers.

Sheila Bair thought neither would do. She told John Podesta, a longtime acquaintance and neighbor, that Obama should "make Paul Volcker his first secretary of the Treasury." She thought that "some of the key decision makers during the 2008 crisis were too close to Wall Street leaders."[15] Volcker had a reputation for toughness. He was willing to reshape, not just restore Wall Street. Obama went along with his advisers. He seriously considered only Summers and Geithner for treasury secretary.

After the election, Summers "was sitting in Boston wondering if I would get a job in the administration."[16] Then he was called to Chicago to interview with President-elect Obama. Geithner got the same call. Obama wanted to see them on the same day, November 16. Inevitably, Geithner ran into Summers in the airport lounge at O'Hare. He

---

15. Bair, *Bull by the Horns*, 141.
16. Summers, interview.

told Summers he had already "urged Obama to choose him as secretary," which didn't really make the situation less awkward."[17]

In his Chicago office, Obama met with Larry Summers first, then Geithner. Geithner wrote in his memoir that Obama "looked less relaxed" and asked "tougher questions" than in October. He asked what "I would do about housing." Geithner said he didn't know, but would do more "than we're doing now." He asked "what I thought of Larry." Geithner told him, "There is no one better at exposing the flaws in an argument." [18] That perfectly defined a staff adviser, but not a crisis-managing treasury secretary.

Geithner was closer to the president's age than Summers was and more closely resembled a fellow basketball player. He had a towel-snapping, wise-cracking style. He expressed himself more succinctly, and, like Emanuel, punctuated his comments with obscenities. Obama might submit to Summers's seminars but enjoyed being with Geithner.

Appointing Geithner would comfort Wall Street. Obama wanted them quiescent. His advisers had convinced him to impart confidence by his words, decisions, and personnel choices. Critically, he must not seek reform of the financial sector at that time. Banking executives had enough to worry about already.

Obama also must have liked the fact that Geithner had a nonexistent public profile. He was the inside guy who knew how to improve the balance sheets of the big banks. Obama's administration would have only one major actor on the big stage of government: Obama himself. By contrast, Summers inevitably would chew the scenery when on stage before Congress, media, and business audiences.

In the security line at O'Hare on his return trip, Geithner took a call from Rahm Emanuel, who asked if Geithner would "run the National Economic Council" if not "named treasury secretary." Geithner said no. He thought NEC was "more about framing and coordinating decisions than making or executing decisions." He would not "abandon" the New York Fed "during the crisis to take a role like that." At Treasury, he would

17. Geithner, *Stress Test*, 249.
18. Ibid.

"be more directly responsible for finishing what he had started, and then trying to fix the broken financial system."[19] Summers obviously would take NEC. Geithner's answer guaranteed him the Treasury.

The day after his interview with Obama, at the *Wall Street Journal* CEO Council meeting in Washington on November 17, 2008, Summers nearly doubled the size of the stimulus that had been in Furman's memo. Perhaps he knew he had lost the Treasury job and wanted to stake out his authority on macroeconomic advice. In any case, he was catching up to published opinions by other economists. He called for $500 to $700 billion in stimulus.

Summers said the mantra needed to be "speedy, substantial and sustained. I think we're going to need some impetus for the economy for two to three years."[20] Congress needed to authorize the spending right away. That S resembled the "timely" in the earlier alliteration of the three T's. But "substantial" and "sustained" could suggest an appropriation to build bridges or highways—or a new clean-energy generation and distribution system—if construction could commence two or even three years after the Congress acted. These S's implied planning, alternative designs, bidding, permitting, and time-consuming interplay between federal, state, and local authorities.

Battling the Great Depression in his first year as president, Franklin Roosevelt's administration created the Public Works Administration. It provided money necessary to complete the long delayed Triborough Bridge linking the boroughs of Queens, Brooklyn, and Manhattan. But the bridge was not opened until 1936, in Roosevelt's fourth year in office. Anthony Dominick Benedetto—known better now as Tony Bennett—sang at the ribbon cutting. That project cost about $1 billion in current dollars, easily affordable within the Obama stimulus. If "speedy" or "timely" had been the limiting rule for Roosevelt, there would have been no bridge.

On the other hand, "substantial" and "sustained" could have meant bridge building, and welfare checks, for a good long time. Social Security

---

19. Ibid., 250.
20. Grunwald, *The New New Deal*, 99.

could be increased, or expanded to allow retirements at earlier ages. Unemployment compensation could be paid for longer time periods so that people could eat while looking for work (and, indeed, it ultimately was extended).

When Summers expressed the three T's earlier in the year, the recession appeared shallower and shorter. That framing smacked of more caution. The situation required a different alliteration. The three S's implied that Summers knew the recession was deep, and would deepen. "Substantial" implied more spending than "targeted." "Sustained" was the opposite of "temporary." Soon enough the stimulus would prove to start with either S or T.

Before Thanksgiving, Obama Outlined His Economic Recovery Plan

The three S's did not surface in Obama's radio address on November 22. As if he already were the president, he said he would spend some taxpayer money to save the financial sector and to restructure Detroit's automobile industry. Obama also said he would soon outline stimulus spending and tax cuts that "created" 2.5 million jobs.

The number begged a question. What were his goals: full employment or an unwillingness to incur a deficit beyond a particular amount? It could have been either one of these opposite directions.

In any given year, about 20 percent of all employees quit their jobs or are fired. If only 19 percent find work, then unemployment goes up 1 percent. As shown in the chart on the following page, at the end of 2008 quits and fires greatly exceeded job openings.

At the time Obama stated his 2.5 million goal, quits were dropping and layoffs rising. The gap between these two and hiring equaled the number of people who needed a job and could not find one: it approached a million in January. In addition to swelling the ranks of the jobless, the Great Recession caused many to stay in jobs they wanted to quit, or took work they did not like. The recession greatly impaired the quality of the work experience for most adults.

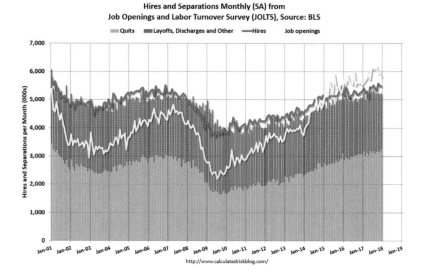

**Hires and Separations Monthly (SA) from
Job Openings and Labor Turnover Survey (JOLTS), Source: BLS**

*Graph 1 from Bill McBride, "BLS: Job Openings 'Little Changed' in February,"
Calculated Risk, April 13, 2018, http://www.calculatedriskblog.com/2018/04/
bls-job-openings-little-changed-in.html. Used with permission.*

Besides, did Obama mean that 2.5 million new jobs would be created, or that 2.5 million would not be fired who otherwise would have been? Did he mean that just for a year 2.5 million new jobs would exist, but after that the private sector would deliver a 3 percent growth rate—the growth necessary to reduce unemployment? Or did he mean the 2.5 million-job boost would last for a couple of years? His talk answered none of these questions. Even if the number encouraged some, decision makers needed to address its ambiguity.

And what sort of jobs would be created? The stimulus money, Obama explained in the radio address, would be spent on roads, bridges, schools, wind farms and solar panel installations, and fuel-efficient cars. Many of those laid off lacked skills for these openings. Nor were the categories easy to visualize. The president-elect had selected what strategists call a "string of pearls" or "portfolio of initiatives" plan for job creation. In this respect he followed the advice Furman, Lew, Steiner, and Daley had given him in their memoranda.

Shaping the stimulus were the three T's with their focus on quickly turning on and off the money faucet. The admirable S's had not gained purchase on policy making.

In his 1993 stimulus proposal, Bill Clinton also spread money across unemployment benefits, education grants, highways, other public goods, summer jobs, and community development block grants. Different congressional figures were supposed to like each of the ideas, and thus vote for the proposal. The Democrats then had a 57-to-43 majority in the Senate but decided to use the conventional approach that required 60 votes to pass the bill. Despite the string-of-pearls methodology, none of the spending ideas attracted a Republican vote. By April, Clinton's $20 billion proposal died.

Scarred by their experience with Clinton, the veterans on his team feared his stimulus could suffer the same fate as Clinton's. Yet they adopted a similar strategy. As was the case with Clinton, Obama had nothing in the bag of spending that he could explain as a compelling vision for the country. David Warsh, an experienced journalist on the economics beat, said, "The stimulus was described as something in economics textbooks for people who'd taken economics but it had no counterpart in the real world. There was no project associated with it that was capable of commanding widespread assent: We weren't going to the moon, we weren't going to tackle climate change, we weren't really going to build new highways, we were going to stimulate. That didn't carry meaning to people."[21]

A week after the November 16 interviews, Emanuel asked Geithner if as treasury secretary he would be "willing" to work with Summers at NEC. Geithner said yes, and a "few days" later Obama called to give the Treasury post to Geithner.[22] Geithner had perfectly played the appointment game. He had repeated the dire warning that the financial crisis was not over. That made him more valuable. He also failed to explain what he thought was "broken" in the financial system. But fixing something broken was repair work. He implied he knew how to do it. Summers, by

21. David Warsh, interview with author.
22. Geithner, *Stress Test*, 250.

contrast, had come across as an architect more than a builder. Geithner communicated also that achieving rapid economic growth and transformational change needed to be someone else's job, not the treasury secretary's mission. In that way he propelled Summers to the NEC.

When Bair heard Obama had selected Geithner, "it was like a punch in the gut." Tim Geithner had been "the bailouter in chief" and "had been responsible for regulating" the firms "whose activities had gotten us all into trouble." She believed that Bob Rubin had pushed Geithner and the rest of the "hit parade" in the Clinton Treasury team into the Obama administration.[23]

Summers, of course, took the runner-up job, the NEC chair that Geithner had deftly defined for him. Perhaps if Summers helped Obama end the recession, he would become Fed chairman in 2010 when Bernanke's term ended. Bernanke, after all, was a Republican appointed by Bush. In any event, in 2009 the fate of the Western economies would be decided in the Oval Office. Summers needed to be there. Constantly meeting with the president gave one power. That, coupled with a confidence in his persuasiveness, gave Summers the conviction that he would take purpose and joy from the task.

Summers happily welcomed Christy Romer, a big brain and potential female ally, to run the Council of Economic Advisers. During the transition, Mike Froman emailed her saying that he wanted to discuss the Obama transition. She didn't recognize his name. Her husband googled it and said, "I think you want to call him back."[24] Later Rahm Emanuel told her, "You were an expert on the Great Depression, and we thought we might need one."[25]

Obama interviewed her in Chicago not long after the election. He opened, she recalled, this way: "The Fed is out of bullets. We've got to do something to get the economy going again. I'm thinking of a big fiscal stimulus. What do you think?"

23. Bair, *Bull by the Horns*, 142.

24. Christy Romer, interview with author.

25. Maureen Burke, "The $787 Billion Question: Maureen Burke Profiles Christina Romer, Former Chair of the U.S. Council of Economic Advisers," International Monetary Fund, March 2013, http://www.imf.org/external/pubs/ft/fandd/2013/03/people.htm.

She answered, "I don't think the Fed is out of bullets." Only later did she realize that the first words out of her mouth to the president-elect were in essence, "You're wrong."[26]

Nevertheless, before she left, Obama asked her to chair the Council of Economic Advisers. She accepted on the spot. This occurred about a week before Thanksgiving. Obama persuaded Austan Goolsbee to back up Romer on the CEA and chair it when she returned to Berkeley in two years.

The third and last major job on the White House economic team is the budget post, director of the Office of Management and Budget. Peter Orszag, another member of the School of Rubin, was then heading the Congressional Budget Office. He was in particular an expert on the budgetary impact of healthcare costs and on the economics of that industry. A week after the election, one of the president-elect's representatives told Orszag that the OMB job was his.

Two years earlier, after I had successfully arranged the meeting between the Gores and Obamas in Nashville, Obama told me he was running for president. I asked for a meeting. He said, "Oh, you're one of those. You have to have a talk."

We had lunch at a four-star hotel in an anonymous part of Northwest D.C., nowhere a reporter would see him. One after the other, people from different countries came out of the kitchen to bow, nod, or just have a look at their hero. He acknowledged every one of them. Not many would be able to vote but they were the foundation of his personal myth. For them, as for a majority of voters in November 2008, he personified the American Dream.

Orszag too wanted a meeting before saying yes, even though of course he was going to say yes, just as I was sure to support Obama's candidacy. He told the job-offering caller, "Well, that's great, but if he has the time, I'd also love to speak with the future president." They had met only occasionally during Obama's brief stay in the Senate.[27]

---

26. Romer, interview.
27. Peter Orszag, interview with author.

Orszag flew to Chicago the night before "just to make sure" he was on time for the morning meeting. When he landed, he got a message saying, "We're going over the president-elect's calendar for tomorrow. He really doesn't feel like you have to fly out to see him. I mean, he's good. Decision's made."

Orszag responded that he was already in Chicago, having dinner with Austan Goolsbee. Did the president-elect want him to fly back to D.C.?

Staff checked with Obama, then called Orszag back. Under the circumstances, since Orszag was already in Chicago, the president-elect would make time to see him.

The next morning the two of them talked for an hour, principally about the stimulus and the health bill, the "two key decisions." They discussed "some of the ways you could design a stimulus" of between $200 billion and $300 billion. This range was not much below the November 12 memo's estimate. They discussed "variation" in healthcare practices across the United States. Then they talked about D.C. schools.[28] Orszag also explained that his two children attended Georgetown Day School. They did not much discuss Orszag's budgetary views. Obama sent his kids to Sidwell Friends.

Holding estimable degrees (Exeter, Princeton, Ph.D. from the London School of Economics), Orszag had made his bones in D.C. by studying the economics of healthcare. By selecting him as OMB director, Obama was signaling that he would fulfill the Democratic master planners' dream of health insurance for everyone.

As Orszag put it, at OMB "you're a member of the cabinet and you're Senate-confirmed, but you're still effectively a West Wing staffer."[29] His particular staff job was to predict the future of economic growth and manage the myriad department and congressional requests for money. He would assemble the president's budget by about February, and then get Congress to adopt it. However, everyone wanted the stimulus to get through Congress on or before inauguration.

28. Ibid.
29. Ibid.

The bigger it was, the harder was Orszag's challenge in projecting a balanced budget at some point in the future. Orszag would not want to lose his reputation as a budget hawk, a true Rubin acolyte in his aversion to deficits. In hiring him, Obama was tilting toward a fiscally conservative presidency, or possibly planning to use Orszag as a beard for a new liberal agenda. No one knew for sure.

Axelrod, in effect producing the Obama TV series, cast Orszag as if he were Montgomery Clift in the administration's movie—concerned, conflicted, and quietly courageous. Like Clift, he was hatched-faced and smooth-skinned, the way a 16:9-aspect-ratio, high-definition television screen likes its pixelated people. The White House, Orszag learned, wanted to "use him a lot for external media."[30] Orszag was cast as the lead in a narrative about saving capitalism while husbanding taxpayer dollars.

The Tuesday before Thanksgiving, Obama completed the announcement of the economic team by stating that Peter Orszag would run OMB. Like the stereotype of a Hollywood star, Orszag found a comely bride from the high-heeled media ranks, and dished on his rival actor Summers. He would be the first cabinet member out, after only 18 months in.

People Choices Are Policy Choices

None of the top advisers on economic issues came from business, much less from banking. I had asked Jamie Rubin, Bob's son, who had worked for me at the FCC, to look for a business leader to add to the team someone who was not an economist and not part of the Clinton Treasury. He shrugged. Presumably others in a country of 300 million might have had the chops for the key jobs, but Obama did not want to spend the time looking for new faces or fresh ideas. During his abbreviated rise to power, he had not assembled a long list of mentors, loyal supporters, and creditors of the favor-bank kind.

30. Ibid.

Besides, even if Obama were to have tried to recruit famous investors, bank presidents, or professors, he would have discovered that most lacked the breadth of experience that matches the range of topics critical to White House policy making. Nor do stars of business and academe commonly understand the complex structure and functioning of the federal government. Even when they learn the ways of Byzantium, they may struggle to adopt their views to the president's political decisions. The most prominent people, in any case, almost always have full-time jobs they are reluctant to leave. Geithner, Summers, Romer, and Orszag were brilliant and available.

The incoming president was known as "No Drama" Obama. He was cool and calm, and also inclined to keep his concerns and thinking within a small group. His personal style helped him in the campaign for nomination. He kept mistakes to a minimum, made decisions quickly, and delegated effectively. After the election, the same style limited his access to information about what was happening in the economy. He had no way to hear ideas that the Clintonian neoliberals did not endorse. He began announcing decisions before diagnosis of the situation could be completed.

New presidents do not understand that, instead of holding the reins of power, they are lashed to their advisers. In choosing his team, Obama was embracing neoliberalism. Markets occasionally fail. Then governments fix the machinery, after which they just watch it hum.

That philosophy, or framework for policy, did not account for the long-term trends shrinking the middle class, nor did it call for an active government to address the diverse victims of the recession, the financial crisis, globalization, and technological change. The forceful critiques of conventional neoliberalism mounted by Paul Krugman, Joe Stiglitz, and Robert Reich would have pushed Obama in a different direction. The Clinton circle had rejected that cranky trio (each of whom, if placed in a fuzzy daguerreotype, would look vaguely Marxist). They were too critical of Wall Street.

As the cartoonist James Thurber said, "He who hesitates is sometimes saved."[31] But Obama thought decisiveness was leadership, and everyone told him that the country desperately needed new leadership.

"By hiring essentially Bill Clinton's economists, Obama was already at odds with the campaign he had run," said David Warsh. Obama was endorsing bank bailouts, inflation risk, budget-balancing, and trust in markets. He was relinquishing populism to his critics. He was, said Warsh, "where the Republicans wanted to put him."[32]

The rule of priorities is to have one. However, before reaching a conclusion about prioritization, the essential preliminary step is diagnosis. The newly selected advisers lacked the staff, time, and models to dive deeply into an analysis of the forces affecting the economy. Each had views. Yet none asked for, or did, a deep dive into the economic situation. McKinsey consulted to the transition team but the firm was not asked to make calls to CEOs or gather data about the contours of the economic collapse. The hundreds of people in the transition team could have produced copious studies. None were asked to do that, and anyone writing something long had no readers. Nor did anyone in the Bush administration have a memo or computer model to share. You would have thought the entire Bush administration operated on the basis of conversation instead of reading. (Bush preferred the former mode; Obama the latter.) The transition team would have had to reach out to the academy and private sector. The nation's tenured professors, CEOs, and experienced market analysts needed only a phone call and they would race to the transition headquarters with advice about how to save the country. Every leader in the country was deeply worried, for themselves and for the system. Many had a sincere, patriotic desire to help.

With unemployment as high as it was when Obama was elected, the Clinton transition also received boundless offers of opinion. Anyone and everyone generated analyses and recommendations. In an economic summit held in Little Rock in December 1992, Bill Clinton boiled the

31. James Thurber, "The Glass in the Field," *New Yorker*, October 31, 1939.
32. Warsh, interview.

ocean to cause opinions and ideas to float to the surface. Ira Magaziner's trawling alone netted hundreds of pages of advice. By contrast, Obama counted on a small group to tell him the truth about the situation. They did not know what they did not know.

7

The Courtiers Gathered

The strategic inflection point is the time to wake up and listen.
— Andy Grove, *Only the Paranoid Survive*

Each of the new nobility, the courtiers to the king, the key advisers, took an office in the recently renovated but eternally drab D.C. transition headquarters, formerly occupied by the Securities and Exchange Commission. Steps away from each other in the tiny spaces that the General Services Administration deemed adequate for prospectus reading, a couple floors below the top (where the president-elect had his rarely visited secure location), clustered at the bleak northeastern corner, a small group studied how to shape Obama's legacy. They quickly learned how much they disagreed with each other. Geithner said of the "marathon meetings with Larry and the economic team" that "some were more productive than others." There were "tensions" with Orszag, who was "trying to establish early dominance over fiscal policy." Romer was "trying to establish her credibility with the president-elect, and was understandably wary of being eclipsed by Larry."[1]

All transitions revolve around what the president should do and when each action should be taken. Chief of Staff Rahm Emanuel would assemble a day-by-day plan. As NEC chair, Summers was to compose the economic policy plan. He might have wanted to dictate it, but he had

1. Geithner, *Stress Test*, 266.

to delegate the various topics to the people appointed to posts with the legal authority to act on the matter: banking went to Geithner, budget to Orszag, stimulus size to Romer, and so on. Summers could lead the drafters to their assignments, but he could not tell them exactly what to write. Only by disquisition and editing the final version could he leave his mark on history.

Obama was in Chicago, discovering that after the election every powerful person in the world wants time with the winner. Emanuel was still in Congress. Phil Schiliro was in the transition team headquarters with Summers, Geithner, Orszag, and Romer. The group did not physically meet on a regular basis until early January. The incoming administration team had many well-informed contacts on the Hill. All of them reported a great deal of anxiety about creating long-term deficits. The spending that had to occur in the immediate present was unprecedented except in wartime. Soon after the election Schiliro toted up the list of items in a lengthy discussion with the transition team leadership: the second half of TARP, the stimulus, appropriations bills, the budget for the next fiscal year, and a wartime spending bill all added up to nearly $3 trillion of spending that would increase the total federal debt because it was not offset by existing or new revenue-raising taxation or budget cuts. Of these items, the two most susceptible to debate were the second half of TARP and the stimulus. Geithner convinced everyone that Treasury needed the entirety of the TARP money. That left the size of the stimulus as the variable.

To kick off his team's policy formation, Obama organized a conference call with the Washington group. Geithner wrote in his memoir: "President-elect Obama wanted to discuss what he should try to accomplish in his first term. I responded first. 'Your accomplishment is going to be preventing a second Great Depression.' 'That's not enough for me,' he shot back. 'I'm not going to be defined by what I've prevented.' He wanted to reform healthcare, education, and the financial system…reduce our dependence on foreign oil and other carbon-emitting fossil fuels. He wanted to give the poor and the middle class some tax relief while asking the wealthy to pay a bit more…but during the worst economic meltdown in 75 years, I didn't think they could be our top priorities. 'If you don't prevent a depression, you won't be able to do anything else,' I said. 'I know. But it's not enough,' the president-elect repeated."[2]

In this elliptical conversation Geithner obtained Obama's tacit assent to his own policy preferences. It had three components: First, Obama would get Geithner the second half of the TARP money as soon as the new Congress convened. Second, Geithner would not put any depositors or lenders to banks at risk of a "haircut"—Bair's more popular, and populist, approach was rejected. Third, Geithner would not want to punish bankers, or even put their bonuses in jeopardy. Obama would spend his political capital on playing nice with Wall Street.

In the inevitable sequence of planning, the decision maker faces nearly insurmountable difficulty in undoing or altering initial concessions or failure to question. This initial conversation translated directly to the priorities in the economic recovery plan presented on December 16. Obama took decisions critical to his prospects and legacy before he could have fully understood the ramifications of Geithner's policies.

Geithner's immediate ambitions were dominated by the "imperatives of the crisis." That included fixing "the broken financial system," crafting a "large fiscal stimulus package," saving "the dying U.S. auto industry," and dealing with "the escalating housing crisis in order to protect millions of families at risk of foreclosure." This transition would be "consumed by the economic emergency." To get through that, Geithner "would carry most of the burden of the financial rescue." While Summers would "take the lead on the fiscal stimulus," Geithner was "worried the world was coming to an end, and not sure we could stop it."[3] The need to inject another $20 billion in Citibank only days before Thanksgiving had scared Geithner into thinking the bank runs were about to begin again. He was worried Merrill Lynch would be the next to fail. Already 13 of the 25 biggest banking firms in 2009 had gone through some major restructuring.[4]

The United States did not face war or pestilence, flood or famine. Geithner's "world" was the system of capitalism as he knew it. That was

---

2. Ibid., 250.
3. Ibid., 259–61.
4. Ibid., 255–57.

what he feared would "end." In his view, the old regime must survive.

Summers disputed Geithner's insistence on continuity with the Paulson policies. He wrote memos to Obama "full of digs" at the mistakes of Paulson and Bernanke, and by implication, Geithner. Summers urged that the new administration distinguish "the Obama response from the pre-Obama response." Geithner thought, "Larry hadn't been there," and didn't have "the right to second-guess with that degree of confidence."[5] He thought, "Our obligation was not to be different for the sake of being different, but to clean up the mess." As an example, Geithner thought "guidelines pushing TARP banks to lend more or pay executives" were "showy populist head fakes." In any event, these steps would not "make America happy about bailouts."[6]

No-Drama Obama wanted to be responsible and post-partisan. He accepted Geithner's advice.

Summers and the other advisers chose to prepare a single economic recovery memorandum to the president-elect that addressed all the major economic problems: banking, stimulus, budget deficit, housing. In the advisers' view, the president-elect needed to decide the entire plan within two or three weeks after he had formed his new team. Then the new White House team could send Congress a plan when it assembled in January 2009, before the inauguration. No incoming president in history, except Abraham Lincoln in 1860, ever intended to make so many decisions before taking office.

Largely absent from the economic recovery plan, however, were proposals for unilateral executive action. The capability to persuade Congress and the public loomed large in the written and accompanying oral commentary. In the 1992–1993 transition, Clinton, Gore and the rest of us adhered to Richard Neustadt's teaching that presidential power comes from the power to persuade others. In the murky weeks of the economy's shrinkage, however, Obama might not illuminate the situation well enough to win support other than from loyalists. Besides, if Neustadt was correct in the 90s, which is doubtful, the George W. Bush

5. Ibid., 261, 263–4.
6. Ibid., 261–262.

administration had conditioned Americans to expect the president to act as necessary, with or without Congressional or popular support.[7] This was the new reality of 21st century politics. Obama could do almost anything he wanted about the crisis. His advisers suffered from stultifying discomfort with that power.

Summers owned the stimulus section. He made the core decision that the economic problem was about confidence and demand. "It's the central irony of financial crises that they're caused by too much spending and overconfidence and too much borrowing, and they're only solved through more confidence, more borrowing, and more spending."

When the 2005 and '06 bubbles were building, financial institutions needed to be slowed down. "But," he thought, "the two classic things America had learned from the past 20 years, to reduce the deficit and to prevent bubbles, both pointed toward exactly the wrong direction in the winter of 2009."[8]

As unemployment soared after the week of the financial crisis, most in government or business agreed that public spending had to make up at least in part for the rapid evaporation of private investment. The two big questions were who should get the money and how much they should get. The economists thought that those who would spend quickly should get money—that meant lower-to-middle-income families living paycheck to paycheck. However, they did not make this case for ethical reasons, such as that these families were the victims of Wall Street or the Bush administration blunders. Instead Obama's advisers explicitly said they did not much care who got the money as long as it was spent quickly. Obama had offered the hope for cultural change, but in the crisis his advisers did not present the economic recovery on any moral grounds.

The right direction, as Summers saw it, was for government to spend to increase demand rather than to encourage more supply. Summers explained, "By Thanksgiving I said to Rahm, 'Here's the deal—we need as much money as we can.' He said, 'No fucking way more than 500

---

7. William G. Howell, *Power Without Persuasion: The Politics of Direct Presidential Action* (Princeton, New Jersey: Princeton University Press, 2003).

8. Summers, interview.

billion.' I said, 'It's not enough. You have to do the right thing here.' He still said, 'No fucking way is this number coming anywhere near a trillion dollars.'"[9]

An unemployment rate of 8 percent is the Plimsoll line of electoral politics. If joblessness exceeds that level in the fall of an election year, the party in power typically is sunk. Within a couple of weeks after this conversation, Summers and Emanuel knew that the federal government had to spend, or somehow encourage businesses to spend a trillion dollars more than they had thought. If that did not happen by the summer of 2010, the Democrats would lose the majority in the House in the midterm election. Emanuel's Thanksgiving obscenities should not have been taken as the final word on the upper limit of the stimulus, but Obama, his people, and the Democratic Party struggled to imagine the dimensions of necessity and opportunity that the unprecedented crisis presented.

By contrast, neither in 2001 nor in 2017 did the Republican Congress Party scruple about crafting stimulus packages in the form of tax cuts that added much more than a trillion dollars to the federal deficit. In those initial years of Republican presidencies, the incoming administration favored supply-side stimulus. Summers had spent two decades opposing tax breaks. They were ineffective as stimulus and they eroded the tax base, making a balanced budget harder to achieve. Therefore, his stimulus plan did not propose a lower corporate tax rate, increased depreciation, extra deductions, rewards for bringing back profits hibernating overseas, reduced payroll taxes, or extra credits for research and development. Banks were not encouraged to loan more. Instead, the opposite: Treasury wanted a lower ratio of loans to equity.

Supply-side stimulus has at least three advantages. It can give more bang for the buck—meaning Congress will score a tax break in the amount of revenue lost by the Internal Revenue Service but businesses may spend much more than that to get the tax break. It can impart confidence to the capital allocators of the country, who are the CEOs of the firms that borrow and spend, not the banks who are only their

9. Ibid.

facilitators. And it does not put the government in the position of deciding what to spend money on, a role that inevitably conjures up logrolling and inefficiency.

In the absence of adequate supply-side stimulus, private investment fell far below private savings during the entirety of the Obama administration. By contrast, in 2017 the Trump administration focused on increased investing in the United States. That could be derided as jingoism, condemned as abandonment of global leadership, called shortsighted in an era of globalization, or celebrated as creating full employment.

The Three T's Prescribed

The meaning of "timely" had not changed much since Summers first coined the phrase. It meant the money should be spent rapidly, and the spending bill had to pass through Congress in a hurry. Remembering the initial rejection of TARP, Obama's advisers wanted to avoid a no vote in Congress. They worried that a protracted battle with Congress over spending and tax cuts would undermine business confidence and drag down Obama's high approval rating.

Orszag said the advisers would not propose "things that would clearly get mucked up on the Hill. So, for example, we decided not to create eminent domain for the high-voltage lines necessary to build transmission systems bringing wind and solar from large empty states to big cities. No huge legislative changes were possible."[10]

"Targeted" meant the money should be spent in ways that had the biggest impact on GDP. Dollars directly given to consumers or in payroll would meet that criterion, but Obama's advisers did not want to increase the amount or duration of unemployment compensation or benefits.[11] These policies would be popular and therefore hard to kill. Helping people in the short term might turn into helping them forever. Congress

---

10. Orszag, interview with author.

11. Stanford economist Greg Rosston suggested to Jason Furman that increased benefits from Social Security should be extended for years, and coupled with a modest carbon tax. This idea, like almost all suggestions about long-run tax code change, was rejected quickly on the grounds that big changes were time-consuming and thus undesirable. Rosston, Greg, interview with author.

could not be trusted to pay for them with new taxes. As neoliberals, the advisers had been warning about debt-creating entitlements for years. They were not going to let the crisis affect those opinions.

Direct hiring might have been a sensible tactic. In 2010 Kevin Hassett, named in 2017 to be Trump's head of the CEA, said that if the government had hired directly into the military, the Army Corps of Engineers, or some newly created temporary entity (such as my son Nathaniel at the Department of Interior proposed for refurbishing national parks in 2009), the stimulus could have created 23 million job-years. The employment would have been designed initially to fit existing skills, and then come with training. By contrast, Hassett argued, the actual "stimulus…comes out to a couple million bucks per job created."[12] Hassett in effect was suggesting that the military be about as big as it was in World War II, when 16 million people were in uniform.[13]

Jared Bernstein said, "The president was always interested in the possibility of more direct job creation. But there were a number of reasons why economists in general and economists on the White House team were skeptical. At the time, we worried that the government didn't have the forces in place to efficiently create employment in such a way that we could avoid accountability problems. That we could get the best bang for taxpayer dollars. That we could avoid the political ridicule of creating make-work jobs. Today there's more openness to the idea of direct job creation then there was back then." He conceded, however, that "we had a very large WPA program in 2009 and 2010, which was hiring for the census."[14]

"Targeted" did not mean aiming the stimulus at areas where ill health, drug addiction, and other social problems were extreme. It did not mean promoting manufacturing. By contrast, Trump argued in 2016

12. Derek Thompson, "Conservative Economist: 'Find the Unemployed and Hire Them,'" *The Atlantic*, August 26, 2010, https://www.theatlantic.com/business/archive/2010/08/conservative-economist-find-the-unemployed-and-hire-them/62100/.

13. This was not his first foray into big numbers. In January 2000 Hassett predicted that the Down Jones Index 10 years later would be closer to 36,000 than to 10,000. In January 2010 it was just above 10,000.

14. Bernstein, interview.

and 2017 for bolstering manufacturing. Here is what happened to manufacturing employment from 2007 to 2017 according to the Bureau of Labor Statistics.

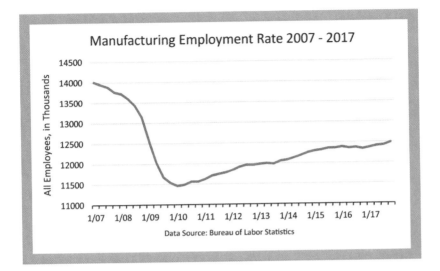

Original graph created by Deborah Nicholls. Data source: Bureau of Labor Statistics, https://data.bls.gov.

The economists thought of aggregate demand as a swimming pool that needed more water. The government would put a hose of money in one corner and the level of demand for goods and services would rise everywhere. Then swimmers (the supply side) would jump in with new investment. However, the swimming pool level did not in fact quickly rise everywhere evenly. As a result of the design principle, the stimulus would produce a geographically uneven recovery.[15] In 2016, the popular vote margin fell below 2 percent in six "swing" or "battleground" states: Florida, Pennsylvania, New Hampshire, Michigan, Wisconsin, and Minnesota. Trump won four, and, as a result, the Electoral College. In

15. See James G. Gimpel, Frances E. Lee, and Rebecca U. Thorpe, "The Distributive Politics of the Federal Stimulus: The Geography of the American Recovery and Reinvestment Act of 2009," Georgetown University, Paper prepared for presentation at the 2010 Annual Meeting of the American Political Science Association, Washington, D.C., September 2, 2010, http://faculty.georgetown. edu/hcn4/SpeakerPapers/Gimpel_Lee_Thorpe_APSA_2010.pdf.

five of these six states the growth rate from 2008 to 2015 also fell below 2 percent.

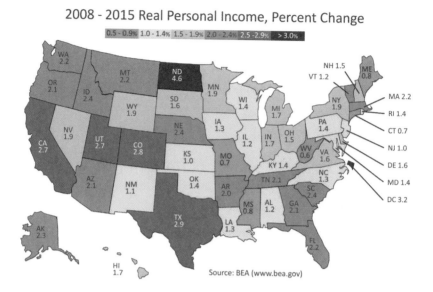

2008 - 2015 Real Personal Income, Percent Change

Source: BEA (www.bea.gov)

Original map created by Deborah Nicholls. Data source: Bureau of Economic Analysis, www.bea.gov.

A successful economic recovery plan had to focus on different solutions for different geographic areas, because skills, income, housing conditions, transportation, education, and other key factors varied astonishingly widely in 21st century America.[16] In the pinch of the post-election weeks, policy makers took a one-size-fits-all approach with the exception of downsizing (but saving) Detroit's automobile industry because of employment in that region.

Public-sector payroll jobs—local, state, and federal—dropped more for Obama than for any previous president back to Carter. The Republicans in the Senate blocked Obama's proposal to help states hire people. In many states Republican governors and legislatures instigated layoffs of teachers and civil servants. "Targeted" did not mean Obama's stimulus sustained public-sector employment.

---

16. Enrico Moretti, *The New Geography of Jobs* (New York: Mariner, 2013).

"Temporary" meant the stimulus did nothing dramatic for businesses involved in digging, erecting, installing, or building for the two platforms 90 percent owned by the private sector: communications and power. Nor did the three T's offer incentive for potential investment in the three platforms principally owned by the public sector: transportation, water, and sewage. Private-sector investors can get a return for privatizing toll bridges, tunnels, and roads, but "timely" did not allow enough time for project developers to present privatization ideas to public officials.

Where state and local bonds provided funds for the platforms, such as for replacing lead-line waterworks or cleaner sewage systems, the federal government might have paid off loans incurred by states and issued new money to start new construction. Neither Congress nor the Treasury Department relishes stepping into the shoes of state and local governments. However, for transportation and education, voters at least in some states will support bonds and other tax measures. In the economic downturn, states lacked the ability to increase their bond issuance. A useful stopgap solution would have been federal money for public-private infrastructure projects. Alternatively, the Treasury could have refinanced state bonds at lower interest rates, paid money up front in return for very low user charges, or simply taken some projects out of the hands of state and local government. That was not the traditional American way: The United States financed only $10 billion of public private partnerships for infrastructure from 1990 to 2006, compared to five times as much in the very smaller United Kingdom.[17]

It followed that construction job loss was severe, as shown in the next chart.

In 2014 Larry Summers would argue for the creation of a federal infrastructure bank, repatriating overseas profits, privatizing more infrastructure, and running a higher deficit.[18] In 2017 Summers wrote that

17. Diane Whitmore Schanzenbach, Ryan Nunn, and Greg Nantz, "If You Build It: A Guide to the Economics of Infrastructure Investment," Brookings, February 9, 2017, https://www.brookings.edu/research/if-you-build-it-a-guide-to-the-economics-of-infrastructure-investment/.
18. David A Graham, "Larry Summers's 4-Point Plan for Saving the Economy," *The Atlantic*, July 2, 2014, https://www.theatlantic.com/business/archive/2014/07/larry-summerss-4-point-plan-for-saving-the-economy/373849/.

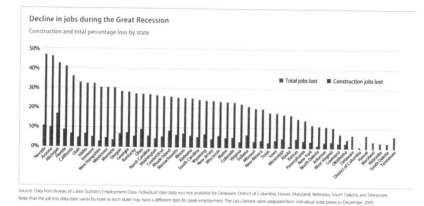

Source: Data from Bureau of Labor Statistics Employment Data. Individual state data was not available for Delaware, District of Columbia, Hawaii, Maryland, Nebraska, South Dakota, and Tennessee. Note that the job loss data date varies by state as each state may have a different date for peak employment. The calculations were prepared from individual state peaks to December 2009.

Chart 2 from Bracken Hendricks and Matt Golden, "Taking on the Tool Belt Recession," Center for American Progress, March 3, 2010, https://www.americanprogress.org/issues/green/reports/2010/03/03/7442/taking-on-the-tool-belt-recession/. This material was created by the Center for American Progress, americanprogress.org.

"public investment in infrastructure, human capital and science" was "inadequate" and gave the economy a "weak foundation."[19] In 2008, by contrast, he thought: "There were only so many infrastructure projects you could get started and get going and get done over a two-year period. The governors were telling Obama they could spend $200 billion. OMB and CBO said infrastructure could only get 40 percent of its money spent in the first two years. Otherwise they will spend it on projects they were already going to spend money on. Nothing extra would be added. The Department of Energy had great difficulty moving the money for energy infrastructure. We planned to spend 75 percent in two years. The last thing we could do would be pumping up spending all through the president's term."[20]

"Temporary" meant that the stimulus probably would not support much innovation. A software start-up needs a year to persuade Apple to

19. Lawrence H. Summers, "The Economy Is on a Sugar High, and Tax Cuts Won't Help," *Washington Post*, December 10, 2017, https://www.washingtonpost.com/opinions/the-economy-is-on-a-sugar-high-and-tax-cuts-wont-help/2017/12/10/6d365950-dc51-11e7-b859-fb0995360725_story.html. In 2017 one respected commentator said that a decade after the beginning of the financial crisis, government still relied for economic growth too much on "liquidity and leverage" from private financial institutions and central banks and still had not made sufficient "investments in infrastructure, education, and human capital."
20. Summers, interview.

put its application on the iPhone. From concept to production of a computer chip, many years will pass. A government grant or loan typically helps a business that is on the verge of production or scaling up.

Tesla was an exception to this implicit bias against earlier-stage innovation. At the exact moment the stimulus became law, Elon Musk was raising capital for building a manufacturing facility. The Department of Energy's half-billion loan to Tesla saved the company and made Musk famous and wealthy. He got money from the government much cheaper than the offers from wary private-sector investors.[21]

The economists understood the deficit would rise. Orszag was delighted and proud of his flexibility on this point. "I think one of the things we got right was not to demand budget neutrality over 10 years. The most important thing was to move pretty quickly to reduce the inside lag, which is typically the core problem in discretionary fiscal policy." Inside lag? "How long it takes to actually enact something.... The typical problem with something like the stimulus is by the time Congress enacts it, it's too late. We avoided that problem. Insisting that the cost be offset by passing revenue-raising taxes at the back half of the upcoming 10 years would have slowed down congressional passage."[22]

Orszag did not favor government loans. As a budget-scoring expert, Orszag knew that a congressional appropriation to a governmental unit could permit the recipient agency to loan many times the scored amount. For example, by appropriating $10 billion to the Department of Energy for loans, Congress could enable DOE to loan $100 billion at the rock-bottom rates set by sales of treasury bonds. Using this technique, if a stimulus capped at $500 billion consisted of loan authorization, it could cause $5 trillion to be loaned to private-sector firms.

Despite this advantage, the advisers disliked government loans for at least four reasons. First, government can borrow more cheaply than any other lender (because it has the power to print money and tax in order to pay interest on debt). Therefore, it can lend at a cheaper rate than any

---

21. See Scott Woolley, "Tesla Is Worse than Solyndra," *Slate*, May 29, 2013, http://www.slate.com/articles/business/moneybox/2013/05/tesla_is_worse_than_solyndra_how_the_u_s_government_bungled_its_investment.html.

22. Orszag, interview.

commercial entity. As a result, banks cannot compete with government in the business of making loans. Geithner wanted to help banks make money. Pushing banks out of any market for lending contradicted Treasury's overriding imperative of helping them make money.

Second, if borrowers face difficulty in paying back loans, they ask the lender to help them out in some way. When the lender is government, the borrower may be tempted to ask government to change a rule so as to help pay off the loan. A conflict will arise between government as lender, who wants its money back, and government as regulator, who orders the business to incur the cost of complying with safety, environmental, labor, or other commercial regulations.

Third, in order to expand private-sector lending to small businesses, students, exporters, and many other kinds of borrowers, the government commonly guarantees that the borrower will repay. Similar guarantees were chickens that had come home to roost in flocks that darkened the government balance sheet: the Fed and the Treasury were absorbing trillions of dollars of obligations by credit unions and the housing lenders Fannie Mae and Freddie Mac. Summers, Orszag, and Geithner wanted government to avoid adding to these guarantees.

Fourth, the advisers did not believe the federal government had the acumen or flexibility to drive the hard bargains that commercial lenders do. Nor can government negotiate the way banks do, varying the terms from deal to deal according to their judgment about the viability of each business. To avoid the appearance of favoritism, government tends to prefer rigid, unchanging formulas, and it minimizes risk by imposing high up-front costs on borrowers. It requires volumes of proof of the wisdom of the borrower's plans. In short, it is a persnickety, officious, frustrating lender. Best for it never to be in that role at all.

By shunning loans, the planners passed on the chance to refinance student loans. They left this market to the private sector. Inevitably, as the next chart shows, a generation of young people who could not find work then had to assume a huge debt burden in order to get educated for the jobs that the slow-growing, rapidly changing economy offered them.

The advisers knew that under CBO accounting rules some spending could expand in practice without being counted by Congress as

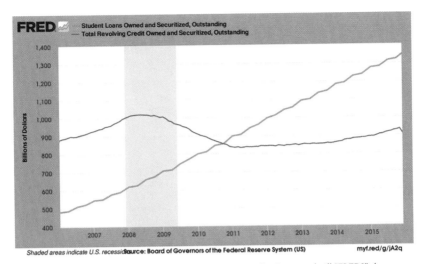

increasing. For example, if Congress created a tax credit, such as for owning solar panels, CBO would estimate a volume of installed solar panels based on past trends. If solar panel costs dropped and state regulators adopted programs encouraging solar installation—both of which events occurred—homeowners would install more panels than predicted. The granted tax credits would exceed the budget score, but Congress would not count the increase. The advisers did not adopt this useful tactic either.

Obama's people accepted that the stimulus could not be scored close to the *t* of a "trillion." Perhaps they correctly assessed the congressional reluctance to pass that big a stimulus. But other motivations, derived from earlier years, caused them to reject ways to spend that would not be scored by Congress in full or in some cases at all.

Interlude 1

Pitching an Idea

In December 2008, past security at the entrance, anyone could wander anywhere inside the transition headquarters. By pretending to have a meeting on the northwest corner, a mendicant could walk past the offices of the potent ones on the northeast corner. That stroll might find Marne Levine, Summers's de facto chief of staff and temporary scheduler for all the economic advisers, in her windowless cubbyhole on the interior of the corridor. Because Obama had not yet filled most posts, the puissant did not have many people to meet with. They could not bear talking to each other 10 to 15 hours a day, so they had gaps in their schedules. They might gain a reputation for humility by taking a meeting with one of the unappointed. Ask the affable Marne for a time. How long? Fifteen to 30 minutes. One-on-one preferably.

I got on the calendars of Summers, Geithner, and Orszag.

To each I came at the appointed time bearing three three-ring binders containing proposals to create three infrastructure banks, one each for financing clean energy generation (wind and solar), efficiency measures for buildings (like insulation and multi-paned windows), and new transmission networks (power from the Great Plains to the great cities). A couple of dozen people from the underutilized economic review team, and other savants known to me from the outside, had created what we called the GRIP: the Green Recovery Investment Plan. We wanted the stimulus to get a GRIP on climate change: by chartering and capitalizing three green banks. Each would loan public money to stimulate clean power investment.

Coal combustion accounted for about 40 percent of electricity generation. To take out this century-old technology and put renewable power in its place, someone had to fund 300 to 400 gigawatts of wind and solar capacity. Each gigawatt would cost about $2 billion. Investors in generation capacity would be paid back, slowly, over a long time, by utilities that bought the power and sold it to end users through the local monopoly distribution grid. Developers would need time to design and gain local regulatory approval for their projects. However, the resulting work would probably go to some of the construction workers laid off in the housing market. Moreover, because the government can borrow money at low rates for long terms, it can afford to loan at only slightly higher rates, and at slightly shorter terms. Low-cost, long-term lending suited most power projects. Typically they require high front-end spending but provide low risk, steady return on investment.

The generation green bank would combine its public money with private capital. The public-private investment would have a cost of capital low enough to keep the electricity prices for payback as or more affordable than current rates. By offering $100 to $200 billion of public money we could pull into the combined public-private lending at least a trillion dollars of private investment into the various projects that replaced carbon power with clean power. Because utilities and consumers would not pay more for clean power, they would make the switch to clean power painlessly. We believed that the pace of climate change called for a rapid move to the clean power platform, but the recession was a horrible time to impose higher electricity bills on consumers. If Congress passed a climate change bill, that could extend emissions reductions beyond electricity to transportation and agricultural power uses. This was a liberal (not neoliberal) idea: use government to deliver a benefit to everyone, protect consumers, stimulate investment and job growth, return capital to the taxpayers over the long run.

A different green bank would finance transmission lines. Carrying electricity from a point of generation, like a power plant, to a utility's distribution network accounts for about half of the price consumers pay. By offering transmission line developers cheap public money, that green bank would reduce the prices needed to pay the projects' costs. The goal was to bring wind and solar-generated power from the Great Plains to points of consumption like Dallas, Denver, or Chicago at affordable prices. An efficiency bank for building renovations.

Every good or service includes the cost of power that is part of production. Lowering power prices while moving to a renewable platform reduces the cost of everything. GRIP would benefit consumers and cause productivity gains.[1] Providing public capital to reduce energy bills also redistributes income and wealth from higher-income payers to the middle-and lower-income classes, from those who are indifferent to the utility bill to those for whom it is a worrisome but necessary expense. That was a good liberal policy anytime, but especially during the recession.[2]

Could I please have the capital to start these green banks? Then we could prove the merit of these models. Perhaps $10 billion each would be enough to get these banks up and running.

Geithner listened, then asked, "Where is this coming from?"

I said, "I'm a policy entrepreneur."

He smiled and said, "I like that phrase."

That was the end of his time for the topic, and hence the end of his interest in it for his term as treasury secretary. His job was to save the existing banks, not create new ones.

Orszag responded, "What do you want me to do?"

I said, "Put in the budget the money for capitalizing these three banks. If you don't like 'banks,' call them finance authorities."

---

1. Ideally, all utility platform outputs should be as efficiently produced and priced as low as possible.
2. "The strongest argument for redistribution is when redistribution boosts economic growth and benefits all or most of society....The second strongest argument for redistribution is that it is sometimes intrinsically better if a poor, needy person has a resource, as opposed to a wealthier person having that same resource." See Tyler Cowen, "Is There a Rawlsian Argument for Redistribution as a Form of Social Insurance?" Marginal Revolution, September 22, 2017, http://marginalrevolution. com/marginalrevolution/2017/09/rawlsian-argument-redistribution-form-social-insurance.html.

He seemed amused. To him, the idea appeared small. He was moving around much bigger pieces of furniture in designing the stimulus and the budget.

He said, "This really isn't my expertise."

Summers cordially received me, saying, "I looked at the proposals. They are what I would have expected from you. Very well thought through."

"Thank you."

"But the problem is that you are talking about creating more debt. Our economic problem is that the country has too much debt."

I had to give Larry credit for instantly elevating his opposition to the level of macroeconomic theory when hearing a modest proposal. That was an argument from authority. I responded, like any lawyer, with a distinction.

"Larry," I answered, "there's too much *bad* debt. This is good debt. There's not enough of that."

I went on, "Money loaned to build generation, upgrade or expand transmission, and install efficiency measures always gets paid back. No one would be borrowing the money unless the projects could be shown to be productive. Utilities would pay for transmission and generated power. Building owners would pay for the efficiency gains out of their savings on power. Government lending into productive investment is the best possible stimulus. You can never have too much of it."

Summers moved to the second string of rebuttal, pragmatism: "It would take too long to create these institutions. It would take time for people to develop the projects. The funding would continue for years. Much of the money would go to materials."[3]

---

3. I sent him a short memo later in which I explained that the Nixon administration implemented wage and price controls for the entire economy in a few weeks. I thought new institutions were a good idea. In a brief interview with *ProMarket*, Anat Admati said: "Acemoglu and Robinson argued in *Why Nations Fail: The Origins of Power, Prosperity, and Poverty* that 'man-made political and economic institutions…underlie economic success (or lack of it).'" See generally Anat R. Admati

Summers was saying no. In Silicon Valley they say the second best answer is no. That means at least you have an answer.

Summers concluded with inversion. He endorsed my motives, but not my methods. He said, "Don't think I'm not concerned about climate change. I was an advocate of cash for clunkers. You and Al Gore rejected that idea."

In the Clinton transition of 1992 he endorsed a policy called "cash for clunkers." The federal government would subsidize the purchase of a high-miles-per-gallon car if the buyer traded in a low-miles-per-gallon car. Al Gore and I thought it was small potatoes compared to the carbon tax we wanted. Later in Obama's first term, Summers persuaded the Department of Energy to adopt his idea, with debatable results.[4]

"What a grand memory you have," I said.

I struck out on the three pitches. A couple days later I persuaded Mark Gallogly, an experienced private equity manager and early Obama supporter, to join me in asking Carol Browner to put GRIP into the energy portion of the stimulus. Gallogly explained that equity and debt compose the capital structure of any infrastructure project. He said the stimulus could provide some of each, in flavors like preferred stock, debentures, and so forth. The government could attract private investors if it operated an infrastructure bank independent of the existing government bureaucracy. Browner understood Summers rejected the creation of new institutions, but she convinced Summers to put money for loans, loan guarantees, tax credits, and cash grants in the stimulus. These were tools a green bank would have used.

Browner also put some green bank techniques in the hands of the Department of Energy. Unfortunately, DOE mummified its loan and

and Martin F. Hellwig, *The Bankers' New Clothes: What's Wrong with Banking and What to Do About It* (Princeton, NJ: Princeton University Press, 2014).

4. See Kevin Robillard, "Brookings: Cash for Clunkers Failed," Politico, October 30, 2013, http://www.politico.com/story/2013/10/brookings-cash-for-clunkers-program-barack-obama-administration-cars-stimulus-099134.

loan guarantee programs with layers of red tape. Billions of dollars were never spent. Nothing transformational happened. If Obama had created the green banks, we might have succeeded over two terms in greatly increasing investment in clean power alternatives to the carbon platform on which the economy still mostly rests.

8

December's Dark News

If you're gonna bring me something
Bring me something I can use
But don't you bring me no bad news
— *"Don't Nobody Bring Me No Bad News,"*
lyrics by Charlie Smalls (from *The Wiz*)

Addressing the National Governors Association in Philadelphia on December 2, President-elect Obama said he would pass "an economic recovery plan…that jumpstarts our economy, helps save or create two and a half million jobs, puts tax cuts into the pockets of hard-pressed middle-class families, and makes a down payment on the investments we need to build a strong economy for years to come." If he meant the jobs to last only a year, then his stimulus amounted to about $250 million, assigning $100,000 for one job-year. At about the same time, 400 economists signed a letter calling for only $300 to $400 billion.[1]

Obama spoke too soon. In early December Summers and Furman circulated to the president-elect and his close advisers a four-page memo suggesting that Obama push for a high number. Romer explained the methodology: "The main variable is GDP. Then you use Okun's law to figure out what the behavior of GDP means for employment or

---

1. Warsh, David. "One Thing Obama Could Have Done Differently," Economic Principals, January 29, 2012, http://www.economicprincipals.com/issues/2012.01.29/1335.html.

unemployment. Usually GDP 1 percent above trend for a year lowers the unemployment rate by about half a percentage point. So if you can raise GDP by a percent, that can shave half a point off the unemployment rate."[2] The Summers and Froman "American Economic Recovery Plan" called for a stimulus of $580 billion, 16 percent higher than the $500 billion that Summers had publicly bandied about earlier. Roughly, that stimulus equaled 4 percent of GDP, so would lower unemployment by 2 percent. This estimate begged two questions: How high was unemployment going to rise, and by how much did Obama want to lower it?

Meanwhile, China, a country that needed to guarantee full employment in return for one-party autocratic control of the state, announced a $600 billion stimulus program in November. That equaled 15 percent of annual economic output, spent over two years.[3] If Obama had proffered a similar program, it would have totaled about $2 trillion.

Apparently reflecting the advice in the Summers-Furman memo, on December 5 Obama said in a statement that the country needed "an economic recovery plan that will save or create at least 2.5 million more jobs *over two years*." Adding the phrase "over two years" effectively doubled the size of the stimulus he described to the governors, because five million job-years required $500 billion of funding.[4] But again, Obama spoke too soon.

The first week of every month, the Bureau of Labor Statistics' first cut at the previous month's number came out. The December 5 report stated that 533,000 jobs were lost in November. Romer thought, "My God, this may be terrible."[5] That compared to October's 240,000. In the two weeks since Obama named his economic team, the economy had shrunk

---

2. Romer, interview.

3. Simon Rabinovitch, "China's $600 Billion Stimulus Is Dotted with Questions." *Reuters*, November 10, 2008, https://www.reuters.com/article/us-china-financial-stimulus-sb-idUSTRE4A91NW20081110.

4. About $100,000 of spending creates about one job-year of employment, because about $50,000 goes to equipment, health insurance, and other expenses associated with an employee, and about $50,000 is the average income per employee. So after estimating the desired reduction in unemployment, multiply the number of desired job-years times $100,000 and the result is the size of the spending. Divide the stimulus by $100,000 and you get the number of job-years it promised.

5. Romer, interview.

far faster than his experts anticipated. A $500 billion stimulus would leave the unemployment rate very high.

Romer calculated that the downturn would lead to "missing demand of about $1 trillion a year for two years."[6] That meant 20 million job-years would evaporate.[7] The economists quickly understood that by relying on their earlier advice, Obama had committed himself to a stimulus number far short of what was needed to achieve tolerable unemployment. From a different perspective, Geithner worried that the deteriorating economy might cause more bank runs.

As shocking as the December 5 announcement was, the truth was almost twice as bad. In later revisions, BLS reported true job loss in October as nearly 500,000 and in November more than 800,000. In the months to come, some of Obama's advisers excused the calculations of late 2008 on the grounds that the BLS provided accurate numbers only months later.

However, even the initially understated report of the November job loss was bad enough to scare not only Romer but also other economists with whom she consulted. She asked Mark Zandi, a well-known forecaster, for his predictions. They were awful. She called many in the academy and business. Everyone was alarmed.[8]

In Peter Orszag's view, "one of the key problems throughout all of this was the macroeconomic and macro-model perspectives from the Econ-Ph.D. world were lagging behind reality at each stage of this downturn. The practitioners, many of my friends and mentors from New York, even in early '08, were saying, 'This is bad. I mean, you don't understand, this is really bad.' The macro guys were saying, 'Eh, it will be okay.' In November and December of 2008, we were in a little bit of catch-up in terms of the depth of the problem."[9]

The advisers got plenty of advice over the telephone and from meetings with CEOs and academics. "But," said Orszag, "the problem with the sort of phone-call approach is it's anecdotal, and against that you've got

6. Ibid.
7. $100,000 equaled one job-year.
8. Romer, interview.
9. Orszag, interview.

the massive machinery, which might be misleading, of the macro-econo-metric models of the Federal Reserve projections, which all look pretty on paper and are well-specified and rigorous and what have you. It takes a lot to overcome that with a couple of phone calls."[10]

Despite the difficulty of diagnosis, and without yet knowing the BLS report of November unemployment, on November 29, 2008, Joe Stiglitz wrote in the *New York Times* that the stimulus should be more than $1 trillion spread over two years.[11] Jamie Galbraith said the right number was $900 billion in one year.[12] Krugman called on his blog for $600 billion of stimulus to be spent in one year, writing, "You really, really don't want to lowball this."[13] At $500 billion over two years, Obama's proposal either assumed a more rapid recovery or tolerated much higher unemployment than these economists thought wise. The first BLS esti-mate made Obama's shortfall stark, and the later revision would reveal it to be woefully inadequate.

Physicist Werner Heisenberg taught the impossibility of knowing both the location of a particle and its momentum at the same time. Obama knew neither the actual unemployment nor the trend. He had a double Heisenberg of a problem. He needed to create optionality. Instead, Obama tied himself to a specific job-creation number that in turn implied a specific size for stimulus and a specific prediction for unemployment.

In a radio address on December 6, Obama stuck with his target, repeating that he would ask Congress to pass a stimulus that saved or created 2.5 million jobs. He must have heard the BLS news, because he mentioned the November job loss number—533,000. He used the new statistic only to bolster his case for the now less-adequate size of the stimulus.

10. Ibid.

11. Joseph E Stiglitz, "A $1 Trillion Answer," *New York Times*, November 29, 2008, https://www.nytimes.com/2008/11/30/opinion/30stiglitz.html/.

12. "Trillion-US-dollar Stimulus Now on the Radar," *Sydney Morning Herald*, December 4, 2008, https://www.smh.com.au/business/trillionusdollar-stimulus-now-on-the-radar-20081204-6rgb.html.

13. Paul Krugman, "Stimulus Math," *New York Times*, November 10, 2008, https://krugman.blogs.nytimes.com/2008/11/10/stimulus-math-wonkish/.

Perhaps Obama's legislative advisers told him Congress would balk at going much above that $500 billion level, regardless of the depth of the recession. However, Congress collectively had no better idea of the severity and duration of the recession than anyone around Obama. Senator Majority Leader Harry Reid and House Speaker Nancy Pelosi probably believed Obama's economists were best placed to calculate the size of the stimulus necessary to let them hold their majorities in the 2010 elections.

In his radio talk Obama also again endorsed the hodgepodge approach to spending. Obama proposed a "massive effort to make public buildings more energy efficient." He would make "the single largest new investment in our national infrastructure since the creation of the federal highway system in the 1950s." He would "modernize and upgrade school buildings" and connect "schools and libraries to the Internet."[14] He would move doctors and hospitals to electronic healthcare records.

Here then would be the stimulus program in action. The government would insulate the walls of its own buildings. A school would let a contract to do a renovation that might close the school for a year, shunting students elsewhere. A doctor would sit at a desk typing a diagnosis on the keyboard of a personal computer. (The iPad was not introduced until 2010.) Ten days later Obama complained to his advisers about the difficulty of explaining such a shapeless program, as he had learned in trying on December 6.

Most newly elected presidents let the outgoing president own bad news that might arrive between election day and inauguration. By contrast, Obama outlined his jobs plan on the radio the same day as the incumbent president's traditional radio address. On his radio appearance, Bush said that he was at the Army-Navy game, and that he had reached agreements with Iraq that enabled some troop withdrawal.

Perhaps since the meeting in the Roosevelt Room after the Lehman debacle, Obama had been convinced the nation wanted a president with

---

14. That was a continuation of the program Al Gore, Senator Jay Rockefeller, and Congressman (now Senator) Ed Markey got Congress to pass and the FCC to implement in 1996–7, pursuant to which the FCC spent about $2 billion per year in the previous 20 years. Not until Obama's second term did the FCC expand the size of the funding significantly.

a plan for recovery and that he was de facto that person. Power abhors a vacuum. He had filled the void left by the absent George W. Bush. Perhaps also Obama thought his public statements would calm business and decrease the risk of bank runs. In any event, as if already inaugurated, Obama continued to explain his proposals in public. On December 7, 2008, Obama told Tom Brokaw in an interview[15] that passing a short-term economic stimulus was his top priority. He said that spending would be on "shovel-ready projects." "Shovel-ready" meant "timely." Obama had adopted Summers' three T's.

"Getting Rahm's Head Around the Situation"

The economic and political advisers wanted to speed the stimulus rather than wait to understand the situation. They wanted Obama to approve the final recovery plan before he left for a two-week vacation in Hawaii on December 17. The decision meeting was pushed to the last possible day—December 16 in Chicago. Summers designed the event to encompass the entire economic recovery program. The ambitious agenda would have called for days of meetings in the business world, but Summers sought only Obama's general assent to the directions the team would recommend. Then Summers himself would complete the proposal that the staff presented to the Democratic congressional leadership.

To gauge and set the decision maker's expectations, Summers and Romer went to Rahm Emanuel. Romer said, "Larry and I wrote a memo to Rahm before the meeting, trying to soften up the ground Larry felt needed softening up, getting Rahm's head around the situation, saying, 'We know you're thinking a smaller number for the stimulus package, but it's going to need be bigger.'"[16] Chiefs of staff in government typically decide what their boss will see. Some also inform briefing teams what the leader will decide before the briefing takes place. Emanuel told Summers that Congress would not quickly pass a stimulus measure starting with a *t* for "trillion."

15. Barack Obama, interview by Tom Brokaw, *Meet the Press*, NBC, December 7, 2008.
16. Romer, interview.

Early the next week, on December 9, Al Gore met with Obama in Chicago. Gore told Obama that he guessed "the stimulus number was $650 billion or something like that." Obama did not dispute him. Then Gore asked, "If you don't mind, where did you get that number?"

Obama said, "It's the figure that is the most politically feasible."

Gore replied, "Well, with all due respect, I would urge you to make it significantly larger, and I would urge you to realize that the political difficulty of having a number that is too low and then dealing with the consequences of it is going to far exceed whatever is the difficulty of passing a bigger number now. Because you're at the peak of your powers coming in, and you need to fix this economy right out of the gate."[17]

Romer, Summers Agreed

With the decision meeting less than a week away, Romer shared with Summers her updated conclusion about the desired size of the stimulus. She said, "I remember it was around December 10 and the stimulus was supposed to be basically a done deal and I finally decided to say, I really think this is too small and it needs to be bigger. I showed Larry the analysis and he was very sympathetic."[18] Moreover, Summers "thought Romer was too optimistic about the underlying path. I thought the country was in big trouble. I didn't believe we were getting to 5.1 percent unemployment in the time frame she predicted. I thought the risk was on the side of doing too little because I thought the forecast maybe won't come true. Obama called me Dr. Kevorkian. They were always making jokes about how pessimistic I was. Unfortunately, I was mostly right."[19]

The mathematical calculations showed that the economy needed $1.7 trillion of additional spending in order to produce full employment. However, the neoliberals in the Obama advisers group could not construct a $1.7 trillion package without including tax cuts, or in other words moving to supply-side measures. They declined to propose large

17. Al Gore, interview with author.
18. Romer, interview.
19. Summers, interview.

tax cuts because they held the dream of balancing the budget in years to come. Summers said, "I did tell Christy we don't know how to spend $1.7 trillion and it will just freak the room out, so it's a better idea to leave this out."[20]

Romer was flying in from San Francisco to be in D.C. two or three days a week. She had never done anything in government before and she had not been working on the campaign. She had no staff, no ability to order work done for her by the hundreds of people in the transition team headquarters. She could not specify how $1.7 trillion would be spent. She had little familiarity with existing programs. She did not know how the budget rules permitted actual spending to reach the level she wanted without triggering a score nearly that high. The disfavored methods of loans and increased entitlements are such techniques, but Romer also did not take advantage of the ten-year rule that the Republicans used to lower the deficit score in their 2001 and 2017 tax cuts. Congress measures revenue in (taxation) and spending out (appropriations and tax cuts) over a ten-year period. Therefore, if Congress cut taxes for five years and raised them for the next five years, the result would count as zero for budget purposes. Alice Rivlin suggested Obama use this method. Then the administration could stimulate in the first term and balance the budget in the second term of the Obama presidency.

Similarly, spending planned for the back half of the decade could be accelerated into the front half. For example, Marty Feldstein of Harvard thought the Defense Department should buy equipment earlier than scheduled. In the budget that would not count as new spending as long as the total over a 10 year period remained constant.

Orszag and Furman knew these scoring tricks. But Romer had no budget mavens helping her. She stuck with the macroeconomics she knew.

"For my section of the big memo we were writing for the president for the December 16 meeting," Romer decided she "wanted to say here's where we think the economy is headed. Let me show you three scenarios —what happens if we do $600, $800, and $1,200 billion of stimulus.

20. Ibid.

If you wanted to keep unemployment below 8 percent you did $800 billion. But if you wanted to get it down quickly to below 7 percent, you needed to do something really big like $1.2 trillion."[21] However, the rest of the team did not want her to frame the choices this way.

She explained that "Peter Orszag had to do a budget. So he was saying he didn't want to go that big [because the deficit would be so large]." Geithner also was reluctant to offer Obama the option of spending $1.2 trillion. According to Romer, "Tim often said, 'There's more fiscal stimulus in financial rescue than in the fiscal stimulus.' But I said, 'There's more financial rescue in the fiscal stimulus than in direct measures to help the financial system.' He would say, 'Let's heal the banks. That would be good for the economy.' I would say, 'Let's heal the economy. That would be good for the banks.'"

She said, "Larry was conflicted. On the one hand he believed deeply in fiscal stimulus. But I think he also thought of himself as a political person who could figure out the most Congress would go for. So he didn't start first with what the numbers said about how big it should be. It was immediately tempered by what he thought we could possibly get through Congress."[22]

Summers deleted the $1.2 trillion number from the draft of the decision memo for the president-elect. Romer recalled that, "Larry said, 'I don't think we should show the $1.2 trillion.' His argument was, he didn't think we'd ever get that, and he didn't think it was good for the president ever to be seen as losing, so it shouldn't be on any piece of paper. But he did give me a lot of time to make the case and I was to be the first speaker in Chicago."[23]

Summers continued to calculate the possible size of the stimulus by talking "to Rahm every day. I thought it was likely he would be willing to go to $900 billion but if he had said $720 billion I wouldn't have been amazed by that." From the conversations he had with Emanuel and the other political advisers running up to the December 16 meeting,

21. Romer, interview.
22. Ibid.
23. Ibid.

Summers "was left with the impression that, even though the number had been running in the 300s as recently as November, the gravity of the situation was becoming clear to people. The president-elect had been saying, 'We need to pull off the Band-Aid fast, we need to act decisively,' so I had the feeling the $800 billion number was likely to be accepted." [24]

Summers was concerned that the economic recovery planning memo might be leaked. Years later it was. By mid-December, however, plenty of people publicly opined that the stimulus needed to start with a *t*. There were few, if any, secrets worth keeping about the economic situation. "In December 2008," Robert Reich said, "there were a number of people, myself included, who were talking about $1.2 to $1.4 trillion over two years. People were trying to estimate the shortfall in private aggregate demand for 2009 and 2010 and to fill it in whole or in part with government spending." [25]

On December 15, 2008, Alice Rivlin, a former head of both CBO and OMB, predicted unemployment would continue to rise to at least 10 percent, and the recovery period would be long and slow with high unemployment for several years. On the other hand, she did not think that another Great Depression was likely. "We have institutions that prevent that, like deposit insurance. We have a much bigger federal government where automatic stabilizers move against any downturn. The main example is that when people aren't earning as much, they aren't paying as much taxes. The drop in income produces federal deficit spending that in turn swings in the direction of stabilizing the economy. Knowing that, it was not reasonable to think we would have another Great Depression with 25 percent unemployment."

Rivlin also thought Obama could ask for a much bigger stimulus if he coupled it with a "Social Security fix"—meaning some combination of reducing future benefits and raising revenues—"up front in a way that has no effect on the short term economy. The calculation of benefits depends on an index of wages, so you can reduce the increase in benefits slightly in the future by making it less generous to upper-income people.

24. Summers, interview.
25. Robert Reich, interview with author.

This was a good moment to put Social Security on a solid track for the future."[26] However, none of the Obama advisers had the temerity to suggest Social Security reform to Barack Obama in the dismal month of December 2008.

A metric for a depression is a 10 percent drop in GDP. As the following chart shows, the Great Recession would not approach that level. As Rivlin predicted, the real problem turned out to be the slow rate of the L-shaped recovery.

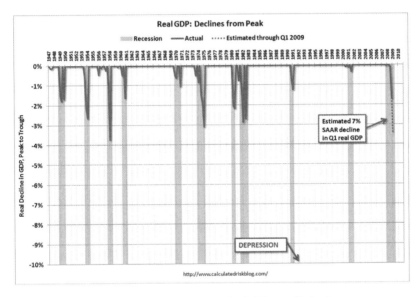

Bill McBride, Calculated Risk, http://www.calculatedriskblog.com. Used with permission.

The advisers agreed that losing 1 percent of gross domestic product led to losing one million jobs and thus would increase the unemployment rate by about one-half of 1 percent. Therefore, the predicted 7 percent drop in GDP would cause unemployment to go to 9 percent for two years. Between the end of 2008 and the end of 2010, the rate would rise to about 9 percent and then fall to 8 percent by 2011. That the advisers called the baseline. Without knowing the actual size of job losses past, present, and occurring in the near future, the advisers assumed that a

26. Alice Rivlin, interview with author.

stimulus of $800 billion would keep unemployment from going higher than 8 percent and would lower it to close to 7 percent by the end of 2010.

Full employment equated to an unemployment rate between 4 and 5 percent. At that point, wages would begin to rise. Very roughly, the advisers calculated that the difference between the trajectory of the recession and a healthy economy was a total of 15 to 20 million job-years. By aiming to close that gap with public spending of $800 billion, they were creating eight million job-years. If they had miscalculated the depth of the recession or if private-sector investment did not fill the hole that the stimulus purposely left, then the American people would not see their standard of living go up for a long time.

The unemployment problem also was certain to be worse for minorities. African-Americans have a higher and more cyclical unemployment rate than whites. They are about half as likely to have a college education. African-American males are about half as likely to be married. The lack of a spouse makes an unemployed person more vulnerable to dire consequences. Therefore the recession hit African-Americans, especially males, harder than other minorities.

All the advisers agreed that unemployment, as Orszag bloodlessly put it, was "a massive waste of resources, of human capital. It's just lost income for the nation as a whole." However, Orszag was also concerned about "writing a budget where we don't blow an unnecessarily large hole in the deficit."[27] He harked back to the rule of the Bill Clinton administration: if the private sector thought the government would run a huge continuing deficit, then lenders would raise interest rates, investment would decrease, the economy would not grow as much over the long term, tax revenues would shrink, and the deficit would go up for that reason too. A vicious cycle would develop and be very difficult to stop. From his perspective, any stimulus should be only enough to curtail the fall of the economy.

Romer, Stiglitz, Krugman, and Reich thought the government had to substitute for the private sector in a big way and for a long time.

27. Orszag, interview.

Summers said he knew "there should have been more stimulus." However, he thought "the project was to get as much money as we could credibly present" in a memorandum to the president and his political advisers. That required "a judgment about how much money we can move and in what form. That was a judgment about what the political process will bear. That was a judgment about maintaining internal credibility. That's what we needed to take this to."[28]

To win their arguments for TARP, Paulson and Bernanke had made histrionic public and private statements. Summers chose not to make his case to Obama the same way. He did not ask to go around Emanuel. He did not try the classic Washington bank shot—tell Speaker Pelosi or Senate Leader Harry Reid what he really thought and let them tell Obama. Summers surely knew Obama required team play.

Summers believed that Emanuel did not want to ask Congress for more than $800 billion. If it were not enough, Summers convinced himself, "it would be possible to pass more stimulus in the fall of 2009."[29]

Besides, Summers had difficulty imagining how he himself would explain a huge stimulus request. The hodgepodge composition adopted weeks earlier caused policy teams to present relatively small proposals. They did not amount to a gigantic number. Moreover, Summers had "spent decades convincing Democrats to be fiscally prudent, and it was hard to sell the opposite message, especially when Obama was not even inaugurated yet."[30]

Chris Van Hollen, then in the Democratic House leadership, said, "House Democrats were not constraining the size of the stimulus bill. That was an artificial cap that came from the White House. Every Democrat would have gone above $1 trillion. I don't think going from $700 billion to $1 trillion would have made a difference for the House vote.

"The political guys at the White House thought that anything over $1 trillion would be politically unacceptable. I don't think that was a judgment made by House Democrats. That was a judgment made by

28. Summers, interview.
29. Ibid.
30. Ibid.

the White House. Very clearly. The White House had the goal of trying to get some Senate Republicans. That was the constraint. Their view was that the only way they could get Republicans on board was to have a somewhat smaller package." [31]

Having decided on a process that required the 60 votes that would pass the stimulus over a McConnell-led filibuster, the Senate Democrats needed two Republican senators to vote for the bill. A possible Republican crossover was Arlen Specter of Pennsylvania. He had been a Democrat from 1951 to 1965, then switched to the Republican Party. He might (and did) revert to his origin. Another vote to get was either Susan Collins or Olympia Snowe of Maine. However, they probably would vote together. So unless and until the Democrats had 59 seats with Al Franken surviving the recount following his close election win in Minnesota, the Democrats had to obtain the votes of the Maine senators for the stimulus. Because the economists emphasized urgency, the Democrats could not wait for the Franken recount.

Only a few members of the House or Senate have both routine access to expert opinion and the experience to know how to ask for and get macroeconomic advice. Most have small staffs. Their committee assignments naturally define and limit their areas of expertise. A congressman like Barney Frank or a senator like Chuck Schumer, both Harvard College and Harvard Law School graduates, could understand the complexities of the financial industry partly because of their innate intelligence but also because they had long held committee positions that required deep knowledge of that sector of the economy. There was, however, no committee with the responsibility or staff that could dig deeply between November 2008 and January 2009 into the causes and remedies of the worsening recession and the financial crisis. In those few weeks, the lame ducks were packing and the new Congress was busy organizing itself.

Under these circumstances, Larry Summers, Peter Orszag, and Christy Romer, even without official jobs or much in the way of staff, represented the most focused and informed strand of decision-making in the

---

31. Van Hollen, interview.

complicated skein of the federal government. As such they had enormous power to influence the thinking of the congressional leadership.

They did not tell the Democratic congressional leadership how much money Romer thought would be necessary to achieve full employment. They certainly did not inform the Republican senators. Perhaps they did not think their math would have persuaded anyone. As a result, in mid-December Congress did not know the calculations that informed the recommendations from the Obama advisers. Emanuel was predicting the congressional reaction to a situation no one had fully explained to the Hill.

Alternatively, Obama might have tried to create public pressure that obliged the Republicans to vote for a stimulus. He would have had to describe the economic condition in very stark terms. He might have alarmed the markets, sparked bank runs. The whole delicate construct of the economic recovery packages' different elements might have collapsed. The terrible economy could grow worse.

Resorting to the court of public opinion, as opposed to fighting a legislative battle inside the Beltway, also would have taken time.[32] Congress, like Nero, might fiddle with the proposal while the economy burned.

Perhaps too Obama wanted to be a post-partisan president more than he cared about adjusting the stimulus upward. He might have wanted to compromise with at least some Republicans in order to vindicate his vision of leadership. Potentially, those same Republicans would join him on other major legislative initiatives, such as healthcare, energy, and financial sector reform.

32. Writers on the right echoed the Republicans in Congress in savaging the stimulus, in part on the cracked claim that Franklin Roosevelt's Keynesian spending had contributed to the Great Depression. Jonathan Chait, *Audacity: How Barack Obama Defied His Critics and Created a Legacy That Will Prevail* (New York: Custom House, 2017), 39–43.

9

The Pre-Meeting Memorandum

*Everything in life is writable about if you have the outgoing guts
to do it, and the imagination to improvise.*

— Sylvia Plath, "Wellesley"

Economists predict wrong most everything in the immediate future, and
in the long run, they are all dead. Surely everyone in the December 16
meeting knew that. Therefore, policies should be flexible, adapted to
events as they occur, and to achieve an objective in an unpredictable
time, excessive resources should be applied.[1] That is what Summers
meant earlier in the year when he wrote the risk of doing too little is
greater than the risk of doing too much. Another way to deal with the
risk of underestimation is to reserve additional remedies, like a general
who waits to see how a battle develops before he commits all the troops.
Lastly, at all times a CEO should engage in experiments in search of the
most effective measures. If the economists could not predict precisely,
Obama needed to apply all three techniques. He adopted none.

Summers wanted Obama to bless a single, comprehensive economic
recovery plan. The situation may have called for contingency but the
process precluded it. Summers explained, "Geithner and Orszag and
Romer told me this has to cohere. They said, 'It's better for you to write

---

1. "The first principle is: act with the utmost concentration…" Carl Von Clausewitz, Michael How-
ard, and Peter Paret, *On War* (Princeton, New Jersey: Princeton University Press, 1976), 127–147.

it from all of us.'" Summers responded, "'That's fine, but you have to agree.'"[2] The memorandum would present a narrow range of choices for the size of the stimulus, and on most topics the president-elect would find only a single recommendation. Obama had to accept it. If he did not like it, or even deliberated, markets might shudder, Congress might cavil, and businesses might quail. The economic advisers did not want a debate.

The Great Khan of China was said to have enjoyed tripartite theological debates among Muslims, Buddhists, and Nestorian Christians. However, as ruler for life, he had plenty of time for learning. Obama's advisers gave their boss only a day for making the most important decisions of a presidency that the Constitution limited to only eight years—a period that proved to be the full length of the economic cycle just commencing.

Summers asked the different advisers to contribute drafts of the sections they would present orally. He and Jason Furman edited the entirety. Complexity and consensus-seeking caused them to do, according to one reporter, 14 drafts of the memo.[3] Apparently they finished the 57 pages the night before the December 16 meeting, and sent it by email to the president-elect—a lot of homework even for a night owl.

On top Summers placed an unsigned five-page executive summary comprising the stimulus bullet points on a single page, then short passages titled "Reforms and Budget Savings," "Medium-Term Budget Outlook and Options," and "Financial Issues." The last topic was two pages, divided into paragraphs on housing, autos, financial stabilization, and regulation.

Some presenters commence by describing who they are, how they prepared, what they did not quite finish, but Summers threw the fastball right over the plate: "In the absence of fiscal stimulus the economy [will] lose three to four million jobs in 2009." That would leave the country "seven million jobs short of full employment" with an unemployment rate "above 9 percent and not projected to start falling until 2011."

---

2. Summers, interview.
3. Grunwald, *The New New Deal*, 116.

"We believe that $600 billion in stimulus over two years would create 2.5 million jobs," but "would leave the unemployment rate at 8 percent two years from now. This had convinced the economic team that a considerably larger package is justified."

Obama could choose the size of the stimulus from four choices "ranging from $550 billion to $890 billion." The range produced an unemployment rate in the first quarter of 2011 ranging from 7.3 to 8 percent.

Obama should aim for an unemployment rate lower than 8 percent, the memorandum stated, but, "It is important to recognize that we can only generate about $225 billion of actual spending on priority investments over the next two years." Transferring federal money to states and cutting taxes were not Obama's "priorities." He needed to commit "to a responsible budget." That was a code word for the neoliberal assumption that public deficits reduce private investment.

Then on page four of the executive summary, in a paragraph Geithner must have insisted upon, fell the fearful hammer: "The scale of potential future losses for the banking sector alone is substantial, and…escalating dramatically." Therefore, "effectively stabilizing the financial system will ultimately require more resources than those currently authorized under the TARP." It was imperative "to decisively stabilize core financial institutions and dramatically increase support to restart the flow of credit." This would require "substantial additional capital injections and dramatic"—the third use of that word—"expansion" of other programs. Obama needed to "support an early January request by the Bush administration for the second tranche of TARP funds" or he could "replace TARP with a program of our design"—but he had to be aware that Treasury would need even more money for bailouts than the two $350 billion tranches of TARP money.

The principal points, as in many summaries to chief executives, were written between the lines in invisible ink. First, the stimulus would have mediocre results, but Obama had to accept this outcome. As Orszag put it, this spending was a small share of the total of $2 trillion of output gap. Moreover, Orszag expected that only about 70 percent of the appropriated money would be spent as quickly as hoped. At the $800 billion level, the actual spending in two years would be $560 billion, or not much more than one-quarter of what was necessary to make up for the economic collapse that came to be known as the Great Recession. Orszag thought everyone knew they were not going to lower the unemployment rate to a low level in only two years.[4] That meant wages would not rise much, or perhaps at all, before Obama's 2012 reelection campaign. The strategic goal was to end the recession, but not to guarantee robust growth and a rising standard of living.

Second, the financial crisis had not ended. Therefore, Obama had to get Treasury the second $350 billion of TARP money very quickly, because much more had to be "injected" into the banks. While high unemployment, and a dreadful slump in housing values, had to be endured by millions of people for a long time, a dozen big banks had to be "decisively" restored to their role of lending at a profit.

Third, the economic recovery plan could not be fused with Obama's goals of building four pillars of the new economy. Financial regulation must be postponed until that industry was on its feet again, and in the three sectors of healthcare, energy, and education, the stimulus would not aspire to major accomplishments. Obama's big legislative initiatives, not the stimulus, needed to drive transformation. Market incentives, rather than public spending, would cause the private sector to construct the pillars. Emanuel had said "a crisis is too good to waste," but this strategy memorandum rejected spending to achieve profound structural change in the economy. This point reflected a key difference between a neoliberal, as opposed to progressive, approach.

Then followed an "Update on Economic Policy Work," a 51-page memorandum concerning stimulus, "reforms and budget savings," "medium-term budget outlook and options," and "financial issues." In her section Romer cited a dozen outsiders who said that the correct, necessary size of the stimulus should be $1 trillion or more over two years. Romer edged toward expressing how big the stimulus should be without violating her promise not to suggest $1.2 trillion as a serious, plausible choice for Obama.

However, the memorandum itself strongly argued against exceeding $1 trillion over two years. It acknowledged: "From the perspective of

4. Orszag, interview.

raising demand and creating jobs there is a case for a very large program of stimulus." But that only seemed to be a good idea. "To accomplish a more significant reduction in the output gap would require a stimulus of well over $1 trillion…which would not accomplish the goal because of the impact it would have on markets." What was that impact? "An excessive recovery package could spook markets or the public and be counterproductive."

Goolsbee explained, "One of our big concerns was whether this much water could fit in the pipe in this kind of time frame. If you were going to rely just on tax cuts, which are essentially unlimited in their potential total size, you could make it as big as you want. But for actual spending stimulus it would be hard to spend the money that quickly. So the bigger the total amount was, the higher the chance that something wouldn't have a high impact. And the larger the total amount, the higher was the chance it might 'spook' people."[5]

Perhaps the most perplexing principle of quantum mechanics is that something causes two widely separated particles to behave consistently in a coordinated way, but the causation is invisible, unknown, and only observable after the pair has jigged and jogged as if joined at the hip. Einstein called this "spooky action at a distance."[6] That's the sort of spookiness in markets that the economists invoked for Obama. They meant the stimulus size connected to inflation fear. At that moment, businesses had far greater worries, such as whether even Christmas buying would evaporate. Nevertheless, the advisers argued just as in 1992 that public deficits could cause investment and job growth to drop. Orszag had to have written that portion of the memorandum. On October 12, 2017, in a paper written with Olivier Blanchard, Summers would repudiate the reasoning in this part of the October 2008 memorandum.[7]

In any case, Goolsbee said, politics severely constrained the proposal: "The thing about getting a stimulus of $1 trillion or more and focusing

---

5. Goolsbee, interview.

6. Albert Einstein, Max Born, and Hedwig Born, *The Born-Einstein Letters* (Basingstoke: Macmillan, 2005), 155.

7. Olivier Blanchard and Lawrence Summers, "Rethinking Stabilization Policy. Back to the Future," Peterson Institute for International Economics, October 8, 2017, https://piie.com/system/files/documents/blanchard-summers20171012paper.pdf.

it on spending—let's call it the Krugman critique—is that getting three Republicans to agree to a number like that would have forced the stimulus to be tax cuts. They would have insisted that it not be spending. As it was, the stimulus was the largest ever and it came down to one vote. Making it even larger and more spending-based was not realistic. It would not pass."[8]

The memorandum did not explain that the miserable economic conditions would deny jobs to the young, and especially to people of color, while encouraging older people to quit the workforce.

The memorandum did not state that a high and rising standard of living would be hard to come by for most Americans until deep into Obama's second term.

Graph 8 from Bill McBride, "Employment Graphs", Calculated Risk, April 5, 2013, http://www.crgraphs.com. Used with permission.

The memorandum did warn that "further negative revisions seem more likely than positive revisions." However, it did not recommend waiting for more information. The reason was the imperative of restoring the financial sector to profitability. "The goal of fiscal stimulus is not

8. Goolsbee, interview.

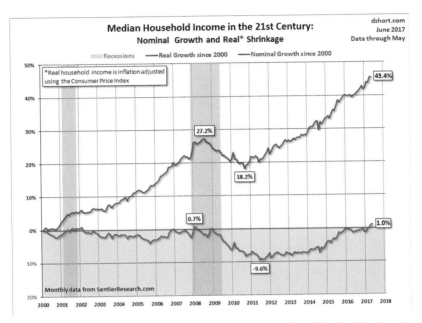

Graph 2 from Jill Mislinski, "May Real Median Household Income Little Changed from April, Last Report," Advisor Perspectives, June 22, 2017, https://www.advisorperspectives.com/dshort/updates/2017/06/22/ may-real-median-household-income-little-changed-from-april-last-report. Used with permission.

just to reduce unemployment and create jobs. It is also designed to be an insurance policy against catastrophic failure of financial institutions and other key industries."

The memorandum stated that the "economic recovery plan will create millions of new jobs by focusing on…critical infrastructure." However, as a condition, there could be "no earmarks," and spending had to be "for ready-to-go projects…obligated within…120 days." The rejection of earmarks—a way to win votes—stemmed from a long-standing neoliberal desire to constrain government activism by eliminating this tactic. The total investment in "repair and restoration" would be less than $40 billion, spread across roads, bridges, wastewater, drinking water, federal building efficiency, affordable housing, and hazardous waste cleanup. This did not accord with the promise in Obama's December 6 radio address.

Human beings as individuals and in social organizations are generally biased against innovation. It is risky, expensive, and drawn out, and can undercut the status of the people threatened by invention. In composing a massive economic recovery plan, Obama could have overcome these innate obstacles to change by funding new institutions on a long-term basis. For example, the Department of Energy's new research investing could have been $5 billion instead of the $500 million funded. The 2008 memorandum proposed to create a "national infrastructure reinvestment bank" with $10 billion in capital. That was as far as my green banks wormed into the plan.

What must have been Geithner's section started at page 38: It stated that "we need to move quickly" to satisfy "the critical imperative of decisively restoring public confidence in the health of our financial institutions." That would require "more resources—potentially considerably more—than those authorized under the TARP." In October the "total need for new capital at banks alone was seen to be in the range of $250 to $500 billion," but that was now at "the low end of what will be needed." The crusher was this: "Private capital seems unlikely to fill the gap." The economic recovery plan might need to be amended not to add more money for job creation, but to increase the bailout funding.

Geithner's fears did not come to pass. The big money-center banks were already borrowing at very low rates from the Fed, and loaning at higher rates. Their relatively high, or very prudent, pricing on loans reduced volume, limited economic growth, and increased their profits. For banks, if not for people, the recovery would be V-shaped.

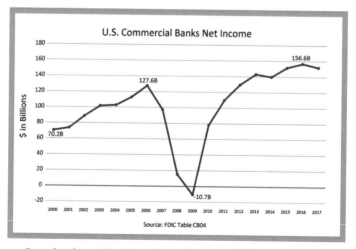

Original graph created by Deborah Nicholls. Data source: FDIC, https://www5.fdic.gov.

Summers injected a critique of Geithner's commitment to continuing the Bush administration's policies toward banks. The memorandum recapitulated Summers's "discontinuity" thesis: We want "to depart in both substance and appearance from the mistakes of the past year and a half." That included "clearer communication with the public" and, Phil Schiliro suggested, possibly "repealing TARP and replacing it with a new program that we design." The memorandum suggested that such a recommendation would be provided in "early January."

TARP Not Amended

TARP could have been improved by inserting the authority for the Fed, FDIC, and Treasury to take over a failing firm and guarantee its obligations as they did with the GSEs. In 2010 this became title II of the Dodd-Frank law. If that had been pushed through Congress in January 2009, then the Fed could have used its essentially unconstrained resources (it can print money) to seize the big Wall Street firms if and as necessary. Obama's Treasury would not have needed to husband the TARP money for the possibility of investing in a failing firm in order to save it. Nor would it have needed a line item for a second TARP in the first budget.

Obama also could have insisted that TARP be amended to impose a financial transactions tax on the big firms and to require a clawback of bonuses paid to bankers in the firms that had played a role in the financial crisis. Taking punitive measures against the banks would have created some space between the Bush-Paulson commitment to preserving the big firms and the Obama administration, which would suffer from the taint of continuing the previous administration's seeming coddling of the banks.

Obama could not easily change TARP by legislation because Democrats on the Hill did not want to vote in favor of it a second time, and the Republicans would vote against it. However, Geithner rejected all ways of separating Obama from the dreadfully unpopular bank bailout. In the meeting and outside it, he persuaded Obama to ask Bush early in January to transfer the other $350 billion to Treasury, the second half of

TARP. There was no "repeal" of TARP, and no break with the "mistakes" of the Bush administration. Geithner kept his new tranche of TARP money in his pocket. His cunning "stress test" of the big banks proved that their balance sheets were satisfactory. From March 2009, less than a month after the stimulus was enacted, their stocks performed well.[9]

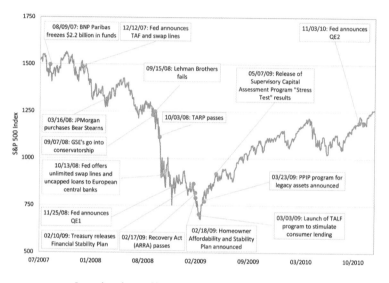

Original graph created by Grace Choi. Data source: S&P 500 index.

If the reader is curious, here is what I would have preferred:

Objective: Get unemployment to 5 percent by 2012, increase workforce participation.

Obstacles: The housing market is destroying value. The financial crisis has alarmed businesses and catalyzed massive layoffs. The combined effect has yet to be fully realized.

9. For an account of neoliberalism tracing its roots to the end of imperialism and emphasizing its hostility to democracy and its trust in efficacious global markets, see Quinn Slobodian, *Globalists: The End of Empire and the Birth of Neoliberalism* (Cambridge, Massachusetts: Harvard University Press, 2018).

Diagnosis: Businesses need incentives to invest and hire. Purchasing (consumption) must increase.

Recommendations:

1. (Supply side) Onetime repatriation of approximately $1 trillion of overseas profits within two years at a 5 percent rate, producing a budget cost of about $50 billion (estimated foregone taxes), contingent on firms also allocating 5 percent to capitalize physical infrastructure banks with $50 billion, leading to $500 billion of public-private investment.

2. (Demand side) Add $200 billion to Social Security and unemployment benefits.

3. (Demand side) Green banks, capitalized with $30 billion, causing $300 billion in public-private investment.

4. (Demand side) Deposit $1,000 in individual tax-free savings account of each child born in America between 2007 and 2017, invest in equity markets through index funds. Total cost $40 billion (4 million births per year). Money would have doubled by at least 2018.

5. (Demand side) Allocate $100 billion of TARP funds to capitalize at least three private-sector banks dedicated to buying underwater homes at full mortgage price, offering to rent them to occupants at affordable rates with an option to buy at full price plus 10 percent.

6. (Demand side) Endow universities, national laboratories, and the National Science Foundation with $100 billion for research into potential breakthrough innovations in clean power, communications, transportation, and health.

7. (Demand side) Refinance all student loans at the government rate of about 1 percent. Estimated cost: $100 billion.

8. Allocate $100 billion to military to recruit and train personnel for army reserves, Army Corps of Engineers, National Park repair and maintenance, and retrofitting of all federal, state, and local buildings to consume power efficiently.

9. Tax reform: impose modest financial transactions tax on big banks. Cut corporate income and payroll taxes. Impose modest carbon tax effective in 2017. Net cost: $200 billion.

10. Create $50 billion sovereign wealth fund for benefit of taxpayers, à la Norway's use of oil revenues. Total cost: $970 billion. Actual boost through public-private partnerships and other leverage (not including multipliers): $1.7 trillion.

10

A Three-Meeting Day

CASSANDRA: *Fool! thus to read amiss mine oracles.*
— Aeschylus, *The Oresteia*, translated by E. D. A. Morshead

In the morning before their meeting with Obama, Summers and Romer gave a preview to Axelrod, Goolsbee, and Emanuel. For weeks, Obama's economists had repeatedly underestimated the magnitude of the problem. Now they had to tell him that increasing the stimulus to $800 billion would leave unemployment rising to almost 8 percent. Goolsbee explained, "Making sure everything is prepared and Axelrod has seen it—that was the purpose of the pre-meeting." This was "without the president-elect, with just the economic team and the message/political people. Axelrod said two things. One: 'The wider country doesn't understand that there's a problem; they think this is a financial problem. Are you saying it's an economic problem?' All the economists say, 'Yes! Oh my God. We're on the edge of a precipice.' And that's when Axelrod is saying, 'Look, America hasn't really had a "holy shit" moment in which it looks at what's happening and says, Holy shit, we need to do something or we're doomed.'" Then the second thing he says is, 'Are you telling me that even if we enact the biggest stimulus of all time—$800 billion, bigger than the New Deal—that the unemployment rate is still going to go over 8 percent? That's definitely going to be a messaging challenge.'"[1]

---

1. Goolsbee, interview.

The president-elect had given the public the inaccurate impression that his promise to "save or create" two to three million jobs by spending $500 to $600 billion would spare the country from a truly severe recession. Axelrod recalled, "Everyone was arguing for a larger stimulus and the question on the floor was, how much would the market, meaning Congress, bear? What was immediately apparent was that we had to both alert the country to the magnitude of the disaster and then hope that we could create enough momentum for fairly prodigious solutions."[2]

Obama could have taken a page from Franklin Roosevelt and in effect declare a national emergency, stating that the economic situation had deteriorated more than expected. Or he could have skated over the difference between his previous estimate of the stimulus's size and the new number that was 60 percent higher. The first option would push the stimulus into the top spot on the priority list. It also required Obama to explain his underestimations, dating back to right after the election. The second enabled him to shorten public discussion, and start spending sooner. The "alert" Axelrod described could be very dramatic, or more in line with Obama's previous erroneous predictions.

No Cake for Carol

The advisers packed the cramped room for the big meeting with Obama. All attendees were men but for Browner and Romer. Maybe a dozen in total. The president-elect came in. Everyone stands when the president or president-elect arrives. He waved everyone back into their seats.

Kings like to call for plates of things to be brought into meetings: the heads of enemies, spoils of war, presents. Obama had a cake brought in. Obama announced that it was Peter Orszag's 40th birthday. Orszag thought this was "nice."[3]

Nobody knew it was also Browner's birthday. There was no cake for Carol—a symbolic representation of the plight of the environmental agenda.

2. Axelrod, interview.
3. Orszag, interview.

In exchange for her agreement not to put $1.2 trillion in the memo-randum, Summers let Romer open the presentation to Obama. Romer had never before been in a decision-making meeting with the chief executive officer of the institution with the world's largest capability to tax, spend, and borrow in its own currency. She wondered how to get her main point across with impact. She needed Obama to endorse the highest number Summers let her ask for.

Summers explained that Romer would begin the briefing, that Gools-bee would cover housing, and Geithner, the ongoing financial crisis. Romer cleared her throat, leaned forward in her seat. She had heard from Axelrod that morning an attention-getting barnyard epithet. She borrowed it for her opening.

"Mr. President, this is your 'holy shit' moment."

Obama turned to the group and said, "Did she just say 'shit'?"[4]

Everyone laughed. Not what Romer hoped would be the response. The male-dominated group had put her on the wrong foot. She retreated to the comfort zone of her numbers. She continued, "Here's our estimate of where we're going, and we think $800 billion will prevent unemploy-ment from rising to a terrible level."[4] "Terrible" was a debatable term. That freighted word went unexamined.

Romer continued, "That will contain a lot of the damage." Then she began selling again: "Let me tell you the two nightmare scenarios you should be worried about. One is Japan. If we don't deal with this defini-tively, we could start a decade of low to zero economic growth like they had in Japan. Second, there could also be another financial crisis.

"If the financial crisis starts again, we spiral down. We have more banks go under. We have loss of confidence. Then you could be looking at Great Depression territory. That would be an argument for why you might do an even bigger stimulus.'"[5] Romer acknowledged that pro-tecting Wall Street against runs was the top priority, which was what Geithner wanted Obama to hear. As she closed her case, some people

4. Ibid.
5. Ibid.

in the meeting heard Romer opine that the odds on reliving the Great Depression were "one in three." She herself did not recall the assertion.

Axelrod, involved in politics for 35 years, had "never thought I'd sit in a meeting with the president-elect and be told there's a one-in-three chance of a second Great Depression. You think of the Depression as something that is part of history. You don't think of it as something that could reoccur."[6]

Romer engaged in hyperbole to make her pitch. Unemployment reached 25 percent in the Great Depression. Only a cascade of bank runs toppling all Wall Street could cause the economy to shrink as fast as it had in the 1930s, and in that event the government would nationalize some of the financial sector, as it had already done for the GSEs.

Romer said without the stimulus it would rise above 9 percent, which "may be an issue for the 2010 election."[7] As Orszag put it, Obama "was informed that unemployment was a very serious problem and that we were sort of falling off a cliff." On the other hand, Orszag said, "There was a lot more confidence that it could be brought down quickly. There was very little discussion that this was going to linger until 2012, much less 2014. It was thought it would be a year or two, not a five- or six-year thing."[8] The advisers had that wrong.

When Romer saw the BLS November unemployment count the first week of December she realized she had underestimated the severity of the recession. On December 16 she made the same mistake, as the January BLS report on the December unemployment statistics would soon reveal. The case for a $1.2 trillion stimulus was stronger than she knew.

6. Axelrod, interview.
7. A 1 percent increase in unemployment equaled about 1.5 million jobs. Quits and fires might range from 20 to 25 percent of the workforce. Roughly, everyone in that category is affected by an increase in the unemployment rate, because they will all have greater difficulty finding employment. Quits and layoffs together ran around five million a month from January 2002 to January 2009. They fell to around four million a month from the middle of 2009 to early 2013. But job openings dropped from 4.5 million per month in early 2007 to about two million in the middle of 2009, and did not exceed quits and layoffs until late 2014. Only when the former exceeds the latter do wages tend to rise.
8. Romer, interview.

If the decision meeting had occurred after the Congress convened, and the December data had come in, that would have been obvious.

In any event, as Romer talked, Orszag thought the president-elect looked as if he were thinking, "Well, this sucks."[9]

Goolsbee said, "The context was we had publicly been for $175 billion of stimulus at the time of the election. Over the course of the transition, with conditions rapidly deteriorating in the economy, the biggest number anybody had seen was around $450 billion. Now we're coming in saying $800 billion. Rahm was there, and when Christy was saying this will be the biggest stimulus ever, Rahm had a very pained look on his face. The president was quite concerned to hear that we needed more."[10]

Did Romer explain that $1.2 trillion was the better choice for the size of the stimulus in her view? Orszag did not think so. Romer didn't tell me precisely that she did. Axelrod thought Romer did mention that number. He said, "Everyone understood that 1.2 was better than 800."[11]

Goolsbee did not recall the meeting exactly that way. He said, "No one in that meeting argued for $1.2 trillion. The only mention of a number bigger than $800 billion was Christy Romer saying, 'We've run the models for a trillion, for $800 billion, and for $500 billion, and we think $800 billion is the right amount. We think $800 billion is a reasonable package and the thing to do.' $800 billion seemed pretty audacious at that moment and the political people were pained at how hard it would be to get $800 billion, much less any bigger."[12]

Phil Schiliro, who had met extensively with Democrats on the Hill, recalled that in October "congressional Democrats met with economists…who talked about having to do a $300 billion stimulus. And the reaction for members…was that was impossible; it was just too big a number. By the time we got to late November, it was clear $300 billion would be woefully inadequate. By the time we got to December…it had

9. Orszag, interview.
10. Goolsbee, interview.
11. Axelrod, interview.
12. Goolsbee, interview.

to be over $700 billion. Then the only debate was how close to a trillion could it be from an economic standpoint."[13]

Schiliro took Romer's "holy shit" to mean the stimulus had to be passed immediately "because the economy was about to slip into a depression." Schiliro heard the advisers tell Obama that "he had to do something big, and he had to do it quick" because "we were on a cliff, about to fall into a depression." If speed mattered more than size, then Schiliro's job was to tell everyone what would pass quickly. Whatever the economists wanted, "we had to balance that with what would pass."[14]

Axelrod said, "I didn't know the Congress well enough to know, but I know that Rahm and Schiliro and some of our legislative guys felt that something between 750 and 800 was about as good as we could get. And that proved prescient, because over time the three or four votes that we needed, including Republicans and Ben Nelson, were absolutely wedded to the notion that it should not go higher than $800 billion. These were political judgments, not economic judgments. There was a high degree of skepticism as there is today about the efficacy of public spending. The economists were Keynesians. Summers's basic argument in that meeting was, there is a hole and we better fill it. How we fill it is less consequential. The other number that was looming in people's heads was the trillion-dollar deficit [in the existing fiscal year]. By the time we got our turn at the presidency it was really up to 1.3 trillion. There was a tremendous public consternation about deficits."[15]

Axelrod acknowledged that Bush's tax cut stimulus had created a bigger deficit than was contemplated by Obama's advisers. However, he said, "the difference between 2009 and 2001 was that when Bush passed his tax cuts we had a $2 trillion projected surplus. Our critics in 2009 were making the argument that you're borrowing against future generations. Bush was making the argument that this is your money, you should have it back. It's a much easier political argument to make.

13. Phil Schiliro, interview with author.
14. Ibid.
15. Axelrod, interview.

"Also, Bush had control of both chambers.[16] We really didn't. When you have a coalition that spans from Bernie Sanders to Ben Nelson it's not a coalition. The president himself would have done more, and frankly when we prodded and poked, the House talked about something more approaching a trillion. We certainly would have accepted that. But we did not think the Senate would accept it. As it turned out, Ben Nelson was the single most difficult person in the group. He said, I cannot vote for anything over $800 billion."[17]

Summers had been preaching for the better part of a year that in the matter of stimulus it was better to do too much than too little. However, at the time of the meeting he thought that "it was a reasonable judgment that if your stimulus target were too big, there was nothing much you could do about it," because you could not get Congress to approve it, "but if it were too small you could pass another jobs bill." Therefore, it was okay to do too little now rather than too much. To that end, "some" of the proposal was "designed" so that it could be expanded later. "For example, we only had one year unemployment insurance, we only had one year of tax cuts. That was designed to avoid sticker shock in the original number and make it essentially obligatory that the stimulus be extended in the second year."[18] However, others thought Summers disfavored extra spending. Goolsbee said, "Larry Summers argued that spending that was to go beyond the two- to three-year time frame ought to be paid for and not thought of as 'stimulus.'"[19]

Romer carried away from the meeting, and all the way back into the academy to which she would return in September 2010, worry about her presentation to Obama on that cold Chicago day, in the winter of economic discontent: "One of the things that I think about is whether a more pessimistic forecast would have led to a bigger stimulus. Suppose I had correctly predicted how bad the recession was going to be. Given

---

16. The Republican control did not last long. The Senate convening on January 2001 was split 50-50. In June Vermont senator Jim Jeffords left the Republican caucus and joined the Democrats, making Democrat Tom Daschle the majority leader. The Republicans controlled the House.

17. Axelrod, interview.

18. Summers, interview.

19. Goolsbee, interview.

where all of the other forecasts were, would people have believed me, or would they just think we were trying to use scare tactics?"[20]

No Moonshot

Obama did not question the size of the stimulus. He certainly did not want to go bigger. Instead, Goolsbee said, Obama and Vice-President-elect Biden argued, "'Look, there needs to be more inspiration, this can't just be a ragtag collection of things that don't make any sense. What if it was one big thing? What if it was bigger but spread out over time?'"[21]

They had discussed possible big things. In their meetings before the presentation, Romer had come up with the notion of a brigade of teacher's aides. Summers suggested free-money debit cards. Despite the brainstorming, the advisers did not present Obama with any "big thing" options.

Looking at the themelessness of the package, Obama asked what he was supposed to say in his ongoing conversation with the American people. Some say marketing boils down to: you are sick, I will make you well. Others say it is: you're not alone, I will help. The stimulus did not suit either formulation. Sensing the problem, Obama asked, "Where's our Hoover Dam?" According to one reporter, Biden also searched "for something big and inspirational but also substantively beneficial."[22]

Obama answered his own question with a suggestion. He said he wanted to pay for an overhaul of the nation's electricity grid so that new power lines could bring renewably generated electricity from the windy Dakotas and the sunny desert to the great urban centers. The federal government would pay for most as it did for the interstate highway system in the 1950s.

Perhaps Gore gave him that idea. Earlier in 2008 Gore sent me as his personal representative to explain to Australian prime minister Kevin Rudd that his government should build high-voltage lines connecting

20. Romer, interview.
21. Goolsbee, interview.
22. Noam Scheiber, *The Escape Artists: How Obamas Team Fumbled the Recovery* (New York: Simon & Schuster, 2012).

the handful of large cities on the coast to serried ranks of solar panels dotting the great emptiness of the interior. The plan Obama put forward was much the same as the tale Gore had me tell Rudd.

Browner said, "After Christy gave her presentation and there was a discussion about what the broad outlines of the stimulus would be, we then had a discussion about transmission, the grid, and investments in the grid. There was a discussion about 'Why don't we look at how much more money we'd be able to spend on energy, and specifically let's look at whether or not there's investments we should make in the grid?' And then out of that we started the work of putting together what became the largest investment we've ever made in energy. The test was job creation, and shovel-ready."[23]

Summers saw that Obama and Biden both "had enthusiasm for the national power grid," but he thought they did not understand that power grids in the United States are funded by the private sector.[24] "They're not like interstate highways. So the government's job is to remove regulatory obstacles. The government's job is to establish a framework. The government's job isn't to pay for the imposition of the grid."[25]

Joe Aldy, Browner and Summers's shared economist, explained, "Highways are almost exclusively publicly funded, whereas for transmission we have a legacy of financing through the setting of rates on both the transmission and connecting distribution lines. We actually wanted to put out a pot of money to create a competition among the states. If any of them could design multistate systems in which they could resolve the siting and cost allocation issues in two to three years, they could get a pot of money for that. That was not enthusiastically embraced by the

23. Carol Browner, interview with author.
24. Summers, interview. The a priori judgment that transmission must be privately funded is not intrinsically obvious. Roosevelt's TVA is evidence to the contrary. Transmission, as Obama suggested, was ripe for new investment.
25. In 2017 Summers and Blanchard wrote: "It may be…that the rate of return on public investment is sufficiently high that public investment should be increased, and financed by debt." When Obama intuited this conclusion, his economic advisers paid him little heed. This can happen to elected officials. Olivier Blanchard and Lawrence Summers, "Rethinking Stabilization Policy. Back to the Future," Peterson Institute for International Economics, October 8, 2017, https://piie.com/system/files/documents/blanchard-summers20171012paper.pdf.

Hill staff. The problem was that you couldn't easily finance transmission through the existing system."[26]

Even though Summers and Browner persuaded Obama not to transform the electricity distribution system, on January 25, 2009, the new president praised the American Recovery and Reinvestment Act on the ambiguous basis that it would "begin to build" more than 3,000 miles of transmission lines. A month earlier he had correctly pointed out that he needed to see the big things that the stimulus would do. He ended up with the notion in his rhetoric, but not in new legislation.

To meet Obama's request, the electricity business would have to change. That was unthinkable. The advisers stuck to their precepts: no big changes in market structure or conduct, no important new legislative authority. The goal was to pump money into the demand side of the economic machine. Reforms would come later in the body of the major legislative initiative called cap-and-trade.

If Obama had wanted a signature item, he needed to insist on a menu of such choices. He had signaled his interest in a new grid, but not demanded options for accomplishing his objectives. Instead he gave Summers and Browner the room to reject his idea. If he had any concerns about the size or composition of the stimulus, he had to ask for more distinct options and a bigger range of choices. To avoid the trap of facing one basic choice presented by the entire staff, the newly elected president, like any CEO, also needed to reserve time for follow-up meetings. Every leader should know that staff is a bully, perhaps well-meaning but stubborn. To get the best advice, the boss has to repeat the same question many times.

Instead, Obama allocated only one big block of time to the critical meeting and then went on his long-awaited vacation. He needed to make his stimulus decision on December 16. Scheduling precluded him from insisting on and receiving a big, bold, brilliant recovery package.

From their perspective, the advisers had a big idea. It was not a thing, like the Hoover Dam or the grid. It was about numbers. Stabilizing finance and incurring a very big increase in the deficit for two years

---

26. Joe Aldy, interview with author.

would end the recession, and then the private sector would deliver growth as it had in the Clinton years. The few dozen specific spending and tax break programs had cognizable features, of course, but overall the advisers cared most about the enormous, if colorless, numbers: $350 billion more of TARP money and $800 billion of stimulus. They paid less attention to flesh-and-blood stories about impact on people or visible, tangible accomplishments.

Obama accepted the strategic objective of stabilizing the finance sector. He did not question the just-short-of-horrible unemployment target. Instead, he plowed through the memorandum, asking questions about the different programs composing the stimulus. Obama and Biden "were interested in the health infrastructure, the health IT," said Summers. "Rahm was very interested in fast rail."[27]

When his turn came, Geithner "warned that credit was still frozen and many major firms were still in danger. The system was broken, and if we couldn't fix it, the economy wouldn't recover no matter how much we spent on stimulus."[28]

Goolsbee said, "Geithner's presentation on financial markets was pretty scary too, because the first $350 billion of TARP was out the door and the Bush administration was saying, 'We're going to need your second $350 billion and we're going to need it now.' Tim went through how extensive the undercapitalization of the banks was, that the markets are going down and the financial markets may continue to collapse. He said we might need hundreds of billions more than what was in the TARP in the coming months."[29]

Geithner had no "strong convictions" about the contents of the stimulus. He was "fine with public works projects," and with "direct aid to the unemployed and other victims of the recession." He "didn't get too involved in the substantive details or the legislative strategy."[30] In other words, he did not believe the unemployment rate or the GDP trend line had much to do with his immediate imperative: no more Lehmans. He

27. Summers, interview.
28. Geithner, *Stress Test*, 260.
29. Goolsbee, interview.
30. Geithner, *Stress Test*, 261.

saw the situation from the supply side of money. He believed that if banks escaped the peril of Lehman-like runs they would start lending again. Low rates would cause businesses to borrow and invest. Hiring would increase and the newly employed would consume again. Christy Romer agreed that the causation went in "both directions," meaning a good economy would help banks and healthy banks would boost the economy. As it happened, the causation went badly in both directions. Economic growth disappointed. Total commercial lending began dropping at the end of 2008 and did not return to that level until 2014.

Geithner did not want Congress to allocate so much to the stimulus that he would have trouble getting the necessary congressional support for the second half of the $700 billion TARP. Paulson and Emanuel had won Democratic votes for that unpopular measure by agreeing to go back for the back half in January if needed. Geithner did not know what the banks might need from the government to build stronger balance sheets, but he wanted at least the next $350 billion in his hands. And what if Geithner needed still more to recapitalize the banks? It was important not to have the stimulus request exhaust the congressional willingness to authorize spending.

Summers pushed housing down in the speaking order, giving it somewhat short shrift, assigning Goolsbee to the topic. Goolsbee began by advising the president-elect, "You have to decide what the goal on housing is going to be: preventing foreclosure, stop overall house prices from falling, what?" He then specifically argued that a "broad policy to help stop the decline of house prices wouldn't work. In a $20 trillion market, even the government won't have the money to do it." He recommended a plan to prevent 1.5 million foreclosures, asking Obama to "understand that even if it succeeds, there will still be five million foreclosures that we cannot prevent."[31] (He underestimated what happened, just as Romer miscalculated unemployment. Between 10 to 15 million households would face the likelihood of foreclosure, and probably more than nine million went through foreclosure or some process like it.)

31. Goolsbee, interview.

Goolsbee's modest suggestion for a housing policy accorded with Geithner's skeptical view about all the "grand plans floating around for universal mortgage refinancing or widespread principal reductions."[32] Obama's advisers believed government help for homeowners would send money to those who did not need or deserve it. Geithner was willing to provide only $50 billion of his TARP money for modifying interest payments on mortgages.

Before the December 16 meeting, Sheila Bair tried to explain to the Obama team that because of "the securitization process," the originators of mortgages did not "collect the mortgage payments." Instead, a few large firms handled "servicing" for owners that were not the same firms that had made the loans. In that market, servicers needed to "go to foreclosure quickly" if they wanted to be "paid immediately, off the top, from foreclosure sale proceeds."[33] Foreclosure doomed mortgage borrowers, but could help servicers. Moreover, securitization created different ownership in mortgages, like a layer cake, where the higher levels had a greater risk of not being paid in the event of default. Investors who had bought only the icing on the cake might tolerate modification. Investors who owned the base layer, the triple-A bondholders, did not want to share in a reduction of the total size of the cake.[34] For these reasons, she said, reducing principal or interest on mortgages required an ingenious policy.

She disliked the one Goolsbee recommended to Obama. He had adopted an idea from Bush treasury official Phillip Swagel. The Treasury would pay "a portion" of the borrower's interest, and lenders would "absorb further rate reductions" if borrowers paid on the "restructured mortgages."[35] Bair was "convinced that it would not work" because it did not address "redefault risk." She preferred to insure modifying firms against excessive loss. Summers and Goolsbee did not report her alternative to Obama, or tell her what they recommended to Obama. Bair wrote later that she hoped "the new administration…would presumably

32. Geithner, *Stress Test*, 262.
33. Bair, *Bull by the Horns*, 60–61.
34. Ibid., 62.
35. Ibid., 136.

bring…a stronger commitment to helping Main Street. But on that score, my expectations proved dead wrong."[36]

After Goolsbee's housing presentation, Orszag "laid out the harrowing budget situation." Geithner "push[ed] strongly for long-term discipline in our overall budget strategy." He felt that he got "pushback" from Romer, Goolsbee, and Bernstein,[37] but Obama took Geithner's side.

In the meeting Geithner thought Obama was "substantive, realistic, and comfortably in command," while he himself personally was "weary and dark…always sucking the hope out of the air in our meetings."[38] Romer thought, "The president-elect was brilliant. I called my husband afterward and said, 'You cannot believe this man.' We were all exhausted and he was still going strong. It was lots of substance, but he didn't really tip his hand. He listened. He asked questions. He obviously heard and understood everything."[39]

As the president-elect rose to leave and everyone stood with him, Austan Goolsbee told Obama, "That's the worst background briefing an incoming president has had at least since 1932, and possibly since Abraham Lincoln." Obama answered, "Goolsbee, that's not even my worst briefing this week." Goolsbee could not remember if the other briefing was a topic like "Pakistan and India are about to go to war," but it was of that nature.[40] As the economy turned out, Goolsbee was right—it was Obama's worst briefing.

Post-Meeting Downsized, Hurried Stimulus

After Obama left, Emanuel held a post-meeting with a few of the participants. Romer remembered it this way: "At the end it was classic Rahm, saying, 'Okay, no way is Congress going over $699. You can't hit the $700 billion barrier.' So we've had all this substantive discussion and it came back to what will Congress bear."[41]

---

36. Ibid,, 139.
37. Geithner, *Stress Test*, 265–6.
38. Ibid., 266.
39. Romer, interview.
40. Goolsbee, interview.
41. Romer, interview.

Goolsbee had a different recollection. He said, "What came out of that meeting was that they decided, 'We're going to shoot at $800 billion as quickly as possible, and it's got to have some themes.' That commenced a 30-day death march getting every aspect of the new government together. Everybody had to come up with stimulus ideas: What are good ideas, and can they get out the door in two to three years?"[42]

Summers agreed more with Goolsbee's memory. He said, "Obama basically had approved what was put before him, in the general way that presidents do, the 800 number." Nevertheless, Summers said, "Rahm afterward decided the range is $675 to $775. Because whatever we come in with they're going to want to add a bunch of stuff. So $675 to $775 is what we should work to develop a package to."[43] In other words, the team would send to the Hill a proposal in the range of $675 to $775 billion, believing that Congress would push it up toward $800 billion.

Romer said, "Meanwhile, outside there was a terrible snowstorm. We all took the train back to the airport. And in the huddle in the subway car, without Rahm, the economics team agreed that $800 billion was the right balancing point between what we could get through Congress and what the economy needed."[44] The number $800 billion was about halfway between the $500 billion Obama had publicly promised before the meeting and the $1.2 trillion that Romer had agreed not to put in the memorandum.

As chief of staff, Emanuel saw prompt signing of the stimulus legislation as the measure of success. The group went along with that emphasis on speed. The economy would begin to grow. The inevitable cycle of recovery would lead to Obama's reelection. Meanwhile, Obama's legacy would be transformational legislation. The legislative initiatives in healthcare and power could not wait, or else they might not be passed. The drawn-out, dilatory Clinton experience with healthcare reform in 1993–1994 taught Emanuel that lesson.

42. Goolsbee, interview.
43. Summers, interview.
44. Romer, interview.

After Obama flew to Hawaii, his team took to the Hill the size and general composition of the stimulus plan. Taking Emanuel's advice, they told the congressional Democratic leaders that the president-elect wanted it to be in the range of $675 to $775 billion and that he also wanted to fund the categories presented as "core." On December 19 the future White House staffers met with each of the various committees in order to explain what one reporter called Obama's "suggested vision" in the six areas: energy, education, healthcare, infrastructure, protecting the vulnerable, and the catch-all of everything else.[45]

Obama's team did not send a definite plan to Congress. In the House the Democratic chairman of the appropriations committee, David Obey, led the drafting process.[46] Each committee in Congress would have flexibility in deciding exactly what programs to fund. However, nothing that required major or time-consuming new legislative authority could be suggested by the Obama team or Congress. Time was of the essence.

Romer said, "After the December 16 meeting the stimulus discussion moved to negotiations with the Hill. At one point the House was at $950 billion, and I remember thinking, 'Oh this is so good.' In the end-game where Snowe and Collins dialed it back, the people who thought Congress wouldn't break the $800 billion barrier may well have been correct."[47]

Emanuel had sized the package in the belief that Congress would add to it, but a week after the Chicago meeting, on December 23, Biden warned in public that the stimulus would not consist of a Christmas tree with lots of presents. Obama's team did not want earmarks—meaning no members could single out specific projects. That limited spending. Summers also worked to cap the spending by arguing Congressman David Obey out of adding $200 billion for transportation projects. (The law ultimately spent less than $50 billion in this area.)

Summers said, "There were only so many infrastructure projects you could get started and get going and get done over a two-year period. The

45. Grunwald, *The New New Deal*, 133.
46. See Carl Hulse, "Defense and No Apologies from Author of Fiscal Bill." *New York Times*, January 27, 2009, http://www.nytimes.com/2009/01/27/us/politics/27obey.html.
47. Romer, interview.

governors were telling Obama they could spend $200 billion. OMB and CBO said infrastructure could only get 40 percent of it spent in the first two years. Otherwise they will spend it on projects they were already going to spend money on. Nothing extra would be added. The last thing we could do would be pumping up spending all through the president's term."[48] Years later, he revised his opinion on this topic.[49]

Sheila Bair said, "The composition of the stimulus was wrong. It was the classic biblical problem of giving people fish instead of teaching them how to fish. At that point, we were all Keynesians. Whether you're spending the money or cutting taxes, we had to increase aggregate demand, right? But we were confronting a major structural problem and we needed long-term sustainable increases in aggregate demand, not just short-term stimulus. We needed job creation, wage growth, not just more cash in people's pockets."

She added, "The stimulus just accelerated demand and front-loaded it. Once it was gone, it was gone. It didn't have ongoing effect. It did not offset the banks' unwillingness to lend money for years to come. We didn't reduce principal on the millions and millions of underwater mortgages. We didn't do significant jobs-producing infrastructure. I remember Larry saying, 'Why do we need to do infrastructure?' The answer was that you need to do infrastructure anyway so let's do it and create some jobs in the process, but Larry didn't want to do that. He said for stimulus purposes we've got to get this money out immediately."[50]

Former senator Trent Lott, Republican from Mississippi, said, "We would have been a lot better off and had a lot more jobs created with a traditional infrastructure stimulus bill: lanes, planes, trains, ports, harbors, water, and sewer. The way typical infrastructure bills are done, they would have had a bipartisan effort, and they would have been doing money for a bridge toward the Mississippi or a water project in Talladega, Alabama, or upstate New York. That would have brought in Republican

48. Summers, interview.
49. Lawrence Summers, "Building the Case for Greater Infrastructure Investment," Larry Summers, September 12, 2016, http://larrysummers.com/2016/09/12/building-the-case-for-greater-infrastructure-investment.
50. Bair, interview.

votes. A lot of people are offended by that, but I'm not. You create jobs on the roads and you get the benefit of tourism, tours, traffic, and the long-term benefits of a sewer system. And safe drinking water isn't where it should be in America."[51]

In 2009 the president's Economic Recovery Advisory Board also recommended an infrastructure bank. Mark Gallogly, a member, said, "Summers and Geithner did not think it was a particularly good idea. They thought that, as structured, the GSEs (Fannie and Freddie) proved the failure of public-private partnerships, and they didn't want to see such failure occur again. They also thought there were more immediate ways to impact the economy and that infrastructure spending, while needed, would take too long. They believed if infrastructure was in demand, private capital should be able to provide it. I thought in a capital crisis, with deleveraging as an overwhelming theme, private capital would not willingly commit to the long term, especially for infrastructure, energy, and some other areas. They believed if it were shovel-ready, it would get done. But the goal was to find important projects that wouldn't otherwise be done."[52]

Tom Mann agreed. "Obama's advisers weren't pressing enough to communicate the economic downturn was worse than they anticipated." If the facts were laid out, Mann speculated, Obama could "have been leading a much earlier and more extended campaign on the investment side of the economy. Really getting out in front on a national infrastructure bank and going full bore on it in spite of the problems some members of Congress have in turning over their authority to allocate funds for favored projects. The investment agenda is crucial to long-term economic growth. Obama had more talk than real serious proposals on the investment front."[53]

Then-Congressman Chris Van Hollen said, "The White House economists were the ones who pushed back on infrastructure. Their argument was infrastructure takes too long to work its way through the system and that we should focus on so-called shovel-ready projects. Every dollar

51. Trent Lott, interview with author.
52. Gallogly, interview.
53. Tom Mann, interview with author.

that was passed had to get into the economic bloodstream as quickly as possible. The counter argument was, add infrastructure in there because there is something to be said for predictability and long-term projects. Saying 'shovel ready' means you are talking about much smaller projects rather than getting people geared up for long-term investment."[54]

Tom Daschle explained that senators in both parties were more reluctant to fund the stimulus than the House Democrats. He said, "Everybody in Congress had sticker shock. There was TARP. Stimulus was sort of round two, and there was a lot of skittishness on the part of many Democrats in the Senate. There was a lack of confidence about whether this was going to solve the problem. You still had a lot of fiscal conservatives in the Democratic caucus who didn't believe that the stimulus would work. They were forceful deniers. You had probably the first clear example of the friction between Democratic leaders in Congress and the White House. It began even before the inauguration. There was just a tension and a friction and a frustration clearly on both sides. The Congress just didn't feel like the president was putting his shoulder to the wheel as much as he needed to on composition as well as on tactics. But there was an agreement that it had to be under a trillion. That was just sort of an arbitrary number picked in part because they thought it was more politically palatable."[56]

The crucial votes in the Senate were Specter, Collins, Snowe, and Nelson. Three were needed. As a practical matter four had to be obtained because no one of them wanted to hold the single last vote that determined the fate of the bill. Too much responsibility! All went along with the size Obama asked for. The bill's composition was about 85 percent of what Obama asked for.[55]

---

54. Van Hollen, interview.

55. "Obama's failure to envelop his economic recovery efforts in a persuasive master narrative ceded the public debate, to long-time conservative nostrums about big government as the enemy of economic growth." Theda Skocpol, Lawrence R. Jacobs, editors, *Reaching for a New Deal: Ambitious Governance, Economic Meltdown, and Polarized Politics in Obama's First Two Years* (New York: Russell Sage Foundation, 2011) 34.

This argument ignores Obama's decision not to try to mobilize public opinion until after he decided and presented his recovery plan in January 2009. He used his rhetorical skills to claim credit, surprisingly successfully, for avoiding a great depression, rather than to sell a more ambitious plan at the get-go.

Daschle said the senators thought, "We've done a lot. Let's see what happens before we do more. It's deficit driven. It's the politics of the moment. The politics were that the government's already committed more than any time in history. TARP was extremely unpopular, a bail-out of the big banks, deficit concerns of growing proportion, all of that created a political climate that made it almost impossible to do more in the stimulus."[56]

Daschle added, "The congressional leaders also thought that above 6 percent unemployment was not politically palatable." However, the economists were predicting that unemployment would rise to 9 percent without the stimulus. Why then didn't the leaders support a bigger stimulus? "Because some of the fiscal conservatives didn't believe the math."[57]

Van Hollen had a different view: "This was a one-shot deal and it was a mistake not to ask for more up front."[58]

56. For a sympathetic, well-reported account of the stimulus from the perspective of the Obama advisers, see Michael Grunwald, *The New New Deal: The Hidden Story of Change in the Obama Era* (New York: Simon & Schuster, 2012). I think this reporting underplays the significance of premature announcements, mistaken assumptions, misplaced fear of deficits, untoward concern for big banks, self-serving assessments, and constraints imposed by non-stimulus considerations, among other things.
57. Daschle, interview.
58. Van Hollen, interview.

Interlude Two

Composing the Stimulus

On December 5 Blair Levin, my chief of staff at the FCC in the 1990s and transition team member, told Peter Orszag, "I noticed that Rahm Emanuel and Nancy Pelosi are talking about broadband being part of the stimulus. If you need some help on that, let me know." Orszag said yes, particularly in light of the president-elect using part of a Saturday radio address to set out specific national goals for broadband. However, Levin said Orszag and Jason Furman told him there was no appetite for "competing with existing private firms. A major concern for the economic advisers was that we not fund competitive entry. The industry too said it was great to have more money for broadband, but 'don't fund my competitor.'"[1] Summers and Furman were both of the view that broadband was fundamentally a private-sector investment story. They were skeptical that the privately owned utilities, like power and communications, should get public funding.

Levin said, "Ultimately, the advisers allocated $7 billion for broadband. I told them there was a gap between what the president-elect said are his goals of universal, affordable service and what the $7 billion will actually pay for. They said, yeah what should we do? I said, just announce that you're going to develop a plan that will chart a path to achieving those goals. They said, that sounds fine, go ahead and write it up. That

---

1. Blair Levin, interview with author.

led to me working with a group to put in the stimulus bill the mandate and funding for the national broadband plan."[2]

Levin became the head of that planning effort. Very few departments and agencies created plans combining spending and regulatory decisions so as to maximize investment. Levin observed, "Fundamentally, the exercise of power is an exercise of choice. You choose this, you don't choose that. For the most part, because it was done in the context of the transition, the choices of allocation of financial and political capital in the stimulus was done by very small groups under extraordinary time pressures with minimal information and often little more than guesses.

"The national broadband plan was a counterexample: the choices were derived from an open, public, multi-stakeholder process. It could and should have been copied in the stimulus spending for power, water, transportation, and other network spending. Doing the national broadband plan from start to finish took less than nine months. There were 70 external hires. Twenty million dollars tops, with half spent on the best gap analysis ever done on rural broadband, a model still being used by the commission. Well worth the money. One signature item, the incentive auction, returned over $7 billion to the government, while moving a lot of spectrum into higher uses. That's a heck of an ROI. Plan beats no plan."[3]

2. Ibid.
3. Ibid.

11

"A Rookie Mistake"

This is perhaps a day of general honesty
Without example in the world's history
— John Ashbery, "Two Scenes"

On January 8, 2009, two weeks before the Inauguration, Obama "urge[d] Congress to move as quickly as possible" to pass the American Recovery and Reinvestment Plan. Speaking at George Mason University, he claimed it would "save or create at least three million jobs over the next few years." The statement sounded similar to the target he had set in November, although the actual stimulus proposed to Congress was much higher. Obama predicted double-digit unemployment unless we "take dramatic action as soon as possible."[1]

Both the jobs number and the unemployment differed slightly from the report entitled "The Job Impact of the American Recovery and Reinvestment Plan," published the next day by Christy Romer and Jared Bernstein, embargoed for the media until January 10. They had the unemployment rate reaching 9 percent in the first quarter of 2010 in the absence of a stimulus. Only a footnote stated that some forecasters saw unemployment topping at 11 percent but for stimulus, as Obama

1. Barack Obama, "Speech on the Economy" (speech, George Mason University, Fairfax, VA, January 8, 2009), NewsOK, https://newsok.com/article/feed/35767/text-of-barack-obamas-economic-speech

175

had said on January 8. The plan aimed to create between three and four million jobs by the end of 2010. A target of four million jobs over two years roughly equaled an $800 billion stimulus.[2]

The economists assumed that the stimulus would be "just slightly over the $775 billion currently under discussion." They said that with this "package," the unemployment rate in the last quarter of 2010 would be "approximately 7.0 percent." The Romer-Bernstein report accurately stated the calculations behind the stimulus. However, it grossly understated the unemployment "in the absence" of stimulus.

On January 9 the Bureau of Labor Statistics reported the December employment numbers. Unemployment had gone from 6.8 percent in November to 7.2 percent in December. In December, 524,000 jobs were lost, following a job loss of 533,000 in November. This report definitely showed that in December Obama's advisers had severely underestimated the potential job loss. The Obama team had concluded three weeks earlier that Congress would not pass quickly a stimulus greater than $800 billion. They had presented their plan to the Democratic congressional leaders two weeks earlier. The Romer-Bernstein report was in reporters' hands. The Obama team would have had to change course, admit error. They chose not to let the BLS numbers change their request to Congress.[3]

On January 10, 2009, Paul Krugman instantly spotted the implication of the new BLS data. He wrote that in light of the December unemployment rate the "estimate of what would happen to the economy in the absence of a stimulus plan seems kind of optimistic." He called the plan "too weak."[4]

---

2. The stimulus would create work disproportionately in construction, manufacturing, retail, leisure, and hospitality. Although women accounted for 20 percent of the decline in employment at the time of the report, they would get 42 percent of the jobs "created by the package." (The desire to make this contention informs the loss of Democratic support from male voters in succeeding years.)

3. "Human behavior is determined not by what really happened but by interpretation of what happened." René Girard, translated by Stephen Bann, Michael Metteer, *Things Hidden Since the Foundation of the World* (Stanford, California: Stanford University Press, 1987, English translation), 78.

4. Paul Krugman, "Romer and Bernstein on Stimulus," *New York Times*, January 10, 2009, https://krugman.blogs.nytimes.com/2009/01/10/romer-and-bernstein-on-stimulus/.

The Romer-Bernstein report destroyed any possibility of persuading Congress to spend more to address the recession in a robust fashion. Reading it, why would budget hawks like Democratic senators Ben Nelson or Kent Conrad want to go above $800 billion? Apparently if Democrats gave Obama all he asked for, the unemployment rate would be safely down in time for the 2010 election. On the other hand, no Republican senator would support a bigger package, one that might achieve full employment in Obama's first term. Such a Republican might get reelected in 2010 but hope Obama would be in trouble in 2012.

At that moment, Obama was, as Geithner wanted, seeking the second half of TARP from Congress. In a letter dated January 12, 2009, Summers wrote to the Democratic and Republican congressional leadership that Obama requested the "authority to implement the rest of the financial rescue plan," meaning the second half of the TARP money, because Obama "believes the need is imminent and urgent." The December 16 meeting had led to the choreography of asking for $800 billion in stimulus, the second half of the TARP money, and a modest program to reduce foreclosures. The felt necessity of urgency discouraged the Obama team from changing the plan because of the BLS data.

Congressional leaders had signaled between December 16 and the first week of January their distaste for conveying the second half of the TARP money unless the new administration spent some of it on the distressed housing sector. Therefore, in a letter to the leadership Summers promised Obama would "work with Congress immediately to implement smart, aggressive policies to reduce the number of preventable foreclosures by helping to reduce mortgage payments for economically stressed but responsible homeowners while also reforming our bankruptcy laws and strengthening existing housing initiatives like Hope for Homeowners."[5] He did not explain that having adopted the Goolsbee plan, the new administration expected to prevent only about a third of expected

5. "Barack Obama: Press Release: Letter from Lawrence H. Summers to Congressional Leaders, January 15, 2009." The American Presidency Project, http://www.presidency.ucsb.edu/ws/index.php?pid=85432.

foreclosures. To address foreclosures, Summers promised to divert up to $100 billion from TARP.

On the same day as Summers's letter, Obama said that he had asked Bush to "trigger the second half of what's known as the TARP program." He criticized Paulson's "absence of clarity, the lack of transparency, the failure to track how the money's been spent, and the failure to take bold action with respect to areas like housing, consumer credit." He said he would focus "on housing and foreclosures,"[6] reflecting, modestly, Summers' advice to seek "discontinuity." Other than the rhetoric, Obama did not differ with Paulson's dedication of TARP to bailing out banks.

On January 16, 2009, Obama stated that ARRA would "save or create three to four million jobs," adhering to the target stated in the Romer-Bernstein report.[7] However, as the following chart shows, on Friday, February 6, the BLS announced that January saw 598,000 more jobs lost. The unemployment rate rose to 7.6 percent, totaling 11.6 million people. By fixing a target of job creation and declining to change that as the economy shrank, Obama's recovery program fell farther behind the needs of the country as job losses mounted. If he had aimed at achieving a certain level of unemployment, as promised by the Romer-Bernstein report, then he would have needed a stimulus that expanded spending as more people were laid off.

Obama's spending probably did create approximately the number of jobs promised. But Congressional Democrats needed the unemployment rate reduced to a level that the American voters would tolerate. If the worsening economy required more job creation to achieve that end, then the stimulus had to include either bigger spending up front or measures that expanded in size as the situation required. Obama's plan aimed at the wrong goal.

"The way I remember it," said Ed Markey, then a congressman from Massachusetts and later a senator, "Christy Romer said the hemorrhaging

6. "Bush Agrees to Obama Bailout Request," *CBS News*, January 12, 2009, https://www.cbsnews.com/news/bush-agrees-to-obama-bailout-request/.

7. "President-elect Barack Obama on His American Recovery and Reinvestment Plan," *U.S. News & World Report*, January 8, 2009, https://www.usnews.com/news/stimulus/articles/2009/01/08/president-elect-barack-obama-on-his-american-recovery-and-reinvestment-plan.

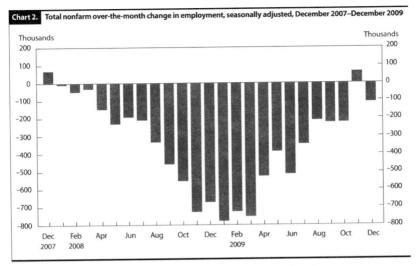

*Chart 2 from Megan M. Barker and Adam A. Hadi, "Payroll Employment in
2009: Job Losses Continue," Bureau of Labor Statistics Monthly Labor Review,
March 2010, https://www.bls.gov/opub/mlr/2010/03/art2full.pdf.*

economy would be cauterized and then in substantial remission by the
time we reached Election Day 2010. Down to 8 percent unemployment
by then. In politics the direction is very important. Success builds upon
success. You want to have an election while showing that your economic theory is working, and 8 percent would be a big improvement over
2009. Many of us wanted the stimulus to be bigger, but at least we
wanted to show that unemployment was down to 8 percent by 2010 and
then down to 6 percent by 2012."[8]

When they issued their prediction on January 9, Obama's economists
had reason to know that they would disappoint Markey and his congressional colleagues. By February 6, they knew for sure that the stimulus
would not achieve the goals that Markey described and that they had
promised Obama in Chicago on December 16. On that day, the BLS
unemployment report stated that 598,000 lost work in January, raising
unemployment to 7.6 percent. The trend was clear.

Romer said, "The whole story of that December and January and even
February was the deterioration right in front of our eyes. I've gotten into

---

8. Ed Markey, interview with author.

lots of trouble because we did a forecast in early December trying to figure out where we were going and how big the stimulus needed to be, and by January it was clear that it wasn't the right forecast.... We'd had long discussions when we first got to Washington about whether the rest of the world would go down with us or would they perhaps help hold us up. Was the downturn going to be synchronized or not? And the main piece of information we got in January was, everybody was going down at least as much as we were if not more. We got the numbers from Japan and Korea and the declines were huge."

Romer concluded, "The stimulus was too small the day it passed in February."[9] Gerry Waldron, experienced Hill staffer and an architect of the climate change bill, said, "If on February 1 when the stimulus was still a work in progress, people had said, 'Wait, you have to change those provisions because we were wrong,' could it have changed the course of it? Yeah, it could have. Going north of one trillion would still have been a politically tough thing to do, but if everybody is out there saying it was necessary, members are not deaf to these things."[10]

Henry Waxman said, "If they realized early that unemployment would exceed 10 percent, why didn't they come up with something to do? We figured that when the stimulus bill was fully in effect, the unemployment rate would drop. We had a little bit but not enough of a pickup. I guess they're geniuses. But if they're such geniuses why didn't they figure out something to do?"[11]

Romer explained, "I think that the thing that bothers me most about Washington is people saying things that they have to know aren't correct. I think you ought to tell people the truth and stand up for the truth. Anyway, we were never allowed to say that the stimulus was too small. So if you ask what was an important strategic decision, I think it was not trying for a second stimulus, early, when we might have had more of a chance. Once the unemployment rate was at 10 percent, it was too easy to say, 'See, the first one didn't work.' If instead we had said early, 'Here's

9. Romer, interview.
10. Gerry Waldron, interview with author.
11. Waxman, interview.

the situation; the recession is much worse than we had anticipated; let's just go back right now and increase the stimulus,' perhaps we could have gotten it.

"Our estimate of the effect of the stimulus on GDP was actually quite good. What broke down was the normal relationship between GDP and unemployment. Unemployment rose much more than you would have expected given what happened to GDP. That's because of a surge in productivity."[12] Our usual rules of thumb broke down.

Orszag had a different retrospective critique: "We didn't put enough weight on the fact that a recession induced by financial crisis could produce a longer downturn than a recession caused by other factors. The reason for misjudging the current state of the economy in late 2008 was battlefield fog; the reason for misjudging the nature of the recovery was partly that the macroeconomic models did not have a detailed financial market incorporated into them and therefore were treating the housing crisis as if it were the IT bubble collapse."[13]

Perhaps a more accurate and dismal description of the downturn's depth would not have caused Congress to spend more or attract more public support for the stimulus. One of the participants in the stimulus negotiation said, "Getting that 800 was very tenuous. It almost fell apart several times. Krugman and everybody are always talking crap. It's fine if you're sitting in Princeton writing columns."[14]

On January 28, 2009, eight days after Obama's inauguration, the House passed a stimulus bill. It closely resembled Obama's request. To get the Republican senators' votes for the 60-vote margin, Obama's negotiators had to accept a reduction in funds for states (that led in turn to big job losses in the public sector), a reduced tax credit for low-income workers, and increased tax breaks for high income and the elderly.

12. Romer, interview.
13. Orszag interview.
Orszag reiterated this point on a panel at the Washington Center for Equitable Growth in late 2016: "Every…macro-econometric model in 2008…was predicting a V-shaped recovery instead of the L-shape that we got, and the reason that that was happening was…they were treating the housing bust as if it were IT bust 2.0."
14. Interview with anonymous source.

The total of $838 billion in the Senate bill passed February 10 equaled the House's $820 billion. In the conference committee where the two chambers' representatives compromised on a final version, the Republican senators used their leverage to push the total below $800 billion, and to shift the mix more toward tax breaks. Obama signed the bill into law on February 17. It totaled $787 billion, but because it included the continuation of the suspension of the alternative minimum tax, it ended closer to $700 billion of new spending, in the range set by Emanuel following the December 16 meeting.

The stimulus package ended as 45 percent spending, 37 percent tax cuts, and 18 percent state aid. The advisers' dislike of tax cuts had limited the size of the stimulus they proposed, but cuts nevertheless composed a goodly part of the package.

As Obama had been saying for months, the plan scattered money across a range of categories:

The American Recovery and Reinvestment Act

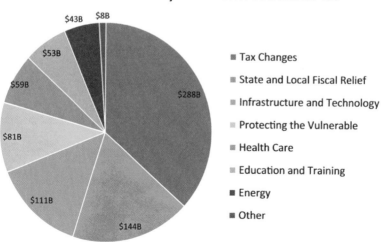

Original graph created by Grace Choi. Data source: www.recovery.gov.

"Political Malpractice"

Almost a century ago, the Copenhagen interpretation of physics cast terminal doubt on systems of thinking and methods of understanding that depended on locality, causation, and objective reality. Niels Bohr believed that one can only know probabilities. Erwin Schrödinger said observation changes a probability into an outcome—the cat in the box turns out to be alive or dead only when the box is opened.

From before the election through January 2009, the Obama advisers reverted to classical Newtonian paradigms. They assumed American businesses would not react to the global downturn. They believed they understood the situation, when they only could guess about probable conditions. They discounted the impact of the opening of the box—i.e., the observation in the negative January and February BLS reports—on the conditions of the cat, otherwise known as the economy.

Gerry Waldron, then working for Congressman Markey, said, "When Romer and Bernstein made their prediction, at the time I remember thinking, 'Wow, they're being frighteningly precise.' At the time it was like, sure, I'll cast the vote if it's an insurance policy against 8 percent unemployment. That's what we were told with statistical precision. The way people heard it was that it was based on serious econometric analysis. So if I take Step X, I have almost scientific certainty that it will lead to result Y, which is unemployment below 8 percent. Bad but politically bearable."

He noted, "They were off by a hell of a lot. There is a profound difference between 8 percent and 9.2 percent. Being off between 4 percent and 5 percent in an unemployment rate is a big difference but they are both close to full employment. Being off from 8 percent to 9 percent is a profound difference because the baseline is 4 percent or 5 percent. So the difference is more like being 20 to 33 percent wrong."

Waldron added, "Later, but still early in 2009, Ed Markey told me someone had told him we are going to have unemployment at around 9 percent all the way through the next election. I said, if that is true, the Democrats are going to lose the House."[15]

Pete Rouse, deputy chief of staff in the White House, said, "We had received overly optimistic predictions of what the effect on unemployment would be. Perhaps we should not have predicted what the unemployment rate would have gone down to. But this is what the economists told President Obama."[16]

Alice Rivlin, funding director of the Congressional Budget Office, former head of OMB, and former vice chair of the Federal Reserve, said, "I've spent my life telling politicians what might happen. If you give them ranges, they don't like it. They want a number. If you give them a range, they pick the midpoint of the number. They need a point forecast, but why their January '09 point forecast was as optimistic as it was is a mystery to me. In that winter things were getting worse at a very rapid rate."[17]

Robert Reich, former labor secretary, said, "It is not a good idea for government to give the public very specific numbers because they aren't reliable."[18]

According to Chris Van Hollen, "This report was the biggest example of political malpractice in the first year. Probably in the entire first term of the Obama administration. I say political malpractice, not economic malpractice, because first of all there's no statistic that was thrown back in our face more than that one. That was a self-inflicted wound. You could make your case without it. You could say instead that the economy is in free fall. 'We frankly don't know how fast it's falling. What we do know is that we need an emergency intervention. We need to do at least this much. We can't predict exactly what unemployment will be. But we know that if we don't do this, things will be a lot worse.' By defining success in the way they did, it set us up for failure on the political argument."[19]

15. Waldron, interview.
16. Peter Rouse, interview with author.
17. Rivlin, interview.
18. Reich, interview.
19. Van Hollen, interview.

Christy Romer said about the memo with Jared Bernstein that included her erroneous forecast, "I don't know who wanted it published. Jason and Larry both went through it and liked it a lot. But there was not some carefully thought-out decision. It was just sort of like it was happening and we were issuing it. It's a shame it made problems for the president because at some level it was well done. We had gotten the best forecasts we could from a variety of reputable sources, we defended our assumptions about multipliers, we ran the simulations, and we made a case. Including the point estimate of the baseline forecast was a rookie mistake. But the estimates of the effects of the proposed stimulus on GDP turned out to be very accurate. I remember Paul Krugman wrote a column saying, 'I don't agree with their baseline, but it's nice to see someone actually doing analysis and putting it out for people to discuss.'"[20]

Unemployment stayed between 9 and 10 percent until late in Obama's first term.

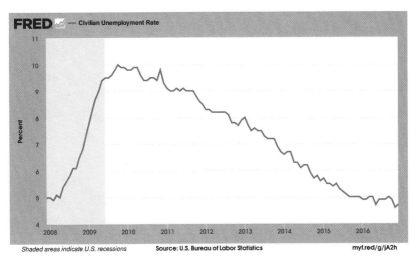

"FRED®" charts ©Federal Reserve Bank of St. Louis. 2015. All rights reserved. All "FRED®" charts appear courtesy of Federal Reserve Bank of St. Louis. http://research.stlouisfed.org/fred2/.

Could Have Beens

Washington political analyst Norm Ornstein said, "The problem of unemployment was never first and foremost for Obama and his team.

20. Romer, interview.

That was a mistake. They made a big mistake by not having Obama use the bully pulpit on a more regular basis to talk about jobs. I sent Axelrod and Emanuel memos arguing for a green bank, an infrastructure bank, and an entrepreneurial fund. They didn't agree. Obama needed to explain to the American audience that we should take this opportunity to unleash the entrepreneurial spirit. For example, we should have created an American version of a microlending bank, creating thousands and thousands of entrepreneurs, which in turn could create millions of jobs."[21]

What could have been done differently? Mark Gallogly thought, "In a deep crisis, decision-making is incredibly challenging and limited by ever-changing political and economic constraints. But the allocation of tax benefits and the relationship between stimulus and burden-sharing by banks could have been better explained. The tone the president set with the American people about the economy could have been communicated differently."[22]

Orszag added, "I think a mistake was not around the size of the stimulus in late 2009 but instead that too little of it persisted in 2011, 2012, and so on."[23] Looking back from 2018 at the stimulus, Orszag thought, "The amount per year in 2009 was not the primary issue; it was instead that the annual flow declined too precipitously. The result, in the end, would have been a larger overall package—but not a larger package in 2009. The best way we could have done this would have been to link many of the payments to the unemployment rate or some other indicator, in a sense temporarily boosting the automatic stabilizers; since CBO projected a short recession, it would have scored the cost as minimal (in an expected value sense). But as they say, hindsight is…."[24] In other words, he wished he had crafted a stimulus that did not score bigger but in fact produced a larger amount of spending. Rivlin shared his view.

Goolsbee speculated later that it might have been better politically to have let the economy grow worse in 2008 and early 2009 before

21. Norman Ornstein, interview with author.
22. Gallogly, interview.
23. Orszag, interview.
24. Ibid.

advancing a stimulus bill. Among other things, that approach would have afforded the advisers time to determine more accurately the condition of the economy. Goolsbee said, "Obama could have said, 'Let's not try to pass stimulus right now and let things get so bad that Congress can't not pass it, then we won't be blamed for anything.' That was in many ways FDR's approach in 1932. But I can't conceive of this president considering that strategy. He'd say, 'If we put this off six months, we could have millions of additional people out of work, right? Well, then, of course we're not going to do that.'"[25]

Romer admitted that April was "the first time I said to the president, 'I don't know how to say this, but we need to be thinking of a second stimulus.' But the consensus was that we couldn't admit that it was too small. I was never allowed to say, 'Yes, it was too small.' That always befuddled me because how could I not say that as I watched the economy deteriorate? I knew the conditions were worse than I had anticipated at the time, and people were asking me to say, 'Nevertheless, we did exactly the right thing.' That makes no sense. Why can't we actually say the truth? And eventually the president did. But not for a year and a half."[26]

Rouse said, "I don't know if asking for a revision would have produced a good result. And it would have weakened him on other priorities he was trying to get through."[27]

What Was Really Happening in the Economy

Austan Goolsbee's view by the middle of 2009 was that "we passed the Recovery Act, now we need a growth strategy. The OMB folks wanted to shift to deficit reduction as the key priority. Personally, I thought the medium run ought to be about getting growth back. We'll never be able to cut our way to a balanced budget if we're growing at 1 percent."[28]

Goolsbee correctly understood that technology destroyed clerical work and stymied wage growth. (See the following charts.) To transform

25. Goolsbee, interview.
26. Romer, interview.
27. Rouse, interview.
28. Goolsbee, interview.

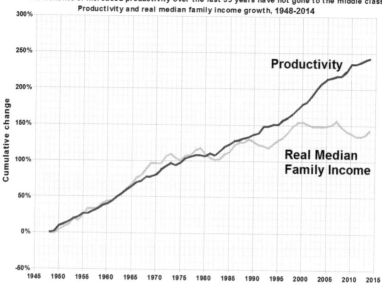

Delphi234. Data Source: Bureau of Labor Statistics and Bureau of Economic Analysis, https://commons.wikimedia.org/w/index.php?curid=32785777 (accessed 11 Feb. 2018).

Original graph created by Deborah Nicholls. Data source: Bureau of Labor Statistics, https://data.bls.gov.

the nature of employment, the government needed to spend hundreds of billions of dollars on teaching science, and deploying innovative power, communications, and transportation platforms. A great part of the existing workforce, including the people who would vote for Donald Trump in 2016, needed a helping hand from government to cope with rapid technologically driven change.[29]

Feminism also played a role in restructuring employment in America. The movement repudiated the ruling postwar paradigm consensus that women should run the homes and men should go to work. From the Second World War to the technology boom of the '90s, women increasingly went to work.

More women have been joining the labor force, peaking at the turn of the century
In 1960, 38 percent of women were in the U.S. workforce. By 1999, that number grew to 60 percent.

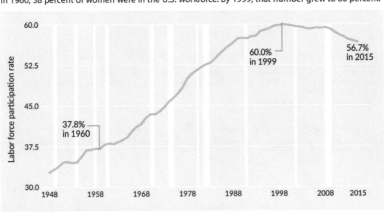

Source: U.S. Bureau of Labor Statistics, Federal Reserve Bank of St. Louis. Shaded areas indicate recessions as defined by the National Bureau of Economic Research.
©2016 Washington Center for Equitable Growth

Fig. 1 from Heather Boushey and Kavya Vaghul, "Women have made the difference for family economic security," Washington Center for Equitable Growth, Equitablegrowth.org, April 4, 2016. Used with permission.

29. "According to…estimates, about 47 percent of total US employment is at risk [of computerization]." Carl Benedikt Frey and Michael A. Osborne. "The Future of Employment: How Susceptible Are Jobs to Computerisation?" *Technological Forecasting and Social Change*, September 29, 2016, https://www.oxfordmartin.ox.ac.uk/downloads/academic/The_Future_of_Employment.pdf.

The work of women accounted for most family income growth in these decades.

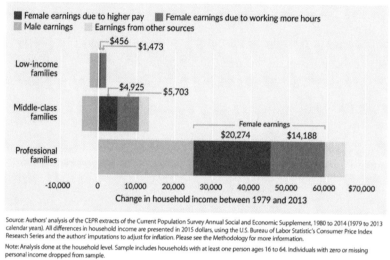

Women are making essential contributions to family incomes

Without women's increasing hours and participation in the labor force between 1979 and 2013, both low-income and middle-class families would have seen an even more negative change or negative change, respectively, in their annual average income.

Source: Authors' analysis of the CEPR extracts of the Current Population Survey Annual Social and Economic Supplement, 1980 to 2014 (1979 to 2013 calendar years). All differences in household income are presented in 2015 dollars, using the U.S. Bureau of Labor Statistic's Consumer Price Index Research Series and the authors' imputations to adjust for inflation. Please see the Methodology for more information.

Note: Analysis done at the household level. Sample includes households with at least one person ages 16 to 64. Individuals with zero or missing personal income dropped from sample.

©2016 Washington Center for Equitable Growth

Fig. 4 from Heather Boushey and Kavya Vaghul, "Women have made the difference for family economic security," Washington Center for Equitable Growth, Equitablegrowth.org, April 4, 2016. Used with permission.

Employers paid women less than men but also moved away from the idea that men should be paid enough to support a family. "Why doesn't your wife work?" became the unspoken assumption at work. The rights revolution had a reaction—all revolutions worth their salt cause a counter reaction. In the domain of wages, the rise of individual identity as the preeminent conceptual unit tended to put each person in a constantly, negotiated, market-set relationship with the world. For males, the result was anxiety.

Education too became a way to demonstrate that winning the genetic lottery guaranteed a high-class education. Really bright students could get scholarships, big loans, decent work. The rest of the country, by definition the vast majority, found that the system charged them far more than they could afford for the education said to be essential to obtaining a rising standard of living.

The advisers thought in large, denatured categories: homeowners, employees, seniors. The nature of the jobs that needed to be created, and for that matter the future of the Democratic Party, could only be discerned from a more granular examination. Anna Burger, a spokesperson for labor, said, "We just didn't do enough to focus on long-term job creation. I just don't think they felt that they could take on the issue of long-term job creation because it was too hard to get measures through Congress. They recognized the societal impact of chronic unemployment. But we didn't see a comprehensive agenda coming out of the administration. Some of it is our fault. We were drumming for him to take on the issue of healthcare, but we also needed to be drumming for him to take on the issue of jobs."[30]

Possible Moonshots

Obama could have achieved a robust recovery if his economic recovery plan had catalyzed a massive private-sector investment boom in platform creation. In 2009–2012 United States needed to imitate the trillion dollars spent to build the modern, digital, wireless communication platform in Clinton's second term. The 21st century called for new platforms: upgraded and well-maintained transportation (roads, trains, airports, hybrid and electric vehicles), the clean power platform (renewable generation, upgraded transmission and distribution of power, efficient consumption), high-speed broadband to every building, and (lead-free!) water systems.

Funding renovation of the entire built environment in 40 of the most downtrodden counties in the country also would have been useful. Possibly a total overhaul of platforms, coupled with achieving very high employment at good wages, could break the pattern of poverty, crime, joblessness, drugs, and despair.

30. Anna Burger, interview with author.

The government would need to plan the platforms, just as Blair Levin's national broadband planning group did. Auctions would award contracts to the lowest-cost bidders from the private sector. The platform construction would put to work those in the job classifications most severely hit by the housing slump.

All the platforms posed similar financing problems. The builder faced high up-front costs and long payback periods. The initial investment might not be recouped. In less densely populated areas, the lower number of customers per mile of build-out reduced the potential revenue. In lower-income zip codes the per capita payments for electricity, broadband, toll bridges, and so forth made the construction less attractive. To address these issues, government could sweeten the market opportunity with public money, just as it was doing to restore the finances of Wall Street firms.

To reduce the budget score, government could fund the platform construction by loaning money on a long-term basis, such as 20 to 30 years, at the same rate that Treasury needed to pay for the debt it was borrowing in the bond market—between 0 and 1 percent. Platform builders could hardly turn down money that cheap. A cable company, merchant power company, or construction builder could reduce its borrowing cost by 5 to 10 percent if it had access to government debt.

Obama's advisers believed that at some point the ratio between total public debt and the size of the economy becomes so high that the economy will not grow fast enough to create the potential for government to extract taxes sufficient to pay the interest on its debts. When the perception of reaching that point becomes widespread, investors take their money to another country, and an economic collapse ensues.

Early in 2009 economists Carmen Reinhart and Ken Rogoff published a book sardonically titled *This Time is Different*. They argued that 90 percent marks the danger zone. Even though history taught that a financial crisis causes a recession to extend much longer than an asset-price collapse, like the dot-com bubble popping that caused the short recession of 2001, governments should not carry a debt burden higher than 90 percent of GDP.

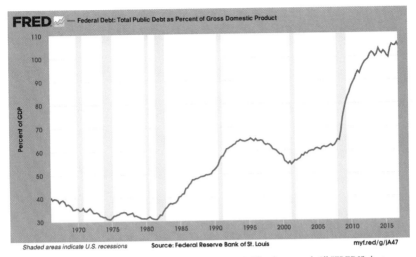

Critics subsequently disputed the accuracy of the mathematics that gave meaning to the 90 percent level. Later still, Summers and DeLong would assert that when interest rates verge to zero government can reduce the deficit in future years by borrowing and spending in the immediate short term at levels that cause the total public debt to exceed 90 percent.[31] Ironically, possibly tragically, in the totally different condition of full employment, Congress and the president in 2017 ignored the possibility that debt might damage the economy.

The advisers also might have addressed income inequality.[32] The stimulus could have included a $1,000 deposit in a personal savings account for everyone in the country born from 2007 to 2017—approximately 50 million people or $50 billion in deposits. Each account would be invested by a trustee like Vanguard in stock market index funds, locked

31. J. Bradford DeLong and Lawrence H. Summers, "Fiscal Policy in a Depressed Economy," Brookings, September 13, 2016, https://www.brookings.edu/bpea-articles/fiscal-policy-in-a-depressed-economy/.

32. The economic recovery program worked well for what Reeves calls the "moneyed upper-middle class." He draws the line at the top 20 percent of the income distribution—household annual income greater than $112,000 in 2014. For everyone below that level the recovery was slow and small.

up for 20 years, and not subject to taxation upon withdrawal either in 20 years or any age after 65. As the next chart shows, below the top quintile in income, few households held any stock at all—even though those assets were poised to rise in value during Obama's two terms.

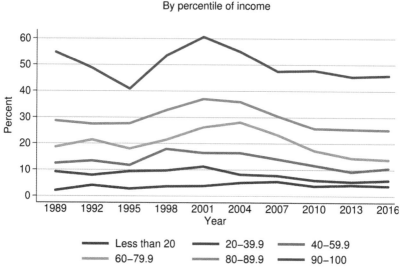

Percent of families with directly held stocks
By percentile of income

Board of Governors of the Federal Reserve, chart "Percent of families with directly held stocks," 2016 SCF Chartbook, October 16, 2017.

The advisers could have proposed a cash payment of $5,000 for every child in a family below the median national income—that would have been about $150 billion in spending. Or the $5,000 could be a onetime bonus paid to anyone who had earned less than the national median in the previous year—that would have been about $350 billion.

For young people, the government could have refinanced all student loans, then about $500 billion, now about three times as large. For the old, it could have increased Social Security payments. And for the unemployed, give them bigger benefits for a longer period of time. All these groups were easy to identify and contact. All would have spent their grants.

The stimulus might have provided a living wage and free tuition for anyone who wanted to go to school. This imitation of the GI Bill might have been coupled with a call to provide national service at a low but reasonable salary. Instead of letting young people suffer high unemployment, an opportunity could have been afforded all of them.

Because neither the 2009 nor the 2010 stimulus bolstered net worth for most Americans, the following chart shows how wealth for those at the top of the income ladder grew more than for the rest of the country.

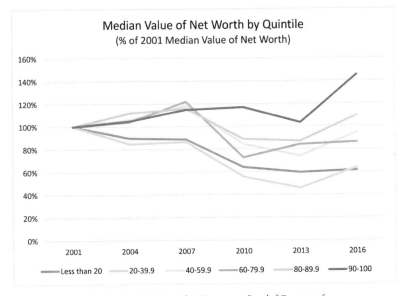

Original Graph by Grace Choi. Data source: Board of Governors of the Federal Reserve, https://www.federalreserve.gov.

As Credit Suisse explained in 2017, "*Mean* net worth is now above the pre-recession peak, while the *median* is not even close. The two indicators have completely diverged."[33]

In other words, the "average" American, addressed routinely by politicians at least since Andrew Jackson's election, now made a lot more money than most people. As the median dropped below the mean, according to one survey, in 2014 40 percent considered themselves lower middle or low income. Because the mean rose, the range for the

33. Lev Borodovsky, "The Daily Shot: Median Household Net Worth Has Languished Since the Recession," *The Wall Street Journal*, December 15, 2017, https://blogs.wsj.com/dailyshot/2017/12/15/the-daily-shot-median-household-net-worth-has-anguished-since-the-recession.

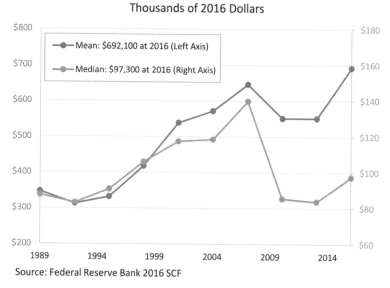

Mean vs. Median Household Net Worth
Thousands of 2016 Dollars

Source: Federal Reserve Bank 2016 SCF

Original graph created by Grace Choi. Data source: Federal Reserve Survey of Consumer Finances 2016, https://www.federalreserve.gov.

definition of middle class shifted up—for a family of four in 2014 it was roughly $50,000 to $150,000 a year.[34] Meanwhile, the top 1 percent saw their income soar much faster than everyone else's. "We are the 99%" became a slogan that inspired the Occupy movement in late 2011. These trends had many causes, but the Obama economic recovery plan contributed. With the barker's cunning for attracting attention, Donald Trump adjusted the gunsights of his message down toward the biggest voting targets, zeroing in on a base that in short order overturned the power structure of the Republican Party and the country's politics.

34. Kimberly Amadeo, "Middle Class Income," The Balance, updated April 24, 2018, https://www.thebalance.com/definition-of-middle-class-income-4126870.

12

"No Greater Exasperation Than Housing"

That the house of every one is to him as his Castle and Fortress
as well for defence against injury and violence, as for his repose.
— Sir Edward Coke, 1604

In the fall of 2008, Hank Paulson at Treasury and Ben Bernanke at the Fed connected to the transition at the level of Summers and Geithner. Sheila Bair, below them in the hierarchy, had to meet with my transition group. I learned later that just then she thought she should be closing Citi, haircutting its creditors, instead of talking to my team about the prospective commercial bank failures that she already knew she could resolve without disturbing financial markets.

Herb Allison, CEO of Fannie Mae, truly wanted a meeting with me. We had served on the Yale School of Management Advisory Council together. He hoped I could tell him how to communicate what he had discovered about the housing market to the powers-that-would-be in the Obama administration. We dined in a quiet place where no one we knew was likely to see us—a dingy Italian restaurant below street level between M Street and the Potomac, where the pasta tasted as if it had been brined in the C & O Canal.

At Fannie for only a few weeks, Allison already had concluded that housing values would continue to drop for two years or more, falling below a reasonable level into a zone of fear-induced prices. That would create a "saddle" on a line graph. Trillions of dollars of wealth would evaporate and not return for years.

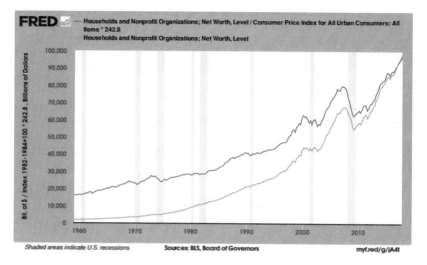

"FRED®" charts ©Federal Reserve Bank of St. Louis. 2015. All rights reserved. All "FRED®" charts appear courtesy of Federal Reserve Bank of St. Louis. http://research.stlouisfed.org/fred2/.

The net worth of all households and nonprofits totaled about $67.7 trillion in the third quarter of 2007. That figure had fallen to $54.8 trillion when Obama took office in the first quarter of 2009. About half the $13 trillion loss came from the stock market, about half from real estate. From 2007 to 2009 the total value of real estate dropped from close to $25 trillion to just above $18 trillion. When the value of a house drops, equity is wiped out. For all homes, owner's equity fell from a little less than $14 trillion to just below $7 trillion. About half of all middle-class savings disappeared.

Only in the third quarter of 2012 did total household net worth return to the 2007 level, at $68 trillion. The stock market valuation returned twice as fast as real estate values, which took a decade to claw their way back up to the 2007 level even in nominal, non-inflation-adjusted

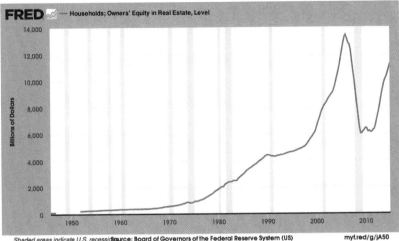

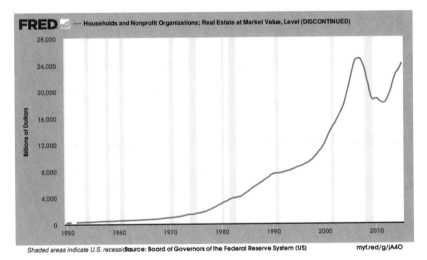

"FRED®" charts ©Federal Reserve Bank of St. Louis. 2015. All rights reserved. All "FRED®" charts appear courtesy of Federal Reserve Bank of St. Louis. http://research.stlouisfed.org/fred2/.

terms. Everyone should have bought stocks in early 2009, just as Barack Obama then said.[1] Only those with cash could take that advice.[2]

1. Elena Holodny, "President Obama Made One of History's Greatest Stock Market Calls in March 2009," *Business Insider*, January 20, 2017, http://www.businessinsider.com/obama-buying-stocks-potentially-good-deal-march-2009-2017-1.
2. Richard Florida, "How Housing Inequality Fuels Economic Inequality," *CityLab*, April 13, 2018: https://www.citylab.com/equity/2018/04/is-housing-inequality-the-main-driver-of-economic-inequality/557984/.

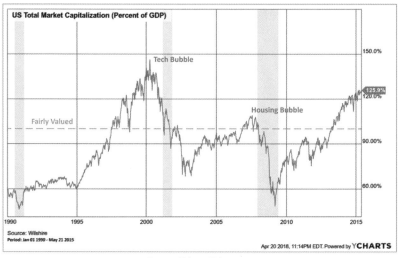

Courtesy Ycharts, Ycharts.com.

More or less about 60 million households lived in their own homes, and about 45 million properties had mortgages: Roughly four out of every ten American households[3] lived in a home they borrowed money to buy. The housing slump pushed between a fourth and a third of these mortgage-debt-owing families into negative equity or near negative equity. That meant about 10 to 15 million families were paying mortgage interest on a house worth less than the mortgage debt on it. By way of comparison the number of people in this situation approximated that of people without health insurance. The foreclosure risk pertained more to the middle class; the health insurance issue, more to low-income people.[4]

For decades, Democratic policy professionals, candidates, and their claques of staff, advisers, and funders had convinced themselves that nothing mattered more than insuring everyone against healthcare costs. When the housing slump shrouded far more people in woe than would need that missing insurance in a given month, no one asked the newly empowered Democrats to reconsider their priorities. New facts rattled uselessly off neoliberalism's dogmatic armor.

3. Assuming there were 117 million households at the time.
4. See Bill McBride, "Q4 Report: 11.3 Million U.S. Properties with Negative Equity," *Calculated Risk on Finance & Economics*, February 23, 2010, http://www.calculatedriskblog.com/2010/02/q4-report-113-million-us-properties.html/.

In the cruel winter of 2008–2009 a typical middle-class household saw its income drop close to $5,000, down below $53,000. What should a family with declining income do if its home was underwater by a large amount? Some would be unwilling to pay the mortgages because they did not want to throw good money after bad. Others would be unable to pay. Foreclosure would ensue.

For a lender to foreclose on a borrower's home was a general disaster. Evicting the family was cinematically cruel (sheriffs, tape, guns). It inflicted on the homeowner untold emotional as well as monetary injury. It also harmed the lender and other homeowners in the neighborhood. The mortgage holder had to slog through a judicial process while the homeowner abandoned the property; no one cut the grass or repaired the drooping gutters. The value of other houses on the street would fall as the foreclosed house, like a contagious disease, infected neighborhood property values.

In that dank restaurant, Allison explained all this to me. He guessed correctly that the drop in real estate collective wealth would be long and deep. In those locust-eaten years, homeowners would spend less than average for a long time. Moreover, the country would see a significant decline in homeownership.

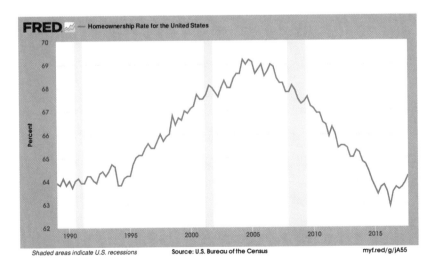

"FRED®" charts ©Federal Reserve Bank of St. Louis. 2015. All rights reserved. All "FRED®" charts appear courtesy of Federal Reserve Bank of St. Louis. http://research.stlouisfed.org/fred2/.

Values fell steeply where speculating developers built many homes in anticipation of incoming migration: South Florida, inland California, Las Vegas. The real estate market in "sand states" would recover more quickly, however, than in colder climes, where layoffs compounded the outbound migration that had been going on for years. Not many new arrivals looked for homes to buy in Wisconsin, Michigan, and Pennsylvania. These states would be fertile territory for Donald Trump in the 2016 election.

Housing market trouble carries over into voting booths. According to academic work published in 2018, John McCain might have won the 2008 election if mortgage credit (a bellwether for the slump) had not shrunk between 2004 and 2008. In swing states affected severely by the housing market downturn, the reduction of mortgage credit supply had five times the negative effect on votes for the presidential candidate of the incumbent party than the increase in the unemployment rate. In 2016 this effect operated against Hillary Clinton and for Donald Trump in the Midwestern states where the recovery remained anemic and the middle class felt they lived in the land of the ignored.[5]

Allison thought the Obama administration should focus specifically on improving the housing market in the most blighted geographies. He believed Fannie Mae could identify the troubled homes and predict the higher prices they would fetch after the dip through the downturn's saddle. Allison saw the situation as a tremendous buying opportunity for government and for taxpayers.

McCain and Obama Proposed Competing Housing Fixes in October

Allison knew why neither Treasury Secretary Paulson nor Obama put housing relief in the TARP legislation. Save banks first, help homeowners later. However, in the second presidential campaign debate on

5. Alexis Antoniades and Charles Calomiris, "Mortgage Market Credit Conditions and U.S. Presidential Elections," *CityLab*, March 2018, https://www.citylab.com/equity/2018/04/is-housing-inequality-the-main-driver-of-economic-inequality/557984/.

October 7, 2008, the Republican nominee, John McCain, suggested Treasury should buy the mortgages from the lenders at face value. The government would pay banks a huge sum in return for assets (loans) worth much less at that moment in time[6]—probably as much as $1 trillion. If Fannie and Freddie guaranteed these loans, the Treasury could use HERA to pay the money. Alternatively, Congress could appropriate two times the TARP amount Paulson had requested. Either way, McCain would increase the total federal debt by about a tenth.

In the debate, Obama sidestepped that proposal, saying only, "Most importantly, we're going to have to help ordinary families be able to stay in their homes." For the previous two years he had followed the lead of his home-state senior senator, Dick Durbin, in supporting legislation that would allow a bankruptcy judge to reduce the size of a mortgage loan in order to strike a compromise between a bankrupt homeowner and a mortgage loan servicer that did not want to negotiate a new payment plan. This was called "cramdown." If the homeowner went into bankruptcy, then a judge would figure out how much the debt owner could reasonably get from the homeowner who wanted to stay in the house after emerging from bankruptcy. The judge would cram the new mortgage amount down the throats of the protesting creditors.

Cramdown also would encourage lenders to be more careful in making loans that a borrower might not be able to pay. If it had been a feature of bankruptcy law in the '00s some of the excesses of shabby lending might not have occurred.

Two days later, speaking in Dayton, Ohio, Obama responded to McCain in detail. He outlined the ways government would reduce the total amount of mortgage debt on the books of investors and help homeowners avoid foreclosure by getting refinanced. In sum, Obama said his treasury secretary would buy mortgages, but only at less than the face value of the mortgage if the mortgage exceeded the value of the house. Paulson had failed to attract sellers with a similar plan earlier

---

6. In February 2008 Alan Blinder in the *New York Times* suggested the re-creation of the Home Owner's Loan Corporation founded by the New Deal Congress at the request of Franklin Roosevelt. It bought mortgages, refinanced, and at one point owned 20 percent of all the mortgages in the United States.

in the year because mortgage holders did not want to sell at reduced values. If Obama's government planned to acquire mortgages and refinance them at lower rates, it would need a way to force the mortgage holders' cooperation. Obama also said he would persuade Congress to allow cramdown.[7]

Obama's Advisers Developed Their Own Views

In the transition, Geithner, Summers, and Goolsbee controlled housing policy. HUD Secretary Shaun Donovan did not participate in the December 16 meeting and joined the White House discussions only in 2009. In any event, he lacked the statutory authority—the spending power—that Treasury had through TARP and HERA.

Strategy consists in large part of deciding not to take certain actions. Before the December 16 meeting in Chicago the team defined the housing problem as limiting foreclosures. They chose not to address these topics:

- The drop in housing values both on average nationally and in severely affected areas.
- The disappearance in savings for the middle class that stemmed from evaporating equity in owner-occupied homes.
- The decline of many cities and towns, especially in the Midwest.
- The inability of the unemployed to make interest payments on owner-occupied houses.
- The impact of falling home values on construction employment.

The Obama advisers worried that the big banks could suffer substantial losses from home equity loans and other residential mortgage-related securities. They built those negative assumptions into the stress tests they applied to the banks in the spring of 2009. Moreover, they understood that the GSEs (Fannie and Freddie), with their unlimited funding, could

---

7. African-Americans and Latinos had more wealth attributable to homeownership than is the case for whites. Neglecting the negative equity problem would have a disproportionately bad effect on racial minorities.

guarantee mortgage lenders from losses stemming from defaults by bor-rowers. Treasury's reluctance to push for major housing policy moves stemmed more from philosophical and practical concerns than from a desire to protect "its" banks. Treasury later was surprised that some big banks took enormous losses from civil lawsuits, GSE put-backs,[8] and regulatory fines,[9] but in 2008–2009 these unforeseen events played no role in setting policy.

At least in the view of Herb Allison, Treasury lacked experience in the sector. It could have used the GSEs to develop policy options. Given the amount of money available from TARP and HERA, and the size of the assets at stake, Treasury could have hired innumerable outside experts or outsourced tasks to consulting firms. Instead, while hardly anyone in Treasury worked on housing issues, they kept a tight rein on policy development.

Although the impact of the housing collapse on family savings and the quality of life in many American cities did not naturally fall into the jurisdiction or expertise of a government agency, Obama chose not to create a task force for the housing sector. Nor, for that matter, did he fashion ad hoc groups to address clean power infrastructure, water or sewage systems, or transportation. Presidents can use such organization-al structures to break jurisdictional silos created by legislation intended for solving different problems in other decades.

Later, worried about deficits, the administration created the Bowles-Simpson commission to address the budget. Similarly, in 2010 the Macondo oil spill led to a rapid organizational change that, quite unexpectedly, produced the energy secretary's valuable insights into how to cap the well. In the transition, Obama chose instead to make deci-sions in small groups that had ample brain power but skinny experience with many of the sectors of the economy.

By staying as the driver for housing policy, Treasury imbued the topic with its values. Institutions have cultures. Their people's predilections

---

8. Required repurchases by lenders of bad loans.
9. James B. Stewart, "Punishing Wells Fargo: Just Deserts, or Beating a Dead Horse?" *New York Times*, April 19, 2018, https://www.nytimes.com/2018/04/19/business/punishing-wells-fargo.html.

shape policy. Treasury as an institution regarded mortgage modification as taking from lenders or an expense for taxpayers. Neither was fair.

The anthropomorphic reference to taxpayers deserves deconstruction. No taxpayer would pay more in taxes. Instead, the total government debt would soar. In Treasury thinking, that would mean eventually someone would have to pay more in taxes to pay off that debt. Congress then probably would fail to raise taxes, and the national debt would go up. More debt raised interest rates, shrunk the economy, reduced tax revenues, made Treasury's job of financing the government more difficult. By vesting Treasury with housing policy, Obama virtually guaranteed that he would never see large-scale, operationally effective, and adventurous policy choices.

What then was the problem that Obama's team *was* willing to address? Austan Goolsbee listed the possibilities:

"There's eight to ten million homeowners at risk of foreclosure.

"We have a household balance sheet crisis, the negative household wealth effect of housing prices went down and people feel less wealthy, and so they're consuming less.

"We have a consumer debt overhang problem from housing where people that owe excessive mortgage debt, even if you give them a tax cut, they won't spend it because they are using anything they can to get their debt down.

"And then you had a group of people saying construction has been a huge part of GDP growth in this country and if we don't have construction, we can't recover, so we should find a way to get more construction people back to work.

"That's at least four major housing problems: foreclosure, negative wealth effect, excessive debt, construction layoffs. What you want to do as a policy depends very much on which of those you prioritize.

"We absolutely thought about and understood that there were a bunch of people underwater and if we could, we'd like to do the write-downs. The only problem was that there was $750 billion of negative equity in housing—the amount that mortgages exceeded the value of the houses. Somebody would have to eat that money. For sure the banks couldn't take $750 billion of losses and for sure the government wasn't willing to give $750 billion in subsidies to underwater homeowners, to say nothing of the anger it would engender among non-underwater homeowners."

Goolsbee added, "We also had the practical issue of the securitized mortgages, which was that people can't get modifications because they can't figure out who actually owns their loan." Finally, Goolsbee concluded, "As the Obama administration comes in, it's fair to say that every single government program tried up to that point had been a total failure in terms of getting people to participate."[10]

Herb Allison thought government needed to tackle a bigger problem than foreclosures. In his view, as long as millions of homes had mortgages bigger than their value, economic growth would not materialize. He wanted to solve what he, as a career-long steward of savings and pension benefits,[11] believed was the most important problem: negative wealth, or underwaterness, the bane of the middle rungs on the American ladder of success.

Jared Bernstein agreed that underwater mortgages created in debtors a deep, enduring reluctance to buy things. He said, "This is an economy that's 70 percent consumption. So unless households are feeling pretty healthy financially, it's hard to get much of a kick." As a result, Bernstein said, "This was going to be a long deleveraging cycle"—meaning consumers reducing their debt—"and that's what it's turned out to be. [Therefore,] this recession was going to be longer and harder to get out of than the average."[12]

Goolsbee disagreed: "There had never been any wealth effect downward before. My argument was, it was a $24 trillion market and it's down to $20 trillion. Let us not try to dye the ocean red; that would be impossible. The government does not have the money to set a price floor on a $20 trillion market. That could cost hundreds and hundreds of billions of dollars."[13]

---

10. Goolsbee, interview.

11. Allison previously was the chief operating officer of Merrill Lynch, and chief executive officer of TIAA, the leading retirement provider for teachers, researchers, and healthcare workers.

12. Bernstein, interview.

13. Goolsbee, interview.

CEA head Christy Romer sided with Goolsbee. She said, "We talked about the negative wealth effect from housing a lot, but it was complicated. There was about $1 trillion of negative equity, and getting rid of it would have helped increase consumer spending and heal the economy. But for the government to just absorb it would have been very expensive. And it is a transfer to the people in the economy wealthy enough to own a house. My view was that if we were going to spend all that money, I would rather use it for fiscal stimulus. That would help the economy directly, and it would focus the help on the bottom of the income distribution and the unemployed, rather than transfer a lot of wealth to the more affluent half of the population."[14]

The Goolsbee-Romer view prevailed. For Goolsbee and Romer, government should attend more to the problems of low-income people than to the middle class. A more well-considered, and electorally astute, political philosophy might have addressed both. In any case, the stimulus did not do much for either. The bill allocated less than $15 billion, about 2 percent of the total, for spending on housing. Goolsbee explained, "My view was that we should not choose a housing program based on what would be best for stimulus. Housing is a reflection of the business cycle. The best thing we can do for housing is get the economy growing. There are 5.5 million vacant homes. We built too many homes. Construction was a big driver of recovery in the past but it didn't need to drive this recovery. We needed to shift more to exports and investment."[15]

Treasury Proceeded to HAMP, Triggered the Tea Party

Goolsbee figured many people valued their "house higher than the outside market price, and so they would be willing to stay there even with negative equity, if the government could help get it affordable. That meant reducing interest payments. We could modify the rate, not the

---

14. Romer, interview.

15. Goolsbee, interview. Congress did pass a homebuyer tax credit for first-time buyers. That reflected the tremendous pressure on elected officials to address falling house prices.

principal, without having to get the approval of other mortgage holders the way a principal reduction would."[16]

The incoming administration proposed to pay lenders for lowering the interest rate on mortgages. The depth of the mortgage underwater did not matter. As long as the owner continued to pay on a nonreduced principal, the subsidy would reduce the interest rate.

On February 6 Sheila Bair met with Summers and others to express her concern about the administration's housing policy. She thought that up to 10 million homes were heading to foreclosure. Roughly, the mortgage debt on those homes alone totaled $2 trillion. Bair disliked the economic team's decision to subsidize mortgage lenders for refinancing paying borrowers.

Rejecting Bair's view, on February 18 the Treasury announced an effort called Making Homes Affordable. Its centerpiece was the Home Affordable Modification Plan (HAMP) that Goolsbee helped design.

Only years later did Bair learn that in the December 15, 2008 economic recovery plan, Summers and Goolsbee had recommended the plan. They had not included her in that decision.[17] She thought the Obama team had only "pretended to listen to her." Bair was "frustrated" with the "arrogance" of Obama's advisers.[18] She did not like one particular "expletive-laced tongue-lashing" and the general "arrogance and disdain" Geithner showed to agency heads, including not only her but also the Fed and the SEC.[19] She did not think that "helping homeowners was ever a priority" for Summers or Geithner.[20]

The day after it was announced, the HAMP plan drew a vigorous condemnation from a screaming Rick Santelli, a regular on CNBC's *Squawk Box*. On February 19, 2009, he spoke from the Chicago Mercantile Exchange trading floor, his normal venue, about HAMP:

"How about this, President and new administration? Why don't you put up a website to have people vote on the Internet as a referendum

16. Ibid.
17. Bair, *Bull by the Horns*, 152.
18. Ibid., 150.
19. Ibid., 191.
20. Ibid., 153.

to see if we really want to subsidize the losers' mortgages; or would we like to at least buy cars and buy houses in foreclosure and give them to people that might have a chance to actually prosper down the road, and reward people that could carry the water instead of drink the water?"

The traders on the floor cheered. Losers lose, winners win! Traders win either way! Let more losers lose!

Santelli continued, "This is America! How many of you people want to pay for your neighbor's mortgage that has an extra bathroom and can't pay their bills?"

The crowd at the exchange, not a fount of altruism under any circumstances, booed the hypothetical guy whose bathroom precipitated his financial ruin.

He concluded, "We're thinking of having a Chicago Tea Party in July. All you capitalists that want to show up to Lake Michigan, we're going to be dumping in some derivative securities."

Back in the studio, Wilbur Ross, later to be named Secretary of Commerce by President Trump, commented, "Rick, I congratulate you on your new incarnation as a revolution leader."[21]

The Tea Party captured the soul of the party of Lincoln and Teddy Roosevelt, Eisenhower and Reagan. Henceforward the Republicans would compromise with Democrats on very little legislation for the rest of Obama's tenure. The fault line of the Grand Old Party started in a TV studio. It ran under Wall Street, where banking executives disliked the government the more they needed it. It ran through largely white, middle-class suburbs where anxious homeowners paying on underwater mortgages despised their handout-taking, defaulting neighbors. Weaker together! That fissure of hatred ran straight in time from 2009 through the Republican presidential nominating process to November 2016, when a political earthquake improbably put Donald Trump into the Oval Office, and the desk made from the frigate *Resolute* became a prop in a wholly unreal reality TV show.

---

21. Rick Santelli, interviewed by Wilbur Ross, CNBC, February 19, 2009.

Reluctantly, Sheila Bair publicly supported HAMP when Obama announced it in Arizona on February 18, 2009, but "cringed" when Obama said the program would spend $75 billion to help three to four million.[22] She thought the top would be just over two million. On this point Goolsbee agreed with Bair: "As soon as we saw that, the economists said, 'We can't spend $50 billion. How could we possibly spend $50 billion? All previous government programs had no participation, almost literally zero participation.' We thought the HAMP interest-rate subsidy would cost $10 billion, maybe $20 billion, but not $50 billion."[23]

Herb Allison said, "They were hell bent on developing what they thought was the right program. Our view, which we put in writing, was that we thought at most maybe 1.7 million people over four years might be helped by this program. So we were kind of mystified, a little frustrated, to see that the president had announced three to four million, which was way above any realistic forecast that we had come up with, even trying to be optimistic. Modifying three to four million mortgages was an impossibility."[24]

HAMP required detailed documentation that homeowners found difficult to provide. In the absence of regulation, many lenders and servicers kept poor records. Nor had all been honest. Moreover, perhaps because it was reluctant to ask Congress for money to hire employees,[25] even on a temporary contractual basis, the administration asked servicing firms themselves to play a key role in implementing mortgage modifications. Anyone who has ever received a phone call from a collection agency dunning on a bill could have explained to the treasury secretary that the skill set and motivations of servicers do not suggest they are good at mediating compromises between creditor and debtor. Servicers before, during, and after HAMP preferred repayment plans—the homeowner

22. Bair, *Bull by the Horns*, 149–150.
23. Goolsbee, interview.
24. Allison, interview.
25. After the Senate confirmed me as FCC chairman in November 1993, I asked the Congressional leadership for extra money to hire economists, lawyers, and other experts so I could do the job the Hill leaders wanted done.

missing a payment would pay a portion of the past due every month in addition to the regular mortgage payment.

The chief economist at Fannie Mae, Mark Winer, thought Treasury had limited HAMP's effectiveness because it was worried "somebody would be getting a loan modification when they really shouldn't have. They should have aimed at helping the people who needed to be helped, and saying if we get a few bad ones in there's no problem. When you're fighting a war, you don't say, 'The first thing we're going to do is make sure no one is doing any war profiteering.' You say, 'The first thing we're going to do is get planes built.' But I didn't win that argument. The Obama team's answer was to make the process of loan modification very cumbersome, lots of paperwork, lots of checks and balances to make sure that you didn't inappropriately offer this benefit to anybody. That was HAMP."[26]

As Jared Bernstein summarized the matter, "Most of what we did was voluntary. We basically said to banks and servicers, 'If you want to join this program, you can.' That's pretty weak tea, but that was where the economics kind of led us."

The economics or the politics? "I would say the political economics."[27]

Moreover, banks played a trick on Treasury. They gave temporary modifications. "They told people," Goolsbee explained, "'Why don't you start paying half of what you were paying' at least for a while—a so-called 'temporary modification.' But then a different part of the same bank would take the fact that the debtor paid 50 percent as a notice of nonpayment. They would launch a foreclosure against the very people that they had given a temporary modification to. It did not cross our mind that the banks would behave like this. That ended up being an Achilles' heel of the program that engendered hostility among some of the beneficiaries. So you would have thought that anyone getting a dramatic reduction in their monthly payment would be happy about the program, but sometimes it ended up the opposite where we had some people saying, 'I got foreclosed on, your program screwed us over.'"[28]

26. Mark Winer, interview with author.
27. Bernstein, interview.
28. Goolsbee, interview.

A month later Treasury announced the Home Affordable Refinance Program, predicting that four million borrowers would refinance. Ultimately, Treasury considered HARP to be by far its best idea for addressing the housing market. It enabled homeowners to refinance if they had not missed any payments.

Goolsbee noted, "The evidence gathered in the years that followed has shown pretty clearly that the HAMP logic was correct. Monthly affordability (which was cheaper to the government) mattered a great deal for people's behavior and default rates, but principal reduction (which was really expensive) did very little."[29] Treasury had limited success translating sound logic into a reduction in foreclosures.

In October 2010 Treasury reduced the Making Homes Affordable effort, which included HAMP and HARP, to $29.9 billion in subsidy payments, down from the $50 billion promised in January 2009. In 2013 the Inspector General reported: "As of September 2011, however, fewer than one million…had refinanced…. As a result…subsequent changes [were] made throughout 2012 and 2013….As of March 2013, 2.4 million HARP refinances had been completed."[30]

From September 2008 to September 2012, almost four million foreclosures occurred. Some unknown additional number went through a negotiated version, such as a forced sale. The total of lost homes approached 10 million in Obama's presidency, one out of ten families, one out of six homeowners.[31] Probably most people whose homes had negative equity at 25 percent or higher lost their property.[32] Some contend that the Obama administration's policies did not reduce at all the

29. Goolsbee, interview; and Austan Goolsbee, email to author.
See Diana Farrell, Kanav Bhagat, Peter Ganong, and Pascal Noel, "Mortgage Modifications after the Great Recession: New Evidence and Implications for Policy," JPMorgan Chase and Co. Institute, December 2017, http://financedocbox.com/Credit_and_Debt_and_Loans/74200853-Mortgage-modifications-after-the-great-recession.html.
30. "Home Affordable Refinance Program: A Mid-Program Assessment," August 1, 2013, https://www.fhfaoig.gov/Content/Files/EVL-2013-006.pdf.
31. In 2015 the *Wall Street Journal* estimated that between 2006 and 2014 more than 9.3 million homeowners suffered foreclosure or gave up their house to a lender or a buyer in a distress sale.
32. Bill McBride, "CoreLogic: '2.5 Million Homes Still in Negative Equity' at End of Q3 2017," *Calculated Risk on Finance & Economics*, December 7, 2017, http://www.calculatedriskblog.com/2017/12/corelogic-25-million-homes-still-in.html.

number of foreclosures and forced sales.[33] Few would argue that Obama's housing programs won gratitude from American homeowners.

Allison's Big Idea

Allison had little sympathy for the Treasury's housing policies. "The Obama administration had extremely bright people in every area that I worked with. Treasury's especially strong. The White House was very strong. But these were not people with practical experience. So the administration tended to come up with elegant, intricate programs, but those programs were not informed by market realities.

"Treasury was a white paper organization. They didn't have operating arms. In terms of operating new programs that would have to reach millions of people, they simply didn't have the experience or the appreciation of the complexity of doing that."[34]

Although thousands of firms participated in mortgage lending, the big banks, led by Wells Fargo, originated close to half of mortgages. However, the risk of default was carried principally by the government entities—Fannie and Freddie, the Federal Housing Administration, and the Veterans' Administration FHA and VA. The banks then would not suffer much if mortgage debtors did not pay interest or principal. The taxpayers would have to make up any losses: because no new tax would be imposed, the result would be an increased deficit. However, bank servicers did count on fees from such borrowers, and they had an incentive to thwart refinancing.

Allison said, "As to the HAMP program, they didn't understand that to implement this program, first of all, one would have to transform the mortgage servicing industry completely. Banks heretofore had been operating back-office collection agencies as servicing arms. They would collect payments and they would foreclose on people who didn't pay. They didn't have the systems to modify mortgages or even to collect

33. Peter S. Goodman, "U.S. Loan Effort Is Seen as Adding to Housing Woes," *New York Times*, January 2, 2010, https://www.nytimes.com/2010/01/02/business/economy/02modify.html.
34. Allison, interview.

the information and process it. They were woefully understaffed. Management didn't have the capabilities in those mortgage servicing arms to be able to handle this task either. So to modify mortgages as HAMP intended you had to reinvent the mortgage industry."

Allison thought mortgage lenders and services occupied no moral high ground, did not deserve the deference Treasury policy showed them. "What also wasn't understood was that a great many of the mortgages issued between 2005 and 2007–2008 were in effect fraudulent. They either did not document income or there was inflated income that was documented. People earning $18,000 a year were given $300,000 mortgages. We were seeing signs that there had been widespread misstatements of income and misstatements of valuations of mortgages."

Allison wanted government to make these bad actors mark their loans to market value. "If the lenders had marked the mortgages to market, they'd be doing refinancing all day long. If mortgages were on balance sheets at their true value, lenders had nothing to lose. They would be voluntarily modifying mortgages to reset the interest and payback periods. The hit on their balance sheets would have been taken. They'd suddenly find the manpower and the systems to do all this." Allison understood that he was proposing a "massive restructuring. It had to be done early on when the Treasury had the power to do it, when the financial sector was on the ropes."

If mortgage holders did not mark the loans to market, then Allison proposed that the government should use the power of eminent domain to condemn the loans. The government can seize property, but under the Fifth Amendment to the Constitution it must pay just compensation. Allison said, "We would condemn the assets [the loans] and take them over at some fraction of the face value. We would offer the owners 80 percent of the upside. The government would take 20 percent of the gain" when housing prices went back up and the mortgages recovered their face value. Meanwhile, we would recapitalize the financial institutions with government investments from TARP." After it owned the mortgages, the government would lower the interest rate the borrowers were paying.

Allison added, "When you control the money supply and you control interest rates, as the government does, you are going to make money if you buy assets. You cannot lose money." He assumed the coordination between the Treasury and the Federal Reserve that everyone believes in and both institutions prefer not to make transparent.

Allison added, "We'd have a different financial sector. It would be lean and lending much more than they are today because their capital would be free and clear of these troubled assets. They could take on new assets by making new loans. They'd probably have new management, probably very much needed.

"This is exactly what was done with GM and Chrysler. By not doing that, we missed a huge opportunity to restructure the financial industry."[35]

Early in the first quarter of 2009 Allison outlined his big idea to Summers and Geithner in a three-page memorandum. He suggested this sequence: make debt holders mark their mortgages to market, use government money to buy the debt and recapitalize the sellers to the degree necessary, and refinance to help borrowers. Then let the banking and housing sectors reestablish profitability from that sound footing.

Outside academics wrote papers supporting the Allison approach,[36] but its vision of activist government contradicted the Obama team's oft-expressed opinion that the private and public spheres should not be heavily mixed in commercial arrangements. The government might create incentives to catalyze private sector actions, but it should not enter into contractual arrangements with private parties. Because government always intrudes on the private sector in some way, this axiom reflected less a principled stance, and more a habit of rejecting proposals for particularly pointed government intervention in markets. Meanwhile, as if it were a bank, Treasury worried about the assets and liabilities on the public sector's balance sheet, hoped that its profit-and-loss statement

---

35. Allison, interview.

36. For a survey written later, see Raymond H. Brescia and Nicholas Martin, "The Price of Crisis: Eminent Domain, Local Governments, and the Value of Underwater Mortgages," *Temple Political & Civil Rights Law Review*, vol. 24, September 22, 2014, https://papers.ssrn.com/sol3/papers.cfm?abstract_id=2498651.

registered as break-even (no deficit spending) at least in some years.[37] Its aversion to meddling in commerce caused Treasury to recoil from Allison's suggestion, even if the surely time-limited drop in housing prices created a syzygy between a shining opportunity to help homeowners rebuild wealth and a brilliant chance to make money for the public fisc.

Goolsbee disliked Allison's idea. "Either we're going to have to commit as the government" to buying the mortgages for hundreds of billions of dollars, if not much more, "or put the losses"—by writing down mortgage amounts—"onto the banks, which will require more TARP money. Either we have to commit to putting hundreds of billions of dollars in write-down to literally get people into positive equity, and recognize that the people who are going to need this are not going to be sympathetic at all, or we're going to have to tailor the program to the issue of just the foreclosures, not the wealth effect."[38]

Obama's team regarded a major write-down of bank loans as too adventurous. Allison acknowledged that "some felt it would be too risky. You'd be taking on these assets and you weren't sure what they would be worth down the road. Secondly, did you want to be so massively transforming your finance sector during the middle of a financial crisis? We're going to try to get through this period. We don't want to appear as though we're socialists. They did not want it said that they were nationalizing anyone. But actually what they got was the worst of both worlds. They acted in a way very favorable to the existing managements and boards of most of the banks and at the same time they were branded as socialists. They got the worst of all outcomes."[39]

HUD Has a View

In January 2009 Secretary of the Housing and Urban Development Department-designate Shaun Donovan entered the debate about housing. Donovan, formerly the housing commissioner in New York City,

---

37. See, e.g.," 2017 Financial Report of the United States Government. Report. U.S. Department of Treasury," https://www.fiscal.treasury.gov/fsreports/rpt/finrep/fr/17frusg/02142018_FR(Final).pdf.
38. Goolsbee, interview.
39. Allison, interview.

"interviewed with friends from New York, Jamie Rubin and Mike Froman, the weekend after the election. That following Tuesday I went to Chicago, exactly a week after the election. The president-elect described how he had been at the White House for the first time the day before. He was stunned by how detached President Bush seemed. Obama was pessimistic about being able to do much in the transition period about how to spend the TARP money. He was very focused on the auto industry and getting a rescue package moving even within those two months. There was also a lot of discussion about the stimulus, about large-scale and long-term goals and balancing them with the short-term stimulus. The president-elect felt we were facing not only an immediate crisis but a longer-term structural set of challenges for the American economy, for the middle class."

Donovan interpreted Obama as framing "the 'long term' as starting with figuring out what are the growth industries of the future that would allow a low or moderately skilled working-class or poor worker to get to the middle class? How are we going to attack wage and wealth inequality? Obama felt that this was an opportunity to do both. He felt that on healthcare, clean energy, infrastructure, housing, on all of these there were opportunities to use this immediate crisis to make big changes. Rahm said, and the president repeated often, that a crisis is a terrible thing to waste."

Donovan himself believed that "in the period of remediating the whole economy, and especially the housing sector, there could be a new focus on rental housing as an alternative. There had been an overinvestment in home ownership. For people in poverty, the public housing model had often concentrated poverty, and cut off those families from opportunity. I had been working in New York on a market-based model to try to create a different kind of housing for the poorest Americans."[40]

Since the middle of the twentieth century, government had favored highly leveraged individual home ownership for providing stability to neighborhoods, creating a tax base for local schools, and generating savings for families. Donovan wanted to move away from these policies.

40. Shaun Donovan, interview with author.

Perhaps the crisis presented an opportunity for radical change—Americans might save in the stock market instead of through home equity, and more easily move in search of better work.[41] Obama might transform not only healthcare and energy, but also the hugely important housing market.

Donovan continued, "About a week and a half later, I was at a very cold and extremely windy soccer game that my then nine-year-old was playing on Staten Island right by the ocean. Wind whipping. Seagulls everywhere. Freezing cold. And my cell phone rang. I could barely hear because of all the wind noise. It was Mike Froman calling to tell me that they were beginning the FBI vet."

Donovan's appointment to run HUD was announced December 13. He did not get on the attendee list for the December 16 meeting in Chicago, but he obtained a copy of the briefing memo. He did not love its housing section: "I felt that we should have gone further on the housing piece. We should have made mortgage modifications mandatory. There was a greater opportunity to use TARP as a lever for mandatory modifications as opposed to the voluntary method that we ultimately pursued.

"At the time, I did not mean necessarily marking to market, but I did want a significant reduction in income to the mortgage holders because of a reduction in interest payments. I did not mean requiring principal reductions in the face value of the mortgage, although I did come to support principal reduction as the full scope of the collapse in home prices became clear. Initially, I meant imposing lower cash flow on the debt holders while resetting interest rates for homeowners' mortgages."[42]

Cramdown Sabotaged

For many years, the mortgage industry argued in court and Congress that mortgage debt should be exempt from the risk of modification even when the homeowner had gone bankrupt. The industry achieved its goal

---

41. According to this vision, globalization and technologically driven disruption would shorten tenure in particular jobs, necessitate retraining, and destabilize communities. Housing policy needed to change in reaction to these trends.

42. Donovan, interview.

in 1993 when the Supreme Court held that mortgages were immune to modification by bankruptcy judges. For years, Obama's fellow senator from Illinois, Dick Durbin, wanted to reverse that decision. As a Senator, Obama endorsed Durbin's proposed legislation before the campaign. Congressman John Conyers, Democratic Chairman of the House Judiciary Committee, wanted cramdown in the stimulus. The path to putting this policy into law seemed clear.

Goolsbee recalled that he wrote in a memo early in the transition, "Let us offer a little amount of money for buying down second liens. These seconds are not worth anything in market" because they are junior to first liens, and when the house's value is underwater they are the form of debt that immediately becomes worthless. "But the lienholders don't want to give them up for nothing. And let us couple that small subsidy with a stick, namely, if they don't take the money in return for writing off the seconds, then we should push for allowing cramming-down the mortgage lender in a bankruptcy proceeding." That meant to him letting judges "write the second lien down to market value, the way they can do everything else in bankruptcy except the first mortgage."[43]

According to Goolsbee, Tim Geithner and Larry Summers were "not very pleased" by the idea of cramdown, largely on property rights grounds. Geithner felt that passing a law that overrode contracts could generate a lack of confidence in the lending system. He was concerned, as he had been in crushing Sheila Bair's preference for "haircuts," that depositors and creditors of banks should trust that banks would preserve and return their money. Goolsbee said that "in the end the political folks argued that putting cramdown in the stimulus could put quick passage of the stimulus at risk."[44]

Some worried also that millions of homeowners choosing bankruptcy to get relief on their mortgages could overwhelm the courts. That might have suggested the virtue of cramdown. Moreover, Congress could have appropriated to the judiciary the money to create a temporary expansion in the capacity of bankruptcy courts in more than a dozen states

43. Goolsbee, interview.
44. Ibid.

(including Illinois) where 25 percent or more of homeowners had negative equity. Judges' salaries do not add up to much.

Here is a 2010 map showing the geographic clusters of the underwater homes:

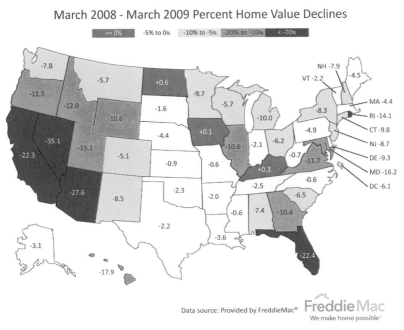

Original map created by Deborah Nicholls. Data source: Provided by Freddie Mac®.

Goolsbee supported Obama's perspective: "Let us take the approach that we're just going to try and prevent the preventable foreclosures, and we're going to just have to eat the facts that house prices are going down, construction's not coming back, the business cycle's not going to go back to what it was. Then you should at least give bankruptcy judges the power to force cramdowns."[45] His CEA colleague Jared Bernstein also supported the measure: "The president talked a fair bit about cramdown during his campaign. He was committed to that."[46]

45. Ibid..
46. Bernstein, interview.

On April 30, 2009, Durbin tried to pass cramdown as an amendment to another bill. That was the moment President Obama could twist arms for the votes Durbin needed. The key vote was Democratic senator Evan Bayh of Indiana. According to Donovan, Bayh thought "this will discourage lending going forward and will raise the cost of lending for the future."[47] In fact Bayh had identified a positive motive for passing cramdown. It would discourage mortgage lenders from making imprudent loans to those who had a shaky ability to pay.

Treasury Secretary Geithner sent a subtly phrased message to Congress that he did not want the law changed.[48] Years later Geithner implied that he sabotaged the measure when he wrote in his memoir, "I didn't think cramdown was a particularly wise or effective strategy."[49] Obama did not intervene. Bayh was enabled to vote no, which he did, fracturing the Democratic coalition. Durbin's amendment lost 45 to 51.

Disappointed, Durbin said about Congress, "Banks own the place."[50] He could have added that at least on this issue the Department of Treasury worked for those who owned Congress, and the White House took a powder. Donovan said, "It's fair to say that Tim and Larry were not as supportive of cramdown as they could have been. I think the president was. I think Austan was. It was extremely difficult to move a set of moderate Democrats, at least in part because of their support from the banking industry."[51]

Bernstein said, "The argument we heard at the time was that we fought for it in the Congress and couldn't get it. I believed that at the time. Since then, I've heard from numerous members of Congress, 'No, you didn't.' I think that's unfortunate."[52]

---

47. Donovan, interview.

48. Tami Luh, "No Bankruptcy Help for Homeowners," *CNN Money*, April 30, 2009, http://money.cnn.com/2009/04/30/news/economy/cramdown/index.htm?postversion=2009043015.

49. Geithner, *Stress Test*, 302.

50. Dick Durbin, quoted in Robert Weissman, "The Financial Crisis One Year Later: The More Things Change, the More They Stay the Same," *Huffington Post*, November 16, 2009, https://www.huffingtonpost.com/robert-weissman/the-financial-crisis-one_b_286974.html.

51. Donovan, interview.

52. Bernstein, interview.

Matt Kabaker, one of Geithner's key team members, said, "Cram-down I think in retrospect was actually quite a reasonable solution that all sides should have embraced. It was fair. It was adjudicated. It was a process. It wasn't an imposition. It allowed a judge to look at a borrower's total ability to pay. Basically it did what should be done in a bankruptcy, which is to treat different creditors the way they're each supposed to be treated. But the banking industry at that time fought it tooth and nail. We were technically for it, but it just didn't happen. And part of it was again the housing policy was not advanced enough in terms of just to say, 'Yeah. Cramdown. Let's go get that done.' There just wasn't enough passion in it on our side."[53]

Romer said, "I do wish we had pushed harder for cramdown. Geithner didn't want to do it."[54]

Goolsbee explained, "Basically what happened is the administration announced support for cramdown but didn't pull out the stops to try to pass it. It was a mistake for us not to do cramdown. Potentially, it might have been a major missed opportunity, but the question is how many people this would have pertained to in the real world."

Goolsbee thought write-downs needed to be all or nothing. He said, "There [were] people arguing, well, let's do a little bit of write-down by arm-twisting banks into some level of mortgage modification. But partial write-down doesn't do much. You've got to eliminate negative equity. It's quite important that you get to positive equity for the person not to default."[55]

In my view, as someone who litigated only a few bankruptcy cases, a general rule would have emerged in a case-by-case adjudication—for example, to reduce mortgages by no more than 20 percent. I suspect Goolsbee's all-or-nothing formulation was wrong. The cram would not have needed to go all the way down to the market value of the home. It would have sufficed to lower mortgages to 120 percent of value. That would have left a fair amount of water that the house's value would

53. Matt Kabaker, interview with author.
54. Romer, interview.
55. Goolsbee, interview.

have to swim through to get to positive equity. However, foreclosure risk drops significantly if a home's value is not more than 120 percent underwater. See this chart from *Calculated Risk Blog* showing how steeply foreclosure risk rises when the loan to value ratio exceeds 120 percent.

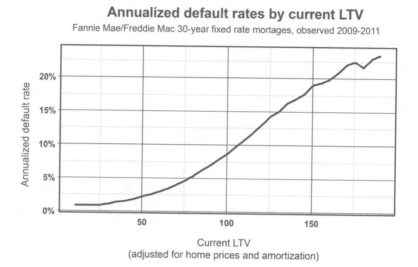

Annualized default rates by current LTV
Fannie Mae/Freddie Mac 30-year fixed rate mortages, observed 2009-2011

Current LTV
(adjusted for home prices and amortization)

Adapted from Todd W. Schneider, "Mortgages Are About Math: Open-Source Loan-Level Analysis of Fannie and Freddie," Todd W. Schneider blog, http://toddwschneider.com/posts/mortgages-are-about-math-open-source-loan-level-analysis-of-fannie-and-freddie/, June 9, 2015.

Perhaps about nine million homeowners were more than 20 percent underwater by early 2009. (No one knew the exact number.) Cramming down mortgages to only 20 percent underwater might require a write-down of 10 percent, or $20,000 per home.[56] Multiplying that number times nine million homes equals $180 billion. That was probably the maximum of total cramdown bankruptcy judges would have forced. That write-down potentially would have helped homeowners at all income levels, although upper-income families would have been less likely to go

---

56. A bankruptcy judge also could have reduced interest rates as opposed to cramming down principal. Research has shown that modifying interest rates is the best way to reduce defaults and foreclosures, rather than trying to reduce negative equity. Kristopher S. Gerardi, Kyle Herkenhoff, Lee Ohanian, and Paul S. Willen, "The Causes of Mortgage Default: Ability to Pay versus Negative Equity," Vox, January 10, 2017, https://voxeu.org/article/causes-mortgage-default.

into bankruptcy. If the banking industry had supported this plan, or if Geithner, who had life-and-death authority over the sector, had pushed, or Obama had insisted that Democrats support the measure, the Senate probably would have passed Durbin's amendment.

Absent cramdown, 31 percent of homeowners with a mortgage owed more than the worth of their homes, leaving owners with no savings in the form of home equity. Zillow reported that in the first quarter of 2016 almost 13 percent of homeowners with a mortgage still were underwater. During Obama's two terms, the geographic center of negative equity moved from the Southwest and Southeast to the rust belt. Chicago had the highest rate of negative equity among large markets—20 percent in 2016. The surrounding states proved fertile territory for Donald Trump's campaign.

The size of the underwater problem stymied Goolsbee. "The fundamental issue is that there was $750 billion of negative equity, and how would you write it down? We weren't stupid. We thought about write-downs and every other potential policy response the critics now bring up. It's that if you sit and look at the magnitude of the problem there's virtually nothing you can afford to do that's up to the magnitude of the problem you're facing."[57]

At this macro level, Goolsbee disagreed with Nobel Prize–winning economist Joe Stiglitz, who said, "It was a mistake not to do something more about homeowners and foreclosure. I said this on one of the conference calls with Obama in 2008 and in meetings with people in Congress. Cramdown was only an example. Economically, if you didn't provide more support to the housing market, prices would likely fall and more people would lose their homes. The dynamic could lead to overshooting and, from a social point of view, disaster. Then politically to be seen at the same time to be helping the banks and not the average American I thought would be a mistake. Later in September 2009 I met with Geithner and emphasized the housing problem. Geithner was not very receptive."[58]

57. Goolsbee, interview.
58. Joe Stiglitz, interview with author.

Fannie Mae economist Mark Winer said, "There were lots of other ways to help people make mortgages more affordable. Expedited short sales, turn ownership into rental, return for turning a house into a rental for some period of time."[59] Another idea was reducing all GSE-owned mortgages by a percentage. Alternatively, Treasury could have contributed $100 billion in capital to a private-sector enterprise that bought homes at a modest discount on the mortgage loan amount, making the lender take a small haircut, and then rented the home to the previous owner, with an option to buy it back if and when the family could afford it. Such firms did spring up, even without government grants, simply because they could borrow at the low rates the Fed established for the entirety of Obama's two terms.

Ultimately Treasury allocated only $46 billion TARP money toward keeping homes from foreclosure, and spent less than that. It used another $80 billion to fund the bankruptcies of GM and Chrysler. Banking investment totaled a little less than $275 billion.[60] More than $200 billion of TARP money then went unused.[61] The July 2010 financial regulation legislation, Dodd-Frank, reduced the Treasury's authority to spend under TARP from $700 billion to $475 billion.[62]

Congress follows this rule: you don't spend it, you lose it.[63] In 2009 and 2010 Obama did not push Treasury to spend all the available money. By

59. Winer, interview.

60. Amy Fontinelle, "Troubled Asset Relief Program—TARP," Investopedia, January 31, 2018, http://www.investopedia.com/terms/t/troubled-asset-relief-program-tarp.asp#ixzz4k1OcKfOh/.

61. By law, no new TARP investments could be made after October 3, 2010. If the Treasury had been confident by the summer of 2009 that the possibility of serious bank runs had diminished, it would have invested the unused $400 billion in TARP money in some activity aimed at contributing either to a recovery in the housing market, possibly in a targeted geographic area, or to a second wave of stimulus. Planners would have had to struggle for a good solution, and one that did not draw political opprobrium. However, that was a lot of money that went unspent.

62. Paul Kiel and Dan Nguyen, "Bailout Tracker," ProPublica, updated June 18, 2018, https://projects.propublica.org/bailout/.

63. As of June 30, 2012, Treasury spent a little more than $450 billion of the authorized $700 billion of TARP money. The principal allocations (rounded off) were:
- $240 billion in bank equity shares
- $70 billion in American International Group (AIG)
- $80 billion in loans and equity purchases to automakers and their financing arms
- $20 billion in mortgage-related securities
- $45 billion in homeowner foreclosure assistance, with only $4.5 billion actually spent.

late 2009 Geithner himself believed the recovery had commenced. He did not want to increase deficit spending or risk congressional criticism of more spending, even if it was already authorized.

The Treasury Department Prioritized Bank Stabilization

Treasury chiefly worried about the colossal magnitude of the big banks' undercapitalization. Somehow, the housing sector caused the financial crisis, but in the wake of Lehman's collapse the Treasury Department focused not on causation, but on effects. To help Geithner heal the big banks, Dan Tarullo, another Clinton veteran on the transition team, asked Lee Sachs to return to Treasury. He had been in charge of capital market oversight during the Clinton administration.

Reporting to Geithner, Sachs was to diagnose and fix the interrelated problems suffered by the big banks: "Capital, liquidity, legacy assets, and functioning markets. If you ignored any one of those, or didn't have a plan that would work for each one of those individually, no plan for stabilizing the system as a whole would have succeeded, and all of them would have failed."[64]

Matt Kabaker, a financial services investor, left the private equity firm Blackstone to work for Sachs. Kabaker explained what he saw and did:

"Paulson had passed TARP, put GSEs in conservatorship, taken initial action with respect to GM, Chrysler, and GMAC, but none of those actions proved to be more than an interim solution. The prime directive for Treasury was to keep banks from pulling back from their core function, which was lending, or leveraging. If you think of the United States economy as basically a levered [borrowing] entity, financed by our financial system [the lenders] and all of its various parts [like the GSEs], allowing that leverage to come down dramatically would basically cause the United States to shrink quite abruptly."

Kabaker continued, "Paulson and his people dealt with a very near-term crisis. We were left with the task of how to get to the end of the crisis. All countries took similar stabilizing actions: A great deal of provision of

---

64. Lee Sachs, interview with author.

liquidity, often times capital into the banking systems. Sometimes firms had to be taken over as we did with the GSEs and other countries did with some of their banks.

"There was never a question as to whether you have to recapitalize the banking system. That was necessary. It was critical to keep banks lending. We had to avoid large-scale deleveraging, because that would be the same as causing a great drop in the GDP and soaring unemployment."[65]

Kabaker said, "The core decision with respect to the banking system was whether to pursue a set of policies that would result in, resolution would be the kind word, nationalization would be the unkind word, of large parts of the banking system, particular very large, complex institutions. Or whether we wanted to create an approach that would allow those institutions to be recapitalized without that level of intervention. Resolution of a bank is the same as recapitalization of the bank. So it's essentially the government taking over the bank, assuming liabilities and then having some portions of the bank reemerge with a cleaner balance sheet. You essentially create capital that way.

"The government could assume liabilities and then the new bank emerges from the shell of the old bank just without all of its bad stuff," meaning assets that directly or indirectly were based on residential housing values, "and that bad stuff is taken on by the taxpayer or the government."[66]

Sachs agreed: "The options ranged from nationalization of the banking system on the one end and at the other end do nothing and take the Lehman Brothers approach—'let the cards fall where they will.' The latter was never really considered."

Sachs said one of the "most complicated" parts of the problem was "to figure out what the magnitude was. How much capital was going to be necessary? As we were entering office, it was clear that we had to get the second $350 billion worth of TARP. Congress had approved $700 billion, but you had to go back for another vote on the second $350

---

65. Summers made the opposite argument when he rejected my GRIP on the basis that the country had too much debt.
66. Kabaker, interview.

billion. The private sector estimates as to how big the hole was that had to be filled ranged up to over two trillion dollars.

"A contingent argued that we should mark the assets to market, force the banks to sell them and recapitalize the banks." That was similar to the Allison view with respect to housing. Sachs considered it to be "effectively nationalization," which "had tremendous potential to start a chain reaction and accelerate the very downward spiral we were trying to arrest." He said its advocates were "largely an unholy alliance of hedge funds, academics, and vulture investors, though there were certainly some voices inside the administration who sympathized with this view."[67]

Kabaker added, "The recap argument was that if you didn't do that then the banks limp along, they don't lend as much, and they don't support recovery to the same degree. The argument for nationalization was that because of the depth of distress on the balance sheet of the banks these things were dead institutions. They were so-called zombie banks.

"Geithner presented the situation as option one, government-driven recapitalization, or option two, private-market driven. I was not offended by the idea of government playing a major role in resolving the financial crisis, but I did think we should be preserving optionality and doing no harm. Therefore, we felt we should try option two, the private-market-driven recapitalization, and if it did not work, you could go to option one later. There was a huge amount of technical detail in executing option two.

"We also thought that by nationalizing, the process of recapitalizing was actually likely to be longer. The idea of nationalization was quick, kill them and get it back out. Our view was that that was hopelessly optimistic.

"General Motors and Chrysler might be pushed through bankruptcy quickly," said Kabaker, "but banks are different because the liabilities don't really freeze when you put a bank in bankruptcy. The liabilities run," meaning that everyone with a deposit or a loan to the bank asks for their money back, "and you either have to fund them, or if you don't fund them, it has a huge chain reaction throughout the entire system."

67. Sachs, interview.

Kabaker explained further, "If you lent money to GM, you're a sophisticated investor and the bankruptcy court will decide if you get paid. And your bond can still trade. You understand that. Your money is at risk. Your bond is not worth the face value. It is worth the trading value. Banks are different. If you lent money to Bank of America by making a deposit there, you think that's money. A dollar is a dollar. Other institutions that lend to each other overnight in a way similar to a deposit think that's money. If you put one of those organizations into bankruptcy, then you suddenly discover that what you thought was currency is not. Money vanishes. That can create major problems throughout a system. Deposits have to be guaranteed.

"We put in place a system in the 1930s, the FDIC, so that we could take individual banks through a bankruptcy-like process without that kind of disruption. But in 2009 we did not have a legal or practical way to do it for a bank holding company."[68]

Mark Gallogly, a private equity investor and informal adviser to President Obama, said, "In a discussion about nationalizing banks after the inauguration, I remember a specific conversation with Larry Summers, Robert Wolf, and David Swensen, chief investment officer for the Yale endowment. Swensen was the biggest bull for nationalizing because he believed a couple banks were economic zombies—unable to play a meaningful role in the economy. I didn't like the idea of nationalization. In that meeting, Larry held his cards close to his vest. Nationalizing would have meant that instead of public shareholders owning a bank, the government would have owned it. The United States would have owned a bank like Citigroup, possibly deciding who would be the CEO and replacing the board. I didn't favor putting the government in charge of decision-making at major banks. While the intervention in the auto industry ultimately proved successful, at the time, I thought government control of banks could have unintended consequences, and that it made more sense to see if other initiatives—ultimately like the stress test— would work instead."[69]

68. Kabaker, interview.
69. Gallogly, interview.

Kabaker said, "From the transition until several meetings with the president in March of 2009, this choice between option one"—resolution by nationalization—"and option two"—using the private market—"wasn't definitively decided. The incredibly difficult part of this period is that the decision on this was so market-sensitive and impacted so many different aspects of the securities markets that the decision-making process was highly insular and very contained. We couldn't have any rumors of any of this discussion get out. And at the same time it needed to be closely coordinated with the Fed, the FDIC, the White House, and a variety of other agencies that were actually implementing different pieces of the policy.

"The decision was outstanding from December to March. In a world where it felt like days mattered, it was a long time. And there was a lot of disagreement on this particular issue." However, in any case, with respect to government-driven resolution—and this was the crushingly dispositive point to Kabaker—"we weren't sure how to fund it without potentially needing to go back to Congress."

The TARP authorization was $700 billion. Kabaker did the subtraction: "Paulson had spent a bunch of that. We committed a bunch of that to autos and to other programs. We needed money potentially available for more investment in banks. When you tallied it all up we felt we only had effectively about $100 billion of spare capacity between December 2008 and March 2009."[70]

Treasury Picked Option Two

Geithner and his team feared that if they put Citi into option one, government-compelled recapitalization, then all banks' creditors would become apprehensive that other banks too would be forced to pay less than what they owed. Haircutting might cascade across the entire banking system. Many businesses would see reductions in the amount of money they thought they had, as if an invisible hand subtracted digits in

---

70. Kabaker, interview.

their balance sheets. The entire economy would shrink in size. Indeed, even if creditors came to believe that government might insist on option one, then they might stop lending to banks immediately. A hint of option one—which was really TARP on steroids—could trigger another financial crisis.

Sachs said, "We thought if we chose option one—mark down the assets on the balance sheets of the banks at that moment in time, and then guarantee the repayment of deposits and loans that had been made to banks—we would need a tremendous amount of capital. But there really was no way to know how much. In fact, because we were unsure of what would happen, it was necessary for the president in his first budget to put in a placeholder for a second TARP of $700 billion."

In this way, Treasury retained the possibility of spending another TARP, $700 billion more, even under option two, the reliance on private markets to recapitalize banks. Sachs explained, "We would tell the banks that if they cannot raise capital privately in six months, to strengthen their balance sheets Treasury will purchase their stock at a 10 percent discount to yesterday's price. That was a floor. That money would come from TARP. We felt we had enough money to back up this promise. But until the stress tests were complete, we couldn't be sure."[71]

The administration did not want to implicate the Fed in another bank bailout. Bernanke may have feared that if he had the Fed once again spend huge sums to save a bank, as it had done for Bear a year earlier, Congress would interfere with his independence. He was in the process of buying trillions of dollars of assets from dozens of institutions. He did not want to risk congressional intervention in his largely clandestine expansion of money supply. Without using the Fed's capability to create any amount of money, the administration either could spend under HERA or go to Congress for money. It did not want to do either.

Sachs continued his explanation: "We thought, for a variety of reasons, that private recapitalization was substantially preferable to a

---

71. Sachs, interview. Stress tests were Treasury's method of determining how much money the big banks needed to raise to preclude bank runs. Geithner chose this title for his book presumably for the double meaning—the government and financial system were under great stress for two years at least; Geithner's technique facilitated private market recapitalization.

taxpayer-funded recapitalization. There are two ways that you can get private money into the system. You can compel it or you can attract it. Compelling it means imposing haircuts on bondholders," reducing payment on money loaned to banks, "because you can't force people to write you a check. Bondholders, creditors have to take less than a hundred cents on the dollar. If you reduce the amount that the banks owe, obviously that changes the balance sheet of the banks for the better. But once you go down this path—even with a couple of banks—it is very hard to stop what could become a devastating downward spiral as depositors and other creditors of other banks withdraw their money in order to avoid a similar fate. We thought there was an unacceptable risk that going down this path would accelerate the run on the system we were trying to stop. And remember, the worse the run became, the further the housing market cratered, the higher unemployment skyrocketed, and the harder it became for businesses and households to borrow. It felt like the economy was coming to a standstill.

"By way of example, GM's creditors were forced to take a haircut. But auto companies are very different animals than banks. And so if we decided to go down the path of forcing these haircuts, basically forcing their creditors to take a haircut," reducing what the banks would pay on their own loans, "which it's not clear we had the authority to do, you had to then convince the world that you were going to stop after bank number one or two."[72]

Kabaker said, "With option one, you might think you are going in to take over only one bank, but when you're in that volatile moment, it could be that many other banks have funding problems, and you end up having to just do everybody. That's the risk. Other countries have found this out."[73]

Sachs guessed a complete markdown could be as much as $2 trillion. Borrowing that amount to recapitalize banking would have increased the debt to GDP ratio to more than 100 percent. At that level, Treasury feared a paradoxical reaction. If the markets thought higher taxes in the

---

72. Sachs, interview.
73. Kabaker, interview. Geithner had rejected "haircuts" in his debates with Sheila Bair.

future would be needed to pay the debt, then interest rates might rise, and housing values and bank assets would fall even farther.

For these reasons, Geithner, Sachs, Kabaker, and ultimately Summers and Obama selected option two, private sector recapitalization. Only if the banks were truly zombies would they have to go with option one.

Sachs said, "So we felt that it was better to focus on the hit for the losses due to nonpayment" on debts owed to banks. "The government would make its determination as to what we thought the ultimate losses due to nonpayment (as opposed to short term mark-to-market losses) could be. That was the stress test." That was the essence of option two. "Then the banks would go out and try to raise capital"—probably selling stock—"privately to fill the hole. If they couldn't do that, we were prepared to step in and fill that hole," which was option one.[74]

Treasury designed option two to unfold in steps. They maximized optionality. They put off possibly bigger government interventions in the hope that the stimulus, the Fed's asset purchases and reduction in interest rates, the government guarantees of repayment by Fannie and Freddie and AIG, and the results of the stress tests would start the recovery and end the possibility of runs on the banks. Then the hole—the banks' undercapitalization—would start shrinking on its own. Government would not have to put in the money to fill it.

Sheila Bair articulated the contrary view: "I didn't believe in a domino effect. If you have a controlled failure, the markets will adjust. There would not be a run on other banks in my view. The difference between what the assets and liabilities are worth is called the hole. If its liabilities exceed its assets, it's insolvent. In a bankruptcy or FDIC resolution process, shareholders and unsecured creditors have to absorb the hole. This is what the FDIC does when it puts a bank into receivership, as it does all the time. But the Fed and Treasury acted as if they thought we could only use government money to fill the hole, meaning restructure Citi. But there was sufficient shareholder equity and subdebt to absorb the losses on Citi's bad assets. The Treasury conversation was based on the

---

74. Sachs, interview.

incorrect assumption that the government was going to have to take on the entire job of filling the hole."

Bair said, "What would have been optimal would have been for Citi and Merrill Lynch to go into resolution. They should have gone into receivership. That's what the FDIC does for smaller banks. But we didn't have the legal right to force that. That could have been in TARP. It wasn't part of designing the TARP legislation.[75]

"The argument against this was that it would run the risk of triggering a run on other banks. We did have a tenuous situation after the Lehman failure, but by 2009 the system had stabilized and we could have imposed more accountability. With Citi, we could have constructed a good bank and a bad bank and said, you know what, debt and shareholders, you're going to fund this bad bank where we're going to put these bad losses. And we're going to take the good stuff and put it in a clean bank and recapitalize it and give you an opportunity to invest in it again. In March we could have done that. We had the time then. We did not have the time in October. The problem was not that they didn't have enough money in Treasury. They said that. It was not accurate. The problem was that they didn't want to haircut their precious bondholders. Shareholders maybe, but bondholders were sacred. They weren't going to make them take a dime of loss."[76]

Sachs responded to the Bair contention: "This was easy to say in theory. Sure, there was some possibility you could have pulled this off. There was no way to know. Treasury believed the probability was low. But regardless of what you thought the chance of success was, the consequences of being wrong were that you could turn the Great Recession into a second Great Depression. It would have been irresponsible to take that risk."[77]

Financial writer Paul Blustein said, "I think it could have had a dampening effect on the economy if they had adopted one of the more draconian solutions of 'nationalize the banks, chuck out the management, bring on the mob, tax them till the pips squeak.' But it would have given

---

75. This authority was what Paulson had passed into law for Fannie and Freddie, but decided not to seek for the big banks in the summer of 2008.
76. Bair, interview.
77. Sachs, interview.

people a sense that the bailouts weren't offensive to their sense of right and wrong. I think people were just shocked to their very foundation by the bailouts. The calculation of avoiding these more punitive solutions was incredibly consequential. The decision not to nationalize was the key. They may have made the right decision. We will never know how dangerous it would have been to do that."[78]

In a White House meeting in March, Treasury finally and definitively persuaded Obama to choose option two: getting the private sector to recapitalize the banks. Treasury thought this plan minimized the risk of bank runs, avoided "socialism" by keeping the government from ownership or control of banks, and did not risk Congressional criticism of spending under HERA or using Fed money. All these constraints led to the normal neoliberal solution: regulate in a way that pushed the industry in a certain direction. The stress tests were that regulation. They required undercapitalized banks to sell equity or otherwise bolster their balance sheets.

To defeat option one, Treasury pointed out that if a big bank went into receivership or resolution (financial industry euphemisms for bankruptcy), then the government probably would have to inject cash in order to meet their obligations to others. If it did not do that, bank runs might start on firms that had loaned to the bankrupt banks. The government had put cash into General Motors, Chrysler, Fannie, Freddie, and others under similar circumstances. The point carried weight. The amount might be much larger than the existing TARP funds. Congress would have to appropriate still more money, assuming Treasury did not spend under HERA authorization or persuade the Fed to fund more bailouts. Sachs said Rahm Emanuel ended the discussion of option one: "At that infamous March meeting, toward the end of that seven-hour meeting, Rahm said, as only Rahm can, 'There's no fucking way that we're getting another fucking dime.'"[79]

While Treasury and the White House agonized over option one or option two, government-supported or private-market-financed

78. Blustein, interview.
79. Sachs, interview.

recapitalization of the big banks, it could hardly have endorsed at the same time a government refinancing of millions of home mortgages. The big banks probably did not carry large mortgage portfolios on their balance sheets. Even if they had, Fannie and Freddie could have held the banks harmless from any mortgage refinancing. But choosing option one for housing and option two for banks would have confused Congress, the financial markets, and voters. Moreover, even if it selected option two for the banks, Treasury still might need more public money for recapitalizing banks, because option two could fail or need a little public-money oil to grease its workings. That was why the second TARP was in the budget. Treasury could not dedicate a big chunk of TARP to housing when it did not know what the recapitalization of banks might require. In short, Treasury followed the sound strategic principle of dedicating all its resources to the primary objective: recapitalizing banks. In the Treasury view, even cramdown, which probably would not have impaired the balance sheets of big banks to any significant degree, could not be risked when Wall Street's foundations shivered and shook.

Perhaps at the end of 2009, when the big banks had passed the stress tests, government could have adopted a version of option one for home mortgages. Possibly if HUD or a housing task force, and not Treasury, had owned the housing policy formation, some advisers would have presented Obama an Allison-like plan a year after the financial crisis. However, in the winter of 2009–2010, some thought the V-shaped recovery had commenced. Housing prices might recover without government intervention. Option two might suffice for both banks and home mortgages.

The "stress test" was the ingenious way that Geithner, Sachs, Kabaker, and a few others at Treasury executed on option two. It tested the value of the banks' assets. It also created clarity and confidence so that business again could depend on the credits maintained in the banking system to represent real, accessible money.

Bair did not applaud. "The stress tests did allow the banks to recapitalize. But the second part should have been to sell the banks' stressed assets into some kind of government facility. That would have gotten the banks to clean up their balance sheets and resulted in principal reductions on a lot of mortgages. Even in 2018, we still have 2.5 million homeowners underwater. After the stress tests, the banks still worried about how many of those second liens would go bad, how many mortgages would go bad that they still had on their balance sheets. The banks were risk averse. So even after the stress tests they didn't loan as much, except to very pristine borrowers. I think we became like Japan. We propped up a lot of inefficient financial institutions so we still had a bloated financial sector. We impeded a natural correction process. There's an old saying in banking, 'your first loss is your best loss.' That did not really happen. So I think that's impeded the economic recovery, the housing recovery and resulted in a very uneven broader economic recovery."[80]

Meanwhile, Bernanke's Fed continued to play a giant, if somehow nearly invisible, role in supporting Geithner's strategy with government money. Bernanke called his memoir *The Courage to Act*. The meaning of the title lay in his largely clandestine decision to triple the size of the

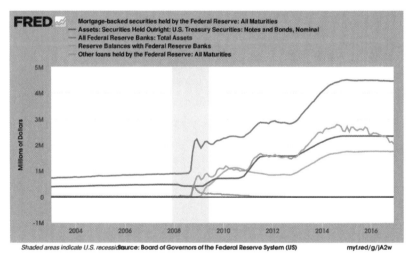

"FRED®" charts ©Federal Reserve Bank of St. Louis. 2015. All rights reserved. All "FRED®" charts appear courtesy of Federal Reserve Bank of St. Louis. http://research.stlouisfed.org/fred2/.

Fed's balance sheet in mere weeks. See:

Eventually, the Fed and Treasury restored the American banking system. The financial crisis had less awful impact on the United States than

80. Bair, interview.

on other major economies that had suffered similar cataclysms. This was perhaps Obama's most important, most invisible, and most unrewarded accomplishment. Probably, the administrations before and after would not have had the acumen and patience to execute on this plan. In political terms, that relative comparison profited Obama nothing. Voters do not consider whether they are better off than people in other countries or earlier eras.

Sadly, having avoided complete collapse, the banking sector did not return rapidly to investing in economic growth. The ratio of commercial and industrial loans by all commercial banks to GDP in the first quarter

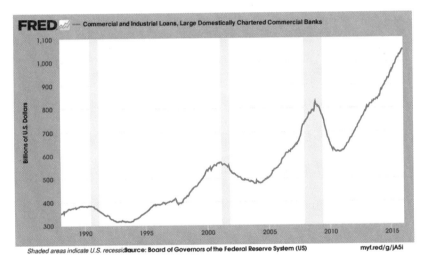

"FRED®" charts ©Federal Reserve Bank of St. Louis. 2015. All rights reserved. All "FRED®" charts appear courtesy of Federal Reserve Bank of St. Louis. http://research.stlouisfed.org/fred2/.

of 2009 was not matched until the end of 2015. Seven lean years.[81]

Sachs saw the positive side of the outcome: "I truly believe that if we didn't structure each part of our plan correctly, the whole thing would have failed. If the Fed didn't do the stress tests right, the whole thing would have failed. If we didn't get the markets working again, the whole

81. Board of Governors of the Federal Reserve System (US), "Commercial and Industrial Loans, All Commercial Banks [TOTCI]," FRED, Federal Reserve Bank of St. Louis, https://fred.stlouisfed.org/series/TOTCI, accessed June 30, 2018.

thing would have failed. But overall the fact that we were able to put out the fire and recapitalize the banking system without spending more taxpayer money, I think it's something everyone involved should be proud of. That includes the bank regulators, the Fed, the president, the Treasury, and importantly our predecessors. While our plan primarily relied on bringing private capital back into the system, those early investments by Hank Paulson and his team were crucial as well."

Sachs added, "People say we coddled the banks. Look, the shareholders of Citigroup suffered almost an 80 percent dilution as a result of their recapitalization. I'm sure some overwhelming percentage of the people would say Barack Obama bailed out the banks. Well, he didn't. He actually didn't put a dime into them. We were never able to figure out a way to communicate this well. I'd say that's one of my biggest regrets."[82]

Kabaker said "the single biggest accomplishment" for him was Treasury's successful recapitalization of the American banking system without extreme involvement of the government. Indeed, precisely because the government was not extremely involved, the recapitalization occurred more quickly. "We used some of the tools we had available to us to try to buttress the banks up and get private capital into them as fast as humanly possible and not have a period where the institutions were actually under government control."

Kabaker observed, "Europe essentially did nothing, and let their banks sit out there, oftentimes with large government investments, for a long period of time." This inaction led to the double-dip recession in Europe that in turn jeopardized the future of the European Union, the security of the continent relative to Russia, and the well-being of hundreds of millions of people.

"The other policy which some countries in much greater distress had to follow—Iceland is an example—was just nationalize everything. Assume the balance sheet. Ireland is another example. Basically nationalize everything. Assume the entire balance sheet of the banking system on the government and then work it out."[83]

---

82. Sachs, interview.
83. Kabaker, interview.

Private equity investor Mark Gallogly said, "The remaining question on banks was: how did the government's treatment of major banks translate to the American people's perception of how they were treated by their government? If we had designed and explained profit sharing so that if the banks' stocks rallied in value, then the American people would have done really well, there might have been a different narrative. The reality was that TARP and other initiatives were put in place to save capitalism and save the American economy. Not to make money for the government. The administration was not fully credited with the success of their programs because it was hard to communicate the dispersed benefits of the success of the stimulus, TARP-like programs, and the bank stress tests, which together rebooted the economy. The narrative was way less successful than the actions taken."

Gallogly said the Presidential Economic Recovery Advisory Board (PERAB) "recommended a SWAT-team focus on housing. The existing structure had key people in various parts of the government working feverishly on multiple problems, including the housing issues. This group could not have eliminated the possible unintended consequences of assisting those with housing issues. However, a more directed approach with a small group tasked solely with the housing crisis might have been able to generate constructive ideas and implement reforms more quickly. I think this SWAT team approach was a good idea. But, in the heat of the crisis, our recommendation did not go anywhere."[84]

In a similar vein, Alice Rivlin said, "I think that the big weakness of the Obama administration's policy was not getting on top of the housing market crisis sooner, and in ways that would work. That does seem to me to be the key to why the recovery has been so slow. Two things are mysteries. One was why they didn't have a better forecast in '09 and the other is why they didn't get focused on the housing crisis faster and better."[85]

Kabaker said, "I feel like housing, at least from a personal perspective, was the greatest piece of undone business of my two-year tenure

---

84. Gallogly, interview.
85. Rivlin, interview.

in Washington. The banking crisis was apolitical in the sense that it was such a technical matter and so serious. But the housing price decline had been going on awhile. Constituencies had developed. The Hill was wanting to do stuff."

So what happened to housing?

"Part of it was that we were principally working on the financial crisis response during the period there may have been political appetite for more radical responses on housing. There weren't that many people there at Treasury. Most of it, though, was that the policy problem was incredibly complex and difficult. Everyone struggled to reconcile the desire to help those most impacted with something that was politically palatable to the vast majority of borrowers who were continuing to pay their mortgages in full. Few remember that the rant by Rick Santelli that launched the Tea Party movement was principally an argument about the unfairness of providing aid to those that could not pay their mortgages. And so for housing essentially we bet on this modification program called HAMP and the more traditional support to homeowners provided by a low interest rate environment which allowed homeowners to refinance at lower rates and save money on their monthly payments. But HAMP was about helping only the people who needed help. We did not undertake a program to restructure the existing base of mortgages in a structural way. There were examples in history, like the Homeowners' Loan Corporation in the 1930s, but we did not decide to follow them."[86]

Although Obama had accepted the modest housing plans presented to him in December and January, as 2009 unfolded he was uncomfortable with the outcomes. David Axelrod said, "I think there was no topic that he raised with the advisers more or with greater exasperation than housing."[87]

Pete Rouse said, "One of the things that has frustrated the president as much as anything was our inability to come up with a policy and a strategy to deal with the housing issue. I was in any number of meetings where President Obama talked to Tim or Larry together and said, 'Can't

86. Kabaker, interview.
87. Axelrod, interview.

we come up with some ideas on housing?' And they said, 'There's just nothing we can do to move the needle. Nothing we can do without legislation.' The scale of the foreclosure crisis was so huge that, without an act of Congress, there really wasn't any program we could implement that would provide homeowners with meaningful debt relief. So that's been a big frustration. Housing has been a very big frustration for the president. I think he would say in retrospect his economic team was never really able to identify a workable solution. They would probably say that there was no good solution available without new authority or a lot of new money from Congress."[88]

Axelrod said, "There were many meetings on housing. The president was never provided with options. He asked for them, he asked for them, and he asked for them. Throughout the two years I was there, I'm telling you that he didn't ask for more on something more often than on housing, and there was not an issue where he expressed greater frustration."[89]

88. Rouse, interview.
89. Axelrod, interview

Interlude Three

"I Think That Went Well"

According to Christy Romer, "It was in the fall of 2009 that conflict among the economics team mattered. You had Tim and Peter saying we need to move to austerity. I'm sitting there saying, the unemployment rate is 10 percent, we absolutely need more stimulus. And I think Larry had a foot in both camps. There was one meeting where I remember saying, 'God I feel like there are three Secretaries of the Treasury here.' I meant there were these three guys saying, we have to get the deficit down. Larry was in agony. A part of him, the Bob Rubin side, cared a lot about the deficit and had a certain sympathy for Peter and Tim's view. On the other hand, Larry does care a lot about unemployment and thought fiscal stimulus would be good. Larry would say, 'I don't like your new jobs tax credit but maybe infrastructure would be okay.' And I'd say 'Infrastructure is too slow.'

"By November, we were in a better place. By that point, I was saying, 'I don't care. We just need something. You can have your infrastructure.' And Larry said, 'Okay fine you can have your new jobs tax credit. By December we were a good team."

Romer recalled specifically "one meeting where Peter Orszag said, 'Well, the unemployment rate is so high. What would another $100 billion of stimulus really do?' And I said, '$100 billion is maybe a million people who will have jobs that wouldn't otherwise.' But the president repeated Peter's argument, got annoyed at me when I again argued for stimulus, and said, 'I can't do that, and stop pushing me on this.' Then we had another meeting a week later and the president repeated Peter's argument again. Larry stood up and said, 'Mr. President, I just think that's wrong.' Afterwards I said to Larry, 'I've never liked you as much,' and his response was, 'Well, if history repeats, that won't last very long.' That was in late November 2009. Then on December 8 Obama gave a big speech at Brookings where he endorsed a new jobs tax credit and $50 billion of infrastructure and substantially more state fiscal relief. He did finally embrace a second stimulus. The House passed a bill providing another big chunk, but then it just died."[1]

Orszag thought it was a mistake not to try for an additional stimulus in late 2009. Orszag also thought that the second stimulus could be accomplished if connected to a deficit-reduction package. Gerry Waldron commented: "That is somebody who does not understand the way that Congress works. Members of Congress have trouble saying, I'm voting for a stimulus package and deficit reduction. Tell me how I explain that to my constituents. Which is it? The average person will say, I don't see how it can be yes and no at the same time."[2]

One observer at a critical meeting in December 2009 reported a vigorous debate on the topic of the second stimulus: "We're preparing the budget for 2010 and we had just been back and forth arguing the same thing between those two camps. Should we declare the era of stimulus will be over in 2011 and we should prioritize reducing the deficit? And Peter and Tim were in favor; Larry and Christy opposed.

"In several meetings they had played out the arguments again and again over which it was. Finally, the president said, 'Look, sit down and figure it out. Tell me what the facts are. What is your economic forecast and what do you forecast would be the impact of policy A versus policy B?'[3]

"But the camps had completely different views on the forecast and on what the impact of the policy would be. At root, that's why they couldn't resolve this. They also did not have any neutral arbiter who could sit

---

1. Romer, interview.
2. Waldron, interview.
3. This illustrated deterministic reasoning. Strategy calls instead for choices of options.

before the president and say, 'Here's the debate and now you can make a decision,' because Larry, who is running the process, has a very firmly held opinion, so he doesn't want to act like this is just a balanced debate that the president can just choose an answer to. So the economic team meets and the two sides reach a tentative peace in which the four principals agree to a tenuous balance of, 'We will all agree on some more short-run stimulus followed by medium-term deficit reduction.' The deficit hawks, knowing more stimulus could not get through congress, would agree to say they were for it for budget-planning purposes. It was a shotgun wedding, though. Everyone said, 'Okay, for the sake of the president, in the meeting we're just going to agree and come in with a united front.'

"So we go into the Roosevelt Room. Orszag presents and says, 'We all agree that you should call for a second short-term stimulus followed by deficit reduction, and here's the briefing document.' The president listens to the presentation and starts picking at the most incongruous parts. 'Wait a minute, how does this make sense?' He says, 'If we think that we need a stimulus in this one year, why do you think we should have such a big cut in the next year if your growth forecast is only modest?' and that sort of thing. Peter breaks down and says, 'You're right, Mr. President, and that's why some of us think we should actually engage in more deficit-cutting sooner.'

"This immediately brings Larry in: 'No, no, we disagree, Mr. President, most of us believe there should be more short-run stimulus.' The tentative peace agreement falls apart under some probing from the president and that leads back to a whole round of exactly the same debate we'd been having for weeks. Finally, the president just slams his pages down, and—it was halfway through a one-hour meeting—he says, 'You know what? This is our fifth meeting on exactly the same topic, with each of you saying exactly the same thing you've said for the last four meetings on this topic, and you aren't making any progress. I gave you an assignment, GO FIGURE IT OUT.' He stands up and walks out. The political people stand up and follow the president out, leaving only the economists.

"The principals—Christy, Peter, Larry, and Tim—pause for a moment trying to process, and then all hell breaks loose. They each start yelling, 'How could you do that? We had a deal! You don't get to dictate things to the president! You deceived us!'

"Then they break off into pairs so that Geithner and Summers are arguing with each other and Romer and Orszag are arguing with each other. As Romer raises her voice, Orszag says, 'I don't have to take this,' and he walks out.

"Geithner, shaking his head trying to figure how the meeting went wrong: 'I still don't understand where we disagreed; we had an agreement, what happened to the agreement?' Then Summers raises his voice at Geithner, 'The leaking has undermined it. We haven't been the ones leaking!' Presumably he is really talking about Peter, but Peter has already walked out at this point, so Summers's anger is directed at Geithner, about negative stories about the NEC that have been appearing in the press. Geithner repeats, 'But where did we disagree?' Romer turns to Tim and yells, 'A billion dollars of fucking stimulus is where we disagree!'

"The principals left the Roosevelt Room.

"Austan Goolsbee turned to the other economic deputies, Jeffrey Liebman, Jason Furman, and Gene Sperling, and said, 'I think that went well.'"[4]

In December 2010 Obama obtained a version of the second stimulus needed for the country and his reelection. The Republicans had won Congress in November. He compromised with them by agreeing to extend the Bush tax cuts on upper-income earners and a reduction in estate taxes in return for extended unemployment benefits, reduced payroll and other taxes, and various tax credits. The budget cost over two years was about $900 billion, about $100 billion more than the stimulus adopted in February 2009. The stimulus of 2009 and the end-of-the-year deal in 2010 amounted to $1.7 trillion of stimulus.

By early January 2009 Obama's advisers knew or should have known the government had to spend that huge sum over several years to achieve full employment in his presidency. Justice delayed is justice denied.

---

4. Interview with anonymous source.

This second stimulus boosted the economy enough to enable Obama to win reelection in 2012. Its tax-cut emphasis contributed to rising inequality in wealth and income. If it had been done as part of the 2009 stimulus, however, it might have saved the Democratic majority in the House. It might have driven the GDP growth rate above 3 percent from 2009–2016, and made Trump's 2016 victory impossible.

It is tragedy, not irony, that in 2017 Trump government committed to about that much deficit spending in the absence of a Great Recession.

13

"Making Healthcare Reform Job One"

"Millions of our citizens do not now have a full measure of opportunity to achieve and enjoy good health. Millions do not now have protection or security against the economic effects of sickness. The time has arrived for action to help them attain that opportunity and that protection."
— President Harry Truman, Message to Congress, 1945

Norm Ornstein, one of the most astute of Washington, D.C., political analysts, thought that Tom Daschle, Democratic senator from South Dakota since 1987 and Democratic leader in the Senate from 1995 to 2005, convinced Barack Obama to make healthcare the administration's top priority. As Ornstein saw it, because Obama prized healthcare reform as his legacy, he hurried to put his economic recovery plan in place.

Daschle wanted Obama to fulfill a liberal or progressive goal sought by Theodore Roosevelt, Franklin Roosevelt, Harry Truman, Lyndon Johnson, and Bill Clinton: decent, affordable healthcare for every person in America.[1] Presidents are prone to think of their place in the history books of the future. Daschle believed healthcare reform could lead the entry on Obama.

Daschle was not alone in identifying Obama's 2004 Democratic convention speech as signaling that he could go all the way. Daschle lost his

---

1. By contrast, the neoliberal goal was to reduce the total cost of healthcare and increase efficiency in providing that service.

251

reelection campaign in November 2004, just as Obama won his Senate seat by a huge margin. Defeated, Daschle contributed his own staff to the fledgling senator. "Our really close relationship started with Barack coming to me and asking whether I could help him recruit Pete Rouse, my chief of staff, to be his chief of staff, which I did."[2]

As the housing market shriveled and the Iraq invasion led to a terrible war, the Democrats gained political advantage coming into the 2006 midterms. Although Obama had not served even a third of his six-year term, Daschle and others wanted him to run for the presidency in the next election. Daschle said, "The Obamas decided to make their annual Christmas visit to Hawaii at the end of 2006 their drop-dead date for deciding to run for president. I argued that it was not too soon, that doing it so soon was more of a positive than it was a negative because number one he hadn't created the image of a Washington insider. Number two he hadn't yet alienated a lot of the factions. He was still able to define himself rather than have his record define him. Third, there still was a memory of his incredible speech in 2004 at the convention. He was hot at that moment. Windows close, as mine did in 2003."

Daschle described Obama as "a student of public service. I'm not sure he was a student of public policy, and I draw a distinction. He was an organizer. But he really never had the opportunity, the luxury, to become a real, solid student of public policy. So, going into the election campaign, there was vagueness about what ought to be on his plate, what ought to be the priorities on that plate, and how he should assess these things."[3] The key to prioritization is to have only one: Daschle wanted Obama to choose healthcare reform.

About 16 percent of the population, about 50 million people, lacked health insurance. About one in four of this number were not American citizens, many of whom were undocumented. The system had gaping holes: many young people went without insurance on the bet they would remain healthy, people with continuing or severe medical problems often could not afford hospital expenses or get insurance. Obama,

---

2. Daschle, interview.
3. Ibid.

like Bill Clinton in 1992, also agreed with economists who generally thought the cost of healthcare had to go down for businesses, government, and individuals. The country, including private employers buying insurance, the government paying for Medicare and Medicaid, and people paying premiums as well as deductibles, spent $2.2 trillion annually for healthcare.[4]

The first healthcare forum for presidential candidates occurred in Las Vegas on March 26, 2007. Obama told the audience that the uninsured needed to be covered but did not outline a plan.[5] Anna Burger, a longtime union activist and a leader of the Service Employees International Union, said, "All candidates laid out a healthcare agenda. In Las Vegas, Obama's was the weakest."[6] Daschle said, "Obama was very, very angry about his performance in Las Vegas and about his lack of appreciation of what he had to do to address the problem in a thoughtful and comprehensive way. That was pivotal. That was a turning point."[7] Burger agreed that Obama responded proactively to develop a healthcare reform proposal.

In amplifying his healthcare proposal, Obama did not adopt the mandate favored by his opponents for the nomination, John Edwards and Hillary Clinton. They wanted the police state to punish anyone who did not buy insurance. Obama did not. Nor did he promise that his government would create its own health insurer, or "public option." He said he would save the average family up to $2,500 per year by using information technology to lower costs, increasing competition among insurers, and making health insurance universal.[8] Eventually, Obama and the Democratic Congress settled on what Paul Krugman later called

4. Barack Obama, "Time Has Come for Universal Healthcare," Families USA Conference, Washington, D.C., January 25, 2007, http://obamaspeeches.com/097-The-Time-Has-Come-for-Universal-Health-Care-Obama-Speech.htm.

5. Nedra Pickler, "Is Obama All Style and Little Substance?" *Washington Post*, March 27, 2007, http://www.washingtonpost.com/wp-dyn/content/article/2007/03/27/AR2007032700472_pf.html.

6. Burger, interview.

7. Daschle, interview.

8. Matthew Holt, "A Detailed Analysis of Barack Obama's Healthcare Reform Plan," The Healthcare Blog, March 21, 2008, http://thehealthcareblog.com/blog/2008/03/21/a-detailed-analysis-of-barack-obamas-health-care-reform-plan/.

the three-legged stool of mandatory insurance, subsidies for low-income families to buy it, and regulation barring insurers from discriminating against certain people, like those with preexisting conditions.[9] In the campaign, however, Obama spoke more generally about objectives rather than methods.

Despite initial vagueness, Anna Burger thought Obama's promise of healthcare reform met the mark. The reason was the implied prioritization. She explained, "He caused us to expect that he had made a commitment on healthcare reform. That it was not going to be a question about when he was going to do it, he was going to do it and get it done.[10] After all, unions, employers, and the Democratic Party all had sought comprehensive healthcare reform for 60 years. A Democratic president whose party controlled both houses of Congress had no choice but to do it."[11]

Obama Chose Daschle and Daschle's Dream

As the former leader of the Senate Democrats and a ten-year veteran of that intractable chamber, Daschle could greatly bolster the Obama administration's capability for passing legislation. He had the bargaining power to extract promises from Obama before agreeing to join the administration. At the same time, Daschle's brother was undergoing treatment for brain cancer at Duke. For Daschle, the personal and political combined in a fateful manner.

Daschle's experience taught him that passing anything required persistent coordination among the White House, the various agencies of the executive branch, and the Congress. To guarantee that he could run the whole effort, Daschle sought both a cabinet secretary's administrative

9. See, e.g., Paul Krugman, "One Reform, Indivisible," *New York Times*, August 19, 2013, https://www.nytimes.com/2013/08/19/opinion/krugman-one-reform-indivisible.html.

10. Burger added, "We also had a belief that he would really support workers' rights to have a union, that he actually believed that workers had a better chance in an economy with the opportunity to bargain and share in prosperity. We thought that we were going to quickly move out on immigration and figure out a path to citizenship for the people who were here in the shadows. Those were the three primary areas that we thought would make a change in the lives of our members."

11. Burger, interview.

power and a White House staff post with direct access to the president's planning, scheduling, and speech-making. Soon after the election, Obama gave Daschle what he wanted.

On November 19, 2008, the press reported that Obama had asked Daschle to take the dual jobs of healthcare czar in the White House and secretary of the Department of Health and Human Services. Ensuring Daschle's influence over the administration's decisions, Pete Rouse, loyal to both Daschle and Obama, would become deputy chief of staff to President Obama. This understanding gave Daschle the confidence to say on December 5 that "President-Elect Obama has made health reform one of his top priorities."[12] For Daschle, "one of" was a polite fiction. With the power of his positions in the cabinet and White House, and a trusted ally as deputy chief of staff, Daschle could make healthcare legislation the top strategic goal in the first year of the first term, when Obama had the most political capital. Exactly what reform remained undecided.

The country's economic calamity threatened to undo Daschle's strategy and preempt his dream. In late 2008 neither the two-thirds of American families who owned their homes nor the millions who worried about finding work thought the primary focus of the newly elected president should be extending health insurance to the 15 percent of Americans who were uninsured. More than 60 percent of Americans obtain health insurance from their employer. For those who could get work, healthcare followed. Americans might well think Obama's top priority should be assuring jobs, not healthcare, for everyone.

The same day Daschle announced that health reform was "one of" the "top priorities," CEA chief-designate Christy Romer saw the distressing November unemployment statistics. In the more benign economic times of 1993, neoliberal economists considered healthcare reform critical to achieving a balanced budget. In December 2008, they regarded economic recovery as the essential strategic objective for the new administration.

---

12. "Press Release: Transition Health Policy Team Leader Asks Americans to Hold Healthcare Community Discussions," The American Presidency Project, December 5, 2008, http://www.presidency. ucsb.edu/ws/index.php?pid=85035.

In government and business, strategy comprises three steps: analysis of a situation, formation and selection among different choices, and irrevocable commitment to the top choice.[13] Although Obama's people did not literally use the three-step framework for strategy, they did reason in a similar way: what was going on, what could be done about it, what choices should be taken in what order of prioritization. In comparison to the previous and succeeding administrations, the Obama administration's strategizing deserved good grades.

In terms of step one, analysis, Daschle could not dispute that the financial crisis and shrinking economy dominated the country's situation. To win his case, he chose to argue that healthcare reform could boost the economy. Obviously healthcare reform would not help recapitalize big banks or mitigate unemployment. However, Daschle believed that the TARP bailout and the stimulus solved both these problems. If they were finalized before or soon after the inauguration, then Obama could turn to the long-term economic problems of the country that he had identified at Knox College and Cooper Union. Chief among them, universal healthcare insurance would give workers the confidence to leave one job in search of another, because their families would remain insured, no longer dependent on the employer for insurance. If everyone paid insurance premiums, costs would drop for everyone, including individuals, businesses, and government. This accomplishment (the maximum risk pool) would benefit America long after the economy had followed the inevitable cycle from downturn to uptick.

Daschle said he wanted Obama to see that "addressing healthcare could be understood in the larger context of addressing the economy in ways that would fit his immediate agenda and his longer-term Obama agenda."[14] Pete Rouse reminded the transition team that the longer-term agenda was "the new foundation. The four pillars were financial reform, education reform, healthcare reform, and energy reform."[15]

13. Richard P. Rumelt, *Good Strategy, Bad Strategy: The Difference and Why It Matters* (London: Profile Books, 2017).

14. Daschle, interview.

15. Rouse, interview.

To build each pillar, Congress had to change conduct in a market. Adhering to the neoliberal canon, government would not alter industry structure in the four sectors. No infrastructure bank would change market shares in the financial industry. No free public schools would retrain workers. Despite much debate in policy circles and Congress, no publicly funded health insurer would compete with private insurers. The government would not expand public investment in clean power. Instead, transformation would result from the response of firms to regulatory carrots and sticks, incentives and disincentives. Government could tip the scales toward firms interested in providing health insurance to those who could not get it from employers, but private markets would choose how and what was to be provided. This neoliberal paradigm excused the relative indifference to implementation that characterized the policies favored by Obama and other Democrats. Execution lay in the private sector's domain. A neoliberal policy could culminate in a model that predicted how non-government agents would respond to incentives and disincentives.

Obama's economists embraced the market-oriented approach to pillar construction, but they did not agree that he should prioritize healthcare reform. According to Daschle, Larry Summers told Obama, "You should really focus on job creation in ways that require your presence with an agenda and a strategy that involves exclusive focus on nothing but the economy. You should make the point with an exclamation point that this is what this administration is all about for the first two years."[16]

Gene Sperling went further in criticizing the prioritization of healthcare. Daschle recalled that he said, "'Look, Social Security has more relevance to our immediate economic issues than healthcare does.' I disagreed with that."[17]

According to Bob Kocher, a former McKinsey consultant and physician helping to design healthcare reform legislation, Rahm Emanuel too said "early on that we have to focus on jobs. He was worried that

16. Daschle, interview.
17. Ibid.

healthcare and climate change and the war efforts post-stimulus were together going to consume all of our political capital."[18]

Vice President-elect Joe Biden reportedly "agreed that large-scale reform was too ambitious given everything else on our plate. He felt we needed to be squarely focused on the economy."[19]

David Axelrod weighed in, "As a political adviser, I told Obama doing healthcare reform wasn't necessarily a good political decision."[20]

Daschle said, "Because my younger brother had brain cancer during this transition time, I was going back and forth to Duke. Trying to participate in meetings by speaker phone, I became concerned that I was losing the argument. Gene and Larry were saying that healthcare reform certainly can address the larger economic issues we've got to face as a country, but for the short term they argued for delay in prioritizing healthcare because it was more important to look at the purely economic questions."[21]

Daschle's fear that he was losing the debate over priority was confirmed on December 7, when on *Meet the Press* President-elect Obama said, "My agenda has changed over the past month and a short-term package is my top priority."[22]

The advocates for prioritizing healthcare reform also had to win out against those who believed the historic Obama legacy should be victory in the battle against climate change. Carol Browner and the environmental organizations had waited a long time for Democratic control of the White House and Congress. The atmosphere was warming, the ice caps melting, and only the president could save the planet.

Environmentalists felt Emanuel and Axelrod were always more inclined to go forward with healthcare than they were on cap-and-trade. Emanuel knew the healthcare issue because he'd been on the House Ways and Means Committee. He hadn't been on the right committees

18. Bob Kocher, interview with author.
19. David Axelrod, *Believer: My Forty Years in Politics* (New York: Penguin Books, 2016), 371.
20. Axelrod, interview.
21. Daschle, interview.
22. "Interview with Tom Brokaw on NBC's 'Meet the Press,'" The American Presidency Project, December 7, 2008, http://www.presidency.ucsb.edu/ws/index.php?pid=85042.

for energy. Axelrod's personal situation, a child with a preexisting condition, made him very aware of the failings of the healthcare system. In addition, with Daschle's leadership, healthcare reform legislation seemed more likely to pass than energy reform. Emanuel and Axelrod wanted to put points on the board.

Carol Browner put the choice this way: "In any White House, you want the president to be successful early on. You could see the way forward on healthcare. In a way, it was more complicated on cap-and-trade, particularly in the Senate where different committees had jurisdiction. It's also fair to say it became clear early on you were never going to do cap-and-trade through reconciliation. There was mechanism for doing healthcare through the budget process using reconciliation," requiring a simple majority. "That was not going to happen on cap-and-trade. Sixty votes were needed. That would be tough."[23]

Bob Kocher, healthcare expert on the NEC, said, "Obama and Summers asked us to flesh out a range of options for prioritization. Probably three-quarters of the NEC team strongly favored a universal coverage approach that included a mandate. The other camp said we should go for ambitious climate change and energy conservation efforts first."[24]

Peter Orszag joined forces with Daschle in arguing to prioritize healthcare. Axelrod said, "Orszag was one of the impetuses for doing healthcare. Peter was one of the most persuasive people in terms of Obama's decision."[25] Orszag felt that unless Medicare and Medicaid costs were reduced, the federal budget could never be balanced. Unless healthcare costs for business went down, economic growth would be hampered.

Daschle had a conversation with Obama in the days following December 7 "about whether or not health was going to remain the top priority."[26] He persuaded the president-elect to execute a finesse—one that militated against changing the stimulus a month later when the December unemployment statistics showed that the stimulus was undersized. The new administration would press for the TARP drawdown and a

23. Browner, interview.
24. Kocher, interview.
25. Axelrod, interview.
26. Daschle, interview.

stimulus bill before the inauguration. By stabilizing the finance industry and ending the recession, job growth would recommence. The economy would recover in a reasonable time period. Then Obama could begin pushing for healthcare reform immediately after inauguration. He would make history by giving all Americans good healthcare from cradle to grave. Success in constructing this "pillar" would create political capital for the other pillars, including energy. Besides, the switch from carbon to clean power required many years of new investment and substitution for coal-fired boilers. Even if the effort were delayed, climate change could still be abated before rising seas drowned Manhattan, boiling summers desertified the Great Plains.

Axelrod said Obama told him, "I think we have a unique opportunity to get healthcare reform done now, and if we don't get it done in the next two years, it's not going to get done in my administration. It might not get done for another generation. Meanwhile the cost of healthcare is going to spiral. We're going to have more people uninsured, more people are going to be dropped. Medicaid and Medicare expenses will soar."[27] Kocher heard Obama react to one presentation of this data by saying: "We have to bend the cost curve down or healthcare will crowd out all our other priorities."[28] Unwittingly, he repeated the arguments Ira Magaziner made in the Clinton transition 16 years earlier.

So "what was not chosen," Daschle explained, "was first the argument that Larry made and Gene made, which was to stay exclusively focused on the economy. Period. That we really didn't have the luxury of diverting our attention to something that would suck the oxygen out of the room like healthcare was going to."[29]

Daschle admitted, "Everybody knew that you take this path, there are going to be trade-offs. One was climate. Others were trade and infrastructure."[30] He acknowledged, "It's unfortunate that healthcare versus

27. Axelrod, interview.

28. Kocher, interview.

29. Daschle, interview.

30. Daschle was not sure infrastructure needed to be traded off. He said, "You did have a lot of pushback from the conservatives in the Democratic caucus concerned about the total amount of spending and the overall price tag of a robust infrastructure agenda. But you also had Republican

climate was viewed as an either/or. I think we probably could have done climate as well. Harry Reid insisted he didn't have the votes for that in the Senate, but he was also very concerned about whether he had the votes in the Senate on health too." In any event, Obama made "an irrevocable, strategic decision" to prioritize healthcare, and Daschle "felt it was the right one."[31]

Sometime between December 7 and 11 Obama reconfirmed to his team that healthcare reform had again become his top priority for transformational change. Geithner would end bank runs. The stimulus would start economic growth. But the historic, long-term transformation of the economy and society would commence with the push for universal health insurance immediately after the inauguration.

Trent Lott, a former Senate majority leader for the Republican Party, was not surprised: "The Democrats want universal healthcare. It's a part of their continuation of the welfare state: Social Security, Medicaid, Medicare, healthcare. They want single payer. They want a more socialistic government."[32]

Orszag explained the decision this way: "Healthcare was personal to Obama. Many people very close to him worked in hospitals or are doctors, like Mrs. Obama and Valerie Jarrett. And also healthcare is more an American problem than a global problem. If you legislate it, you're done, whereas with climate, you can legislate it, and that's nice, but it's global, you're only solving a piece of it, whereas with healthcare it's under your control."[33]

Daschle believed Obama thought the stimulus "was purely an economic necessity, a reactive effort to deal with the crisis and not something to be concerned about with regard to the longer-term prioritization of issues on Obama's agenda as he got into the coming year. The stimulus

---

support for infrastructure. I think you could have done an infrastructure bill. The bad economy was focused and concentrated in some states, but even among conservatives there was fear that this thing could spread. Nobody felt immune from the potential of this thing getting much, much worse."
Ibid.
31. Ibid.
32. Lott, interview.
33. Orszag, interview.

was a deck-clearer. It was something to get done, put behind us, and then move on to the things we need to do. It was the reactive so we can get to the proactive."[34]

Daschle's Victory

With the president-elect's strategic prioritization in place, Daschle then agreed that his nomination and acceptance of the two jobs could be definitively, officially announced. On December 11 Obama explained to the press Daschle's unique, powerful role. Obama said this dual position would help his administration pass a law providing "affordable, accessible healthcare for every single American."[35]

Daschle did not worry that the president-elect would change his strategy in the economic recovery discussion in Chicago on December 16. Geithner would prevail in arguing that banking stabilization was the first part of economic recovery, and Summers would persuade everyone that getting a stimulus bill through Congress in January was the second part. Healthcare reform, however, would be the centerpiece of the administration's legacy-creating agenda.

Obama then asked his advisers to design the healthcare bill. According to Kocher, the "schisms concerning what to ask Congress to pass on healthcare reform were absolutely not worked through in any substance during the transition."[36] Daschle himself had long favored two big ideas. A Federal Health Board would decide what Medicare and Medicaid would pay for. It would drive down government's costs. The insurance industry would support this institution because they could copy government in paying less to healthcare providers.

Daschle also wanted the federal government to offer health insurance to compete with private plans. This so-called "public option" was debated for most of the year.[37] As much as insurers would like the Federal Health

34. Daschle, interview.
35. Robert Pear, "Daschle Will Lead Healthcare Overhaul," *New York Times*, December 11, 2008, https://www.nytimes.com/2008/12/12/us/politics/w11health.html.
36. Kocher, interview.
37. Robert Pear, "Public Option Fades from Debate Over Healthcare," *New York Times*, September 12, 2009, https://www.nytimes.com/2009/09/13/health/policy/13plan.html.

Board, they would hate the introduction into their market of such a parsimonious and well-funded nonprofit actor as the federal government.

Additionally, sick people (those with "preexisting conditions") needed the government to compel insurance companies to insure them if they lost their jobs and the insurance that their employer had provided. Children should be able to stay on their parents' health insurance plan longer, especially because even in their 20s they would find it hard to get employers to hire them, much less pay for their health insurance. No one should suffer from annual and lifetime limits on healthcare.

Kocher explained, "On the broader healthcare policy team there was a perspective held by some advisers that we should just expand children's coverage and allow children to stay on their parents' plans into early adulthood and let that be the building block toward more people covered. These people felt that very comprehensive and highly subsidized coverage was important. The hitch with this plan is that it was almost as expensive as near-universal coverage and covered far fewer. What the president took away from the briefings was an understanding that there were a wide range of policy choices and that paradoxically it didn't cost a whole lot more to cover almost everyone if we used a mandate and designed sensible benefit designs. We ended up being challenged to develop a healthcare reform plan that cost less than $1 trillion, was deficit reducing, and achieved near universal coverage. Besides, Tom Daschle was very clear that he didn't want to be HHS Secretary and czar for healthcare reform unless Obama chose a plan more ambitious than his campaign plan, which was chiefly a mandate for children to have insurance."[38]

As a first step in healthcare reform, Congress passed and Obama signed on February 4 the Children's Health Insurance Reauthorization Act of 2009. Democratic senator Ted Kennedy and Republican senator Orrin Hatch had caused Congress to pass legislation expanding taxpayer-funded health insurance to children in 1997. George W. Bush vetoed two efforts to expand this program from a focus on insuring children in low-income families to a broader demographic target. In 2009, the

38. Kocher, interview.

new Congress took advantage of Bush's departure by adding four million children and pregnant women to the covered group, including "lawfully residing" immigrants.

The stage was set for the big reveal of the Obama plan. However, Daschle decided that the White House would not send to the Hill its own healthcare legislation, avoiding the mistake Ira Magaziner and Hillary Clinton made in 1993. Instead, the Obama team gave the congressional leadership general direction, with plenty of room to cut deals needed for votes. They also did not want the president to be reported as winning or losing on different provisions.

All knew the insurance industry would support reform as long as the government commanded everyone to buy insurance. The insurers wanted more customers. They needed more money to make up for the other obligations that would be imposed on them. They wanted the mandate. They implacably opposed the public option. They believed that would lead to the government providing Medicare to everyone.

The mandate imposed a new and unpopular requirement on all Americans. If previously healthy, the uninsured did not like paying for what they did not need. If sick, the newly insured worried about co-pays and premiums. Moreover, the least popular of all government agencies, the Internal Revenue Service, would enforce the mandate by fining people for not having insurance.

Only low-income individuals got subsidies to cover a portion of the premiums. If the fines and subsidies were too low, the individual would choose to go uncovered. During the campaign, Obama had opposed Hillary Clinton's advocacy of the mandate for good reasons. He thought correctly that only the insurers and neoliberal economists liked it. Nevertheless, to please the economists and win political support from the insurance industry, his advisers insisted the bill include the mandate.

Tom Mann, a scholar at Brookings specializing in Congress, said, "The problem was that healthcare reform looked like really active, aggressive, liberal government and the question is how much could the public tolerate. Obama's approach was to embrace the private sector, private insurance, competition and the like. The liberal appearance was the individual mandate and the public subsidies for the purchase of insurance to low-income families. You are creating the appearance of taking from the rich and giving to the poor, from the so-called 'responsible' working white insured and giving it to the 'undeserving' people. This appearance limited the appeal of the healthcare reform."[39]

The healthcare advisers searched for a theme that Obama could use to sell his reform to voters. They had two points. First, call for sympathy for those with preexisting conditions. Many millions fell into this category. If they lost their jobs and insurance, they might face medical bills that would drive them into bankruptcy or force them to forego treatment. This argument assumed the healthy would want to pay more in taxes to care for the chronically sick.

Second, promise that the reform would lower healthcare costs. Insurers would compete against one another in online marketplaces called exchanges. Competition would produce lower prices for insurance. If everyone bought insurance, insurers also could charge each person less money to cover the same total amount of healthcare. Technology also would make doctors and hospitals more productive, and result in lower prices for each service. This argument assumed most people would pay less in premiums and deductibles.

At the time, no one dwelled on the possibility that a bad economy could harm the health of Americans. In later years, researchers concluded that high unemployment and low wage increases led to increased death by overdose. The opioid epidemic at least partly stemmed from the size and composition of the stimulus.[40] Chris Van Hollen explained, "On healthcare, the idea was that having a secure healthcare system in place would be good for the economy. But the healthcare debate did not focus on the economy."[41]

In January 2009 the Obama team had what Daschle called a "relapse"[42] in prioritization. As the stimulus bill was moving through the House

39. Mann, interview.
40. Michael R. Betz and Lauren E. Jones, "Wage and Employment Growth in America's Drug Epidemic: Is All Growth Created Equal?" ASSA Annual Meeting, December 15, 2017, https://www.aeaweb.org/conference/2018/preliminary/paper/Syhtt452.
41. Van Hollen, interview.
42. Daschle, interview.

and Senate, a strategic debate broke out in the Obama team. Christy Romer, who by then had apprehended the likely failure of the stimulus to achieve the desired reduction in unemployment, said, "I was one of the voices who said to the president, 'I know you came into office wanting to make fundamental changes in the lives of middle-class families like healthcare reform, but the truth is you've been dealt a terrible hand with an economy in free fall. If you manage to turn that around, that would be an accomplishment beyond anything anyone could have hoped for from you. You should not feel that you need to go forward with healthcare reform.'"[43]

Orszag continued to plump for healthcare reform. He persuaded Romer to support him in this advocacy. Christy Romer thought "a huge strategic decision was to move forward on healthcare reform in the spring of 2009. That inevitably took some focus away from a second stimulus. At the same time, I became persuaded that there could be synergies between the two. There was a tension between fiscal stimulus and the deficit, and healthcare reform was intended to be something that helped reduce the deficit by slowing the growth rate of healthcare costs paid by the government. So perhaps health reform could make space for more stimulus."[44]

Looking back, Daschle said that giving top priority to healthcare reform was Obama's "most important strategic decision from an historic perspective, and I would call it as the most important strategic proactive decision. Making healthcare reform job one was an irrevocable strategic decision that I felt was the right one."[45]

Peter Orszag said, "From the perspective of 20 or 30 years, pushing for the health bill may have been Obama's most important decision. If implemented in full, the move toward a quality-focused instead of a quantity-focused healthcare system could be transformative."[46]

Kocher said, "It was decided in a meeting in January 2009 to put in the budget a 'down payment' on healthcare reform. We put $650 billion

43. Romer, interview.
44. Ibid.
45. Daschle, interview.
46. Orszag, interview.

into the budget to signal to Congress that we were committed to paying for the costs of expanding coverage. Half of the down payment was new taxes on high-income people and the other half were Medicare cuts. I can remember Daschle standing up in the room and saying, 'Mr. President, this is fantastic that we're going to make healthcare the priority.'"[47]

Because of reduced tax revenue, recovery measures, and healthcare, the two fiscal years 2009 and 2010 together added about $3 trillion to the total federal deficit, raising it from $14 trillion to $17 trillion. The additional healthcare spending accounted for a fifth of the increase. The bottom 20 percent of the income ladder would benefit.

Daschle's Downfall

Even as Daschle finally won his case for prioritizing healthcare and treating economic recovery as a "deck-clearing exercise," he lost his place in the next administration. A Senate staff review of tax records of the president's nominees (almost nonexistent for the Trump nominees) uncovered a tax problem for Daschle. After the senator lost his reelection in 2004, a cable executive named Leo Hindery provided Daschle a car service. A Senate party leader has free car service. The former Senator had unfortunately taken a continuation of this perk for granted. The IRS did not deem it to be a gift. It was taxable income. Three years of being driven caused Daschle to owe more than $100,000 in taxes that he had not realized he owed.[48]

The Senate might have let Daschle pay the tax and then forgiven his mistake. However, Treasury Secretary-designate Tim Geithner had failed to pay a bit more than $40,000 in taxes. The banks had to be restored to financial health. He had to be put in office to do that job. He was not expendable. The Senate Finance Committee let Geithner pay what he owed, and confirmed his appointment.[49] Geithner used up the Obama

47. Kocher, interview.

48. Robert Pear, "Daschle Pays 3 Years of Tax on Use of Car," *New York Times*, January 30, 2009, https://www.nytimes.com/2009/01/31/us/politics/31daschle.html.

49. Colin Barr, "Senate Confirms Geithner as Treasury Secretary," *CNNMoney*, January 26, 2009, http://money.cnn.com/2009/01/26/news/geithner.senate.vote/index.htm.

political capital allocated to nominations. Daschle withdrew his candidacy on January 30, 2009. Like Robert E. Lee losing Stonewall Jackson to gunfire from his own army, Obama lost the general to lead the legislative and political battle for healthcare reform.

In late January, the week after the Inauguration, Henry Waxman, chair of the House Energy and Commerce Committee, visited President Obama to discuss legislative strategy. Waxman explained that he had beaten John Dingell in the Democratic Party vote for chairmanship of the Energy and Commerce Committee in December by promising the Democratic congressmen that he would write and pass both comprehensive healthcare reform and a comprehensive cap-and-trade bill. Obama made it clear that his "top priority was healthcare."[50]

Other members of the House Democratic leadership agreed with the president. Van Hollen said, "I thought we should move healthcare first. The difference between the politics of healthcare and the politics of energy is that when it came to the politics of energy you had to deal with not just the party issues but regional differences. For healthcare, the primary obstacle was the partisan issue."[51]

However, the Obama team believed it could pass its whole agenda. They thought that healthcare should go first, but would pass quickly. "Our initial sense of healthcare timing was that healthcare reform would be passed in the House in the first 100 days or at least by Memorial Day. And done in the Senate by the Fourth of July," said Kocher.[52]

As he had predicted to Obama, Waxman passed cap-and-trade out of the Energy and Commerce Committee on May 20, 2009, and healthcare on June 14, 2009.

As everyone expected, the Senate side worked on healthcare legislation much more slowly. The Senate Democratic leadership gave committee chairs more leeway than did Speaker Pelosi. The chairs themselves lacked the influence over their party colleagues that the House committee chairs had. Obama needed 60 votes in the Senate for the legislative initiatives that would build his "pillars." Republican leader Mitch McConnell had

50. Waxman, interview.
51. Van Hollen, interview.
52. Kocher, interview.

not been able to stop three Republican senators from voting for the stimulus, but pushed his caucus hard to deny Obama any votes for the pillars.

The Republicans whipped up a frenzy in the media against changes in healthcare. Polls showed most Americans either did not understand or did not like Obama's various explanations of why the bill mattered.

McConnell and the other Republicans treated Republican senator Arlen Specter of Pennsylvania so harshly for voting with the Democrats on the stimulus that Specter switched to the Democratic caucus. (He had left the Democratic Party in 1965.) That gave Democrats 59 votes. In July, Al Franken finally gained the Senate seat in Minnesota, after defeating repetitive, out-of-state-funded Republican challenges to the vote count. At last the Democrats had 60 votes. However, at that time, unlike Henry Waxman in the House, Democratic Senators Max Baucus, Chairman of the finance committee, and Barbara Boxer, chair of the energy and public works committee, still had not gotten the healthcare or cap-and-trade bills out of their respective committees and to the Senate floor.

In August Ted Kennedy died, costing Democrats an iconic leader in healthcare reform and the 60th vote as well. In September, Massachusetts governor Deval Patrick named Democrat Paul Kirk as a temporary replacement. Holding a 60-vote majority again, the Senate Democrats then had to compromise over healthcare with the two most recalcitrant members of their caucus, Joe Lieberman of Connecticut and Ben Nelson of Nebraska. Lieberman, from a state long under the influence of the insurance industry, insisted on the elimination of all versions of a public option as his price for voting for healthcare reform.[53] Nelson sought a special deal for Nebraska, then under criticism scurried away from this legislative blackmail. The Senate finally passed its version of healthcare reform in December 2009.

In January 2010 Republican Scott Brown won the Massachusetts Senate seat. Because the Senate Democrats then lost their 60 votes,

---

53. Trent Lott commented, "Obama was right to back off on single payer. He would get it eventually. Once we get people hooked on mandatory coverage, it's going to go to single payer eventually. Because the government is going to be the only guy in town. You're going to wind up with single payer. I think Obama figured that out." Lott, interview.

no compromise between the House and Senate bills could be passed without obtaining a Republican vote in the Senate. Olympia Snowe, Republican from Maine, was the most likely candidate, but she refused to help Obama and the Democrats. (She never ran for office again, and her unwillingness to fashion a compromise remained mysterious.) Obama's team and the congressional leadership cunningly devised a two-step passage to pass the legislation. First, the House voted for the Senate bill without change. It became law when the president signed it on March 23. Second, the House passed a bill imposing various taxes and funding various healthcare measures. Because the measure concerned only budget issues, the Senate passed it by the reconciliation process that required only 51 votes.[54] This maneuver completed healthcare reform. The president signed the Affordable Care Act ("ACA") on March 30, 2010. The political war over the government role in healthcare would continue to be fought during the regulatory process, up to the Supreme Court, through the 2016 campaign, and into the Trump administration.

Healthcare Reform as a Strategic Decision

The neoliberal market-lovers believed the ACA would and should erode employer-provided healthcare, which they correctly considered to be inefficient. The online markets on which insurers would sell policies (exchanges) would create such affordable, appealing choices that employers would face little employee backlash from cutting back their healthcare benefits. Employees would be happy enough to give up healthcare coverage in return for higher wages, knowing that they could use the money to buy good health insurance on the exchanges. Dr. Ezekiel Emanuel, Rahm's brother, predicted that by 2025 the number of employees obtaining healthcare coverage from their employer would drop by two-thirds, down to only 20 percent of the workforce.[55] Sold on this vision, Obama himself described buying insurance on the exchanges

---

54. This was the technique McConnell used to pass tax reform with a bare majority in 2017.

55. "Zeke Emanuel: Employer-based Insurance Will Die out by 2025," Advisory Board, April 9, 2014, https://www.advisory.com/daily-briefing/2014/04/09/zeke-emanuel-employer-based-insurance-will-die-out-by-2025.

to be as easy as shopping "for a plane ticket on Kayak or a TV on Amazon."[56] As with most neoliberal recipes, the result would be that private market competition and consumer choice produced welfare gains, a rising standard of living.

Competition also would lower employers' cost of employment. Then employers would pay higher wages or hire more people. In addition, if individuals bought insurance in a market, then they could more readily quit a job with healthcare benefits and look for better work elsewhere. Labor would enjoy a freer market, although perhaps one that offered fewer non-cash benefits to workers. One of Obama's transformational goals, the latter concept in particular gave people more anxiety than hope.

If Obama had chosen in 2009 to spend money on expanding Medicare for the old and Medicaid for the poor, and guaranteeing healthcare for those with the most serious conditions, he would have been expanding intrinsically popular programs.[57] This move also could have been part of an economic recovery program, because it would have directly helped the increased number of low-income families and older people who gave up looking for work. By this simpler tactic, Obama would have increased his chance of passing an energy bill.

Rahm Emanuel proposed a similar compromise in late 2009. John Podesta said, "Rahm argued for cutting the healthcare bill in half. Cover 20 million people in August and get out of the debate on the Hill. There are those who don't believe that was really an option. The reason Rahm wanted to cut the deal was not because he didn't care about the other 12 million without insurance. It was that we had to get off of this. We can't have any more meetings with Democratic Senate Finance Committee Chairman Max Baucus. The meat is spoiling here. The opportunity

---

56. Jason Millman, "Even with Obamacare, Shopping for Health Insurance Isn't as Easy as Buying a Plane Ticket," *Washington Post*, July 15, 2014, https://www.washingtonpost.com/news/wonk/wp/2014/07/15/even-with-obamacare-shopping-for-health-insurance-isnt-as-easy-as-buying-a-plane-ticket/.
57. Conservative commentator Megan McArdle advanced the idea that government would pay all healthcare costs above 20 percent of adjusted gross income and provide Medicaid to everyone below 150 percent of the poverty line. Megan McArdle, "A Cheaper, Simpler Obamacare Plan," Bloomberg.com, November 13, 2014, https://www.bloomberg.com/view/articles/2014-11-13/a-cheaper-simpler-obamacare-plan.

costs are huge. Get out of it. I think that would have changed the political dynamic substantially if it was executable. It would have lowered the temperature. It would have set up a different dynamic than the excruciating negotiations that dragged through September, and then Scott Brown came to Washington. It was a big judgment call. I leaned toward cutting the deal and getting out."

Podesta speculated that if Emanuel's slimmer version of reform had been adopted in late 2009, perhaps the Democrats could have held the House. Podesta said, "I think healthcare created the Tea Party, which created the momentum for the Republican victory in the House in 2010, and then was coupled with the lack of jobs."[58]

Van Hollen did not agree: "The biggest decision made in the first term was whether to go for comprehensive healthcare reform or whether after Brown won the Massachusetts Senate seat to retreat into a slimmed-down package. We finished that job. However, I would argue that the overriding issue in the 2010 election was still the economy. The economy trumped everything across the election."[59]

Podesta thought that healthcare reform undercut other goals: "The most important decision Obama made was to focus everything on the Hill. He lost track of the public conversation because everything was focused on passing bills. He became the prime minister. He did get an enormous amount done doing that. He made two big promises in the campaign. Healthcare being at the front of the list. And he said he was going to change the tone in Washington. I'm going to make the dogs lie down with the cats. He was going to be the one.

"He couldn't do both. He could not pass healthcare reform and change the tone. He chose the reform. I think he made the right choice, but he never found a way to bring people together. People were invested in that promise and were disappointed by its failure."[60]

When his team got the Affordable Care Act done in March 2010, Obama surely thought he had accomplished his quest. He had slain the

---

58. John Podesta, interview with author.
59. Van Hollen, interview.
60. Podesta, interview.

Antoine-Louis Barye, Theseus and the Minotaur, 1843, Baltimore Museum of Art. Photo by Nrswanson, https://commons.wikimedia.org/wiki/File:Theseus_Slaying_Minotaur_by_Barye.jpg.

Minotaur, done what no other president had been able to do. In terms of a legislative victory, the battle had been very well fought. In terms of impact, the numbers later showed that a meaningful fraction of Americans were better off. By January 2017, it was generally believed that 20 million individuals had health insurance as a result of the ACA. The ACA thus lowered the percentage of people without insurance from 17 percent in 2013, before the major reforms of the law went into effect, to about 10 percent.[61] By the end of 2016, between 20 and 25 million people remained uninsured. Those with preexisting conditions benefitted from the coverage regulations.

Kocher, one of the architects, said, "I'd give the healthcare reform politically an A. It was the most ambitious thing that was possible to pass. A B+ on coverage expansion. And a B- on cost side because we

61. The difference—7 percent—times the population of 325 million roughly equals 22 million. Mark A. Hall and Michael J. McCue, "How Has the Affordable Care Act Affected Health Insurers' Financial Performance?" July 26, 2016, The Commonwealth Fund, https://www.commonwealthfund. org/publications/issue-briefs/2016/jul/how-has-affordable-care-act-affected-health-insurers-financial

could have done more to strengthen the economic incentives that drive productivity, address drug prices, and limit hospital market power. But overall, I would say an A since it was the most ambitious policy agenda that could be passed and we capitalized on a brief window in time to get it done."[62]

For the great majority of Americans, premiums continued to rise, although probably at a lower rate than would have been the case. Employers, employees, and government continued to bear most costs. Surely the ACA provided better healthcare—not insurance, but actual care—to some number of people. In the 2017 tax law, the Trump government repealed the mandate. Perhaps 13 million people were likely to become uninsured, undoing more than half the increase in the insured attributable to the Affordable Care Act.[63] Cuts in Medicare and Medicaid might follow. Unlike Social Security, the disparate measures of the ACA were not invulnerable to change when political power shifted, although the system remained so complex and critical to most Americans that the Republican Congress could not completely repeal the law.

62. Kocher, interview.

63. Robert Pear, "Without the Insurance Mandate, Healthcare's Future May Be in Doubt," *New York Times*, December 19, 2017, https://www.nytimes.com/2017/12/18/us/politics/tax-cut-obamacare-individual-mandate-repeal.html.

14

"The Moment When Our Planet Began to Heal"

This is the saddest story I have ever heard.
— Ford Madox Ford, *The Good Soldier*

By December 2008 Americans could see that the new president and the new Congress intended to pass sweeping legislation limiting the country's greenhouse gas emissions. The United States led the world in causing global warming. Now it might lead an international battle to stop environmental disaster.

Obama named an environmental leader as a "czar" in the White House to coordinate his administration's response to the crisis of global warming. His economic advisers asked the environmentalists to suggest spending measures for the stimulus. Energy and Commerce Committee Chairman Henry Waxman promised he would pass a bill reducing all greenhouse gas emissions from the United States to the level needed to combat global warming. Speaker Nancy Pelosi vowed the House would pass it. Many business leaders, including some in the electric utility industry, supported the "cap-and-trade" bill. Foundations put millions into a public relations campaign intended to offset coal and oil industries' opposition. Senate Majority Leader Harry Reid and Barbara Boxer, chair of the Senate Environment and Public Works Committee, promised the Senate would pass some form of a cap on emissions. It would meet the House bill in conference, and result in a bicameral compromise approximately when President Barack Obama went to a multinational meeting in Copenhagen in December 2009. There he would urge other countries to imitate the United States by passing similar regulations.

Commodity price trends supported the shift to the clean power platform. The price of natural gas was plummeting, partly because of the recession's impact on demand and partly due to increases in supply from a new technology called "fracking" that involved shattering rock at points deep in the earth discovered by radio waves and computers. Traditionally a high-cost but cleaner fuel, at a lower price natural gas would substitute for coal. Wind and other power prices also headed down as technological and design improvements produced gains in the volume of electricity produced per dollar of cost. If given an adequate tax break, homeowners could save on their power bill by putting solar panels on their own roofs.

The new law would not change the structure of the utility industry. It would only push the fuel of the power business away from carbon to renewables. After dominating energy politics since the 19th century, old King Coal could be toppled. Everything the environmental movement had wanted since the Earth Summit in Rio de Janeiro in July 1992— and had been unable to achieve during the frustrating Clinton administration and the retrograde Bush administration—at last would come to pass. The planet could be saved from devastation.

A decade later the environmental movement's confident hopes had turned into bitter disappointment. In two terms Obama signed no major energy law. His Environmental Protection Agency imitated cap-and-trade in a complex regulatory package, but the Trump administration's EPA administrators dedicated themselves not only to undoing that Clean Power Plan, but dismantling the agency itself. President Trump encouraged Americans to doubt the reality of climate change. He pulled the United States out of the global pact to reduce greenhouse gas emissions that was finally reached not in Copenhagen in 2009 but in Paris in 2015. Natural gas did replace some coal-fired boilers used for generating electricity, but in the first year of the Trump administration coal production climbed.[1] The volume of solar and wind power increased markedly, but renewable power picked up less than five points of market share over Obama's two terms.[2] Out of 100 million new cars sold in the seven years from 2009 to 2016, not even a million were plug-ins.[3] Greenhouse gas emissions in the United States were approximately the same every year from 2009 to 2016, and in 2016 were almost identical to the level in 1993, the first year of Bill Clinton's presidency.[4]

This sad story began long before Obama's election.

From Rio to the White House

Soon after he entered Congress in 1977, Gore contrived to hold hearings on global warming. After his losing race for the presidential nomination in 1987–1988, he dug deeper into the topic. In 1992 he published his dramatic, alarming conclusions in *Earth in the Balance*.

That summer he took me on the congressional delegation's trip to the first Earth Summit, held in Rio. We partied with Yanomami royalty from the Amazon. Then we commenced a sidebar trip with the doomed senator from Minnesota, Paul Wellstone (dead 10 years later, small plane, pilot error, days after voting against the Kuwait invasion and days before voters would have decided whether to give him a third term), to the Atlantic rainforest in southern Brazil. There was I, key grip on a crew filming a documentary movie featuring Gore as narrator of the effects of climate change in critical spots around the world. For one segment Wellstone, the movie director, and I stood dripping in a jungle rain on

---

1. "U.S. Coal Production, Exports, and Prices Increased in 2017," U.S. Energy Information Administration (EIA), February 16, 2018, https://www.eia.gov/todayinenergy/detail.php?id=34992.

2. Solar and wind power went from about 2 percent market share in net electricity generation market to about 6.6 percent in 2016—less than five points of market share increase. "Monthly Energy Review—May 2018," Report, U.S. Energy Information Administration, https://www.eia.gov/totalenergy/data/monthly/pdf/sec7_5.pdf.

3. As of December 2017, cumulative sales in the U.S. totaled 764,666 highway legal plug-in electric vehicles since the market launch of the Tesla Roadster in 2008. https://www.hybridcars.com/americas-plug-in-car-sales-were-their-best-ever-in-2016/

4. "Inventory of U.S. Greenhouse Gas Emissions and Sinks: 1990-2016 Executive Summary," Report, Environmental Protection Agency, https://www.epa.gov/sites/production/files/2018-01/documents/2018_executive_summary.pdf.

the deck of a lumbering tourist boat while several hundred yards away, conning a fast boat across the estuary, Gore stood in a miraculous dry space illuminated by a shaft of sunlight reflecting off the water and up underneath his brave visage, as the camera woman filmed him from the prow below. The director said, "He looks like he's on fucking PT-109."

That was a heady day.

Then Bill Clinton phoned and asked if Gore would meet him to interview for the vice presidency. Clinton and Gore met on an airport tarmac back in the States, and agreed that a pairing of moderate Southern Democrats could move the party away from the failed liberal nostrums championed by, say, Wellstone. They ran on a neoliberal platform of middle-class tax cuts, balanced budget, and a strong military. (Gore had voted for the Kuwait war, unlike most Democratic senators.) To the surprise of many, the next generation ticket defeated the incumbent George H. W. Bush. The flick went into the freezer until thawed early in the 21st century, when one sliver slipped into the award-winning movie, *An Inconvenient Truth*.

In the 1992–1993 transition, Gore had me chair a committee designing a tax on coal, oil, and natural gas. We wanted to give more efficient, cleaner carbon fuels like natural gas an advantage against coal, and keep renewables untaxed. We came up with the British thermal unit tax: fuels with different capability to generate heat would pay different taxes. Energy is an input to almost all goods and services. Therefore, the BTU tax would cause business and residential consumers to pay more for inefficient, coal-based power. In reaction businesses would invest in more efficient, less energy-intense ways of manufacturing, and homeowners would install insulation and double-paned glass windows. When renewable power became commercially feasible, utilities would shift to that source to avoid the BTU tax. These changes would occur over time.

The BTU tax (like the carbon tax) resembled the typically unpopular sales tax, albeit with a point of incidence high up the supply chain. The Democratic House barely enacted our neoliberal, anti-consumer, poorly explained measure over opposition by members from states that had major coal mining industries like West Virginia and Montana. Utilities in the Midwest also told their representatives not to supplant the cheap coal used for at least 40 percent of the fuel for generating electricity nationwide and a higher percentage in the Rust Belt. The bill died in the Senate, killed on the desk of Senator Max Baucus of Montana.

The Democrats voting for the bill lost their seats in the 1994 midterms, and their party lost the House. The Democrats said they had been BTU'd. To their minds, the administration's failed healthcare and energy efforts had given the Republicans control of the legislative body that Democrats had controlled for four decades. After that, Bill Clinton stayed far away from both issues.

If Al Gore had become president in 2001, he was going to make the battle against climate change a central operating principle of his administration. He planned to have all executive departments and agencies develop strategies for accelerating the switch from carbon to clean as the power platform for the country. In this respect, he aimed to imitate the push to move the communications sector in the 1990s from analog to digital, from fixed line to mobile, and from serial TV to the Internet. Toward this goal, he might try to persuade Congress to eliminate the payroll tax on businesses and employees and replace it with a carbon tax, one of his favorite policy ideas. Or he would have used the EPA to regulate greenhouse gas emissions, as Obama did in his second term. At the least he would have persuaded Congress to spend colossal sums on research into clean power technologies.

Cap-and-Trade Versus Carbon Tax

During the Bush administration, those who continued to regard climate change as one of the top two global risks (along with nuclear war) agreed on a neoliberal strategy. They would seek a law that internalized the external cost of carbon combustion, as the economists put it, or "put a price on carbon" in more colloquial terms. The BTU tax would have done that too. However, to avoid looking like a sales tax, environmentalists adapted the regulatory solution adopted in reducing acid rain from sulfur oxide emissions. Greenhouse gas emissions would be "capped," a synonym for "licensed" or "permitted." To burn carbon, a business would need a permit. The government would sell or grant the permits. Businesses could trade them. They would expire annually. Over time the government would grant fewer permits, forcing business to pay more for permits or reduce emissions by adopting efficiency measures or moving to renewable power. The permit market would cause the economy to shift from the carbon to clean power platform in the most efficient, least costly way.

The BTU tax and cap-and-trade had the same neoliberal goal: adjust the price of carbon use, and let buying and selling in power markets make change happen. The government did not need to do much after adjusting pricing in the market.

In political terms, putting a price on carbon meant punishing consumers in the pocketbook for buying carbon power and using it inefficiently. Hit people with this pricing stick to make them buy renewable power and install better heating, ventilation, lighting, and air-conditioning systems. They would pay more to be on the clean power platform but not as much as the price society collectively over time would pay for staying on the carbon platform due to the cost of environmental damage.

Generational debates, the essence of many political debates, typically have a moral dimension. Environmentalists felt that just as parents would step in front of an oncoming car to push their children to safety, so too adults should pay any price to save the next generation from the costs of walling off coastal cities against the rising sea, stopping murderous migrations from drowning lands, halting the spread of desertification, blocking the spread of equatorial pestilence. Committed to paying now to avoid future costs, the green lobby was willing to inflict on Americans 10 to 20 percent increases in the cost of power.

Economists saw the choice between present cost and future harm as a familiar trade-off question. The shift to the clean platform cost money in the present. The carbon platform's cost would be incurred in the future. In 2006 Nicholas Stern concluded that the cost that climate change would impose on future generations approximately equaled the cost the present generation had to pay to avoid it. Therefore, countries right away[5]

5. Nicholas Stern. "Stern Review: The Economics of Climate Change," Report, Government of the United Kingdom, 2006, http://unionsforenergydemocracy.org/wp-content/uploads/2015/08/sternreview_report_complete.pdf.

should begin spending 1 percent of their GDP per year on stopping global warming.[6]

All costs end up imposed on some or all of three stakeholders: taxpayers, businesses, or consumers. Who then should pay for the move to the clean power platform: the government, the relevant industry shareholders, or the consumers? By Stern's reasoning Obama should have spent public money, or forced industry to spend its money, or charged consumers, at a rate of about $100 to $200 billion a year for a decade, for a total of $1 to $2 trillion. That amount would green the American power sector. Consistent with neoliberal thinking, the econo-enviro alliance chose to make consumers pay directly and indirectly, via the cap-and-trade mechanism. They sought utilities as allies, so did not ask their shareholders to pay.

Alternatively, the cost could be covered by the government. That would have been the progressive solution, foreshadowed by the New Deal creation of the Tennessee Valley Authority. Government did not need to nationalize utilities in exact replication of TVA. It could cause clean power to substitute for carbon power by lowering the price of renewables below the lowest price carbon power could charge without going out of business. To lower the price of clean power, it could provide tax breaks, grant subsidies, or offer finance. Any of these techniques could have given a monopoly utility distribution company an offer that could not be refused—buy cheaper clean power instead of more expensive carbon power. Moreover, making consumers better off in the short term guaranteed clean power rapid market penetration and gained votes for political proponents.

By contrast, cap-and-trade used markets to accomplish the switch from carbon to clean at the lowest possible total cost to society. Its advocates toted up all costs whether incurred by consumers, shareholders, or government. Simply buying down the price of clean power might lead to a higher societal price.

---

6. "The final neoliberal fallback is geoengineering [which] gleefully diverts attention to Band-Aids while the patient is dying of heat exhaustion." Mirowski, *Never Let a Serious Crisis Go to Waste*, 340–41.

Neoliberal dogma rejected clean power subsidies as inefficient in an economic sense. Just as with the mandate to buy healthcare, the neoliberal policy for energy aimed to create a market that over a long time did not reduce productivity and welfare gains. This impossibly abstract, distant goal gave Obama very tough messages to sell in both healthcare and energy reform debates.

At the Federal Communications Commission in the mid-1990s we thought that mobile telephony and the Internet should wrap around the world and supplant all previous communications platforms. We directed our policies toward enabling the purveyors of the new platforms to offer services faster, better, and cheaper. We tilted interconnection prices in favor of the innovators, knowingly using government power to transfer wealth and market advantage from incumbents to disruptive entrants. We intended to expedite the substitution of new, better, more useful technologies in place of the soon-to-be-antedated modes of exchanging information. We had the progressive zeal to make the world new, and we trusted the machinations of markets, especially oligopolized markets, less than did neoliberal absolutists. Not everything worked out exactly as intended (Facebook, Russians, etc.), but we did our part in helping mobility and data become ubiquitous, with American firms leading in most countries.

In a similar way, public finance could accelerate the move to clean power by supporting innovative, consumer-delighting solutions. If government intervened with enough money, clean power could not fail to supplement carbon power at least as soon as cellular crushed landline, and the Internet swallowed the old media. By contrast, "trading systems tend to reinforce oligopoly power...to penalize new entrants...[and] to stifle further technological measures to curb emissions."[7] Moreover, although cap-and-trade worked beautifully in theory, in practice its details could be problematic. According to one critic, "Once the framework of permit trading is put into place, the full force of lobbying and financial innovation comes into play to flood the fledgling market with excess permits, offsets, and other instruments, so that the nominal cap

---

7. Mirowski, *Never Let a Serious Crisis Go to Waste*, 339.

on the carbon emissions never actually stunts the growth of actual CO_2 emissions."[8]

Despite the challenge of imposing on voters a system that raised power prices, the environmentalists thought the purpose of political power was to do the right thing at the risk of being ousted from office. Only the ignoble preferred a more politically beneficial approach to change. Nor did the climate crisis afford the time to learn from more modest policy experiments. Sometimes a great notion requires hard votes.

Many forgot in 2008 that similar thinking around the BTU tax had cost the Democrats the House in 1994.

During the primaries, no one knew whether Obama would commit the power of his presidency to pushing cap-and-trade through Congress. However, when in early June Obama's 16-month campaign for the nomination ended with a victory speech in St. Paul, Minnesota, he declared, "We will be able to look back and tell our children...this was the moment when the rise of the oceans began to slow and our planet began to heal."[9] Environmentalists took heart from Obama's grandiloquent promise.

In late August, when he accepted the Democratic Party nomination before 84,000 in Denver's Mile High Stadium in Colorado,[10] Obama seemed to backtrack. I watched Obama's speech with a group of Gore friends on the 20-yard line. When Obama embraced all fuel sources, a politically necessary statement in a carbon-rich state, and evaded commitment to a cap-and-trade bill that attracted no marginal voter, we groaned.

The economy posed a bigger problem for environmentalists than Obama's poll-driven rhetoric. The economic advisers to Obama believed that cap-and-trade could not be put in place until the economy had begun growing again (as they also felt about financial regulation). Cap-and-trade increased costs for business and consumers—it also smacked

8. Ibid.

9. "Barack Obama's Remarks in St. Paul," *New York Times*, June 3, 2008, http://www.nytimes.com/2008/06/03/us/politics/03text-obama.html.

10. "Barack Obama's Acceptance Speech," *New York Times*, August 28, 2008, http://www.nytimes.com/2008/08/28/us/politics/28text-obama.html.

of regulation, the enemy of business, growth, and increasing national income.

The environmentalists argued back that the clean power platform would call for new investment, new job creation. The economists responded that total power consumption would go down, or stay flat, because of the recession. Therefore, emissions would decline, and the move to the clean power platform could be delayed.

On September 9, 2008, John Podesta, whose think tank, the Center for American Progress, led Democratic policy development, countered the economists with a Green Recovery plan calling for $100 billion to be spent by the federal government in two years to stimulate private sector investment in three electricity generation sectors (wind, solar, biofuels) and three construction segments (efficient buildings, efficient electrical grid, and mass transit). This resembled my finance-centered Green Recovery Investment Plan presented in the transition two months later. CAP estimated that $50,000 of investment would create one new job-year, and two million newly employed would reduce unemployment by 1.6 percent.[11] The green movement could recast its program as economic stimulus.

In the first presidential debate, on September 26, Obama touted his plan to increase oil "production at home, but most importantly…starting to invest in alternative energy, solar, biodiesel." Picking up Podesta's investment theme, he said we need "a new electricity grid to get the alternative energy to population centers that are using them."[12] When on December 16 Obama asked the team why his proposal to modernize and reconfigure the grid was not in the stimulus, he might have added that he had called for it nearly two months earlier.

Obama returned to the investment theme in the third and last debate, on October 15, 2008.[13] The government could pass laws compelling

11. John Podesta, "Green Recovery," Center for American Progress, September 9, 2008, https://www.americanprogress.org/issues/green/reports/2008/09/09/4929/green-recovery/.

12. "September 26, 2008 Debate Transcript," Commission on Presidential Debates, September 26, 2008, http://www.debates.org/index.php?page=2008-debate-transcript.

13. "October 15, 2008 Debate Transcript," Commission on Presidential Debates, October 15, 2008, http://www.debates.org/index.php?page=october-15-2008-debate-transcript.

utilities to buy clean power. Already many states imposed renewable electricity standards (RES) that required utilities to buy a certain percentage of renewable-generated electricity. These standards helped project developers raise the capital for investing in new renewable capacity because they guaranteed demand would exist. Money could be spent productively on generation, transmission, and renovation of the utility distribution monopoly, as well as retrofitting 100,000 major commercial buildings in the country to consume less power. At least several hundred billion dollars could be invested in the clean power platform during a two-term presidency.[14]

Gerry Waldron, then the chief aide to Congressman Ed Markey for drafting cap-and-trade legislation, explained that "the energy bill of 2007 increased fuel economy standards. That was the first down payment on battling climate change. We saw the stimulus as the second down payment in that it would put money into financing for clean energy. And the third leg of that stool was the cap-and-trade bill. We thought this would unleash the investment that the country had enjoyed in the 1990s from the high-tech sector."[15]

Investment, however, was a supply-side approach to stimulus. By deciding in 2008–2009 that shortfall in aggregate demand was the problem government had to solve, Summers effectively rejected a grand strategy of investing enough in clean power to replace carbon power. Indeed, if the new clean power platform included more efficient techniques for generation, transmission, and consumption—and if clean power cost less than carbon power—then a supply-side strategy to stop greenhouse gas emissions from growing would diminish revenue from power sales and decrease the size of the economy. This supply-side subsidy would create jobs in new construction projects, and it would enhance productivity, just as any reduction in input cost for any goods or services tends to do. Overall, it would replace the old carbon platform with a better, cheaper power platform than its dangerous, dirty predecessor. Gross domestic product might go down a tad.

---

14. Reed E. Hundt, *Zero Hour: Time to Build the Clean Power Platform* (Odyssey Editions, 2013).
15. Waldron, interview.

Clean Energy Got Stimulated

John Podesta, a true believer in the urgency of meeting the climate change crisis, conjured up the job of a designated senior adviser to the president on energy and climate change. After Thanksgiving weekend, Carol Browner flew to Chicago to interview with the president-elect. Obama had not decided if Summers should have environment as part of his NEC portfolio. Alternatively, the Council on Environmental Quality or Domestic Policy Council might own the topic.

When Gore met Obama in Chicago on December 9, the president-elect already knew that the former vice president was not interested in returning to government. Obama did want to get Gore's view on how to manage the climate change agenda and specifically cap-and-trade legislation. Gore recommended that Clinton EPA administrator Carol Browner be named to a key post in the White House. Obama made her the energy czar, a job that had not existed in the White House since the Ford administration.[16]

Striving for a position of influence in the Obama team, Browner pressed the case that the move to clean power was an economic issue. She tried to avoid the experience of the Clinton administration, when Summers and the other neoliberal economists skeptically challenged her EPA rulemaking and Gore's climate change concerns. Ingeniously allying with the NEC, Browner asked for a single economist to report to both her and Larry Summers.

Joe Aldy won this difficult post, and he played the principal role in designing the energy portion of the stimulus. Aldy said, "We gave the shadow OMB, the group in the transition that Orszag ran, a package of energy and climate provisions in the $30 to $40 billion range, and they said, 'You're not spending enough.' I don't know if OMB staff had ever used those words before. This was in late November or early December. In October we were in the $200 to $300 billion range [for the size of the

---

16. My friend Gore also asked Obama to offer me a particular appointment relevant to the climate change battle. I had expressed interest in a regulatory job, but when Michael Froman called me about it, I said I would rather have the new president ask me to create a new institution of a green bank. That act of lèse majesté disappointed my patron and ultimately left me in the private sector.

overall stimulus package], in the $500 billion range by November, and by the end of December people were like, 'the economy is in free fall. We need one trillion of stimulus.' So by mid-December we were going to be at maybe $60 to $80 billion for energy alone. It ended up at about $90 billion."[17]

Browner said, "The Recovery Act was a jumpstart for clean energy. It was a down payment on the technologies and the jobs that would be important for a different energy future. The stimulus made a financial down payment on clean power."[18]

Aldy said, "There was only one big thing we wanted that was new. It was fixing the energy tax credits because the tax equity market had really dried up. The fix was that instead of taking a tax credit, you can actually elect to get a cash grant in place of it. This 1603 grant was one of the few things that was novel in the clean energy package."[19]

A tax deduction reduces taxable income. It is worth the amount of tax that would otherwise have been paid on the income. For a corporation taxed at a 35 percent rate, a deduction of $100 is worth $35. By contrast, the beneficiary subtracts a tax credit directly from tax otherwise owed. A tax credit of $100 is worth $100. Obviously, developers preferred tax credits. To turn the credit into ready cash, Aldy smartly persuaded the stimulus drafters to allow new firms, who owed no taxes, to take the tax credit as a cash grant. This move ran counter to the advisers' aversion toward new legislation, but greatly boosted clean-power project development. It illustrated how the stimulus might have promoted all infrastructure investment.

Cap-and-Trade Remained the Goal

Despite the "liberal" use of the stimulus to spend on the supply side of clean power, the Obama advisers preferred regulation to create demand for renewables. Browner thought "the long-term success of a clean energy sector would require the right policies because you had to create the

17. Aldy, interview.
18. Browner, interview.
19. Aldy, interview.

demand that would draw in ongoing private investments. To create the demand, you needed clean energy legislation. You needed a renewable electricity standard that required utilities to buy clean power. You needed a price on carbon that raised the price of carbon-based power above the renewable alternatives. Government wasn't going to be there forever to provide tax breaks. We could be there in the near term as in the stimulus, while we sorted through the right policies that would give the private sector the right incentives and opportunities."

Browner took her job knowing that "Summers was very wary of moving forward with the cap-and-trade bill," because by raising power prices it would decrease demand. If some policy were adopted, "Summers and Orszag wanted a carbon tax instead. They thought it cleaner. It was simple. You could achieve your policy outcomes."[20]

Anyone could express support for a carbon tax in order to show sympathy to the long-run concerns about the impact of climate change, while not fearing that any such tax would be proposed by the Obama administration. At bottom, the economic advisers wanted to postpone legislation addressing climate change. Bob Kocher, observing from his healthcare seat on the National Economic Council, said the NEC as a group was "convinced that there was not an energy policy that was not GDP-destroying. Every cap-and-trade scenario would slow investment, reduce American competitiveness, and be a high tax on business. Larry Summers certainly was clear in his convictions that there wasn't a strong counterargument that he found believable."[21]

While the advisers debated the prioritization of policies, Browner won a place for cap-and-trade in the budget. Browner said, "One of the things I was able to do in the budget is provide an assumption of revenues from cap-and-trade. It was an important moment because it becomes the first marker. Budgets are used to demonstrate the president's commitment to particular policies. An example would be that the Bush administration always included revenues from drilling in ANWR. If we hadn't included some revenues from cap-and-trade, environmentalists and the business industry would have thought, they're not real." The budget insertion also

20. Browner, interview.
21. Kocher, interview.

had the advantage of reducing the deficit. As Browner acknowledged, cap-and-trade created "a lot of money, so that helped" get it in the budget.

"And as we went through the election," Browner explained, "there was a coalition of companies under the auspices of the Edison Electric Institute, the trade association of power generators and utilities, who had a very specific proposal. So I don't think anyone doubted that cap-and-trade was the mechanism."

Browner placed cap-and-trade in the sweep of history. "It took about 10 years to get to the passage of the 1990 Clean Air Act. Following that pattern from around 2000 to 2008, environmental leaders like Fred Krupp and Republicans like Boyden Gray, George W. Bush, and Bill Reilly to some degree were coalescing around the idea of using market mechanisms to achieve environmental benefits. So by the time Obama comes to office, it is widely accepted that the cap-and-trade method achieved the environmental goal of reducing acid rain at significantly lower cost than anyone had ever anticipated."[22]

Waxman Entered the Scene

Both the healthcare and cap-and-trade bills fell within the jurisdiction of the House Energy and Commerce Committee. John Dingell was the longtime Democratic leader of the committee. As of November 2008, Henry Waxman had been junior in seniority to Dingell for his entire 22 years in Congress. But Dingell's efforts to pass Hillarycare in 1993–1994 had ended in electoral disaster. And with respect to energy Dingell had long been aligned with the pro-carbon inclinations of the automobile industry in his Michigan congressional district. However, at that moment the survival of General Motors and Chrysler totally depended on whether Barack Obama would pony up the money to recapitalize them. They and their congressman were vulnerable.

Waxman launched a usurpation campaign. He promised Democrats that if he chaired the committee he would pass both comprehensive climate regulation and healthcare reform. At the same time, Obama selected Waxman's loyal staffer Phil Schiliro to be chief legislative counsel,

22. Browner, interview.

signaling a close alliance between Waxman and the White House. The time for maximal, dream-come-true legislating had arrived.

Waxman told me, "While I had been number two to John Dingell for a very long time, and ordinarily would not have challenged him, I just felt I was better able to handle those [two] important legislative items. So I called him up and said, 'This is a very painful thing for me to do, but I'm going to run.' A lot of people said, 'Why didn't you just wait two years for Dingell to retire?' My argument was that these are the two years that matter the most." So we ended up in an election fight, which I won."[23]

Waxman won in the Democrat-only House caucus vote, 137 to 122.

Gerry Waldron said, "On November 20, 2009, Henry Waxman defeated John Dingell to become chairman of the House Energy and Commerce Committee. It was my birthday and a day I will long remember. Ed backed Henry and immediately after the election Henry said, 'Ed, I want you to be the chair of the energy subcommittee in addition to the select committee on climate change chair and I want to make cap-and-trade one of my priorities. I want to get it out of committee by Memorial Day and off the floor by July Fourth.' I was like, 'Wow, that's very aggressive. That's four months to write a massive bill.' Henry said, 'I agree but I think we need to set an aggressive timetable because I want to do healthcare next. I've consulted with Nancy and the notion is we'll get energy out by July Fourth. We'll get healthcare off the floor by the August recess. The Senate can turn to that after Labor Day and then do the energy bill. That way we can have a climate bill largely done by the time the president goes to Copenhagen in December.' The thinking was not that we would have had a signing ceremony on energy by early December but we would be in conference. The Senate would pass climate and energy by October, healthcare in November and December, and then the energy bill could come out of conference in late December 2009 or early in 2010 and the president would sign it."[24]

Waxman thought, "We could move energy and healthcare both and see if we could achieve them both. If we didn't try, we weren't going to

<hr>

23. Waxman, interview.
24. Waldron, interview.

succeed. They were both very important issues. I remember going to the White House and having a meeting with President Obama, and he said, 'Well, I want energy, and I want health reform. I love them both equally, but healthcare really is my first choice.' And I said, 'I understand. But I don't think this jeopardizes healthcare. In fact, I think success leads to success.'"[25]

John Podesta said, "The decision to support Henry Waxman in going forward with the energy bill was not supported by everybody in the White House. Ultimately it went to Obama. Obama said, 'The only way to get both is to have Henry go first on energy.' That decision was made in January. Nancy and Henry were pushing, 'Let us go in front of that. Put the climate bill out of committee by Memorial Day and out of the House by Fourth of July.' And they did that."[26]

On climate change, Waxman said, "Ed Markey and I worked very, very closely. Our staffs became almost one."[27] Markey said, "The signals that were coming out of the Senate indicated that they could find the votes for both climate and healthcare and that we should do our best on both of them. They would deal with healthcare first. We would wind up conferencing both bills before the end of the year and put both bills on the president's desk before the end of the year."[28]

"But," said Waxman, "what do we do with coal? Generally what we agreed to do was have a transition. We agreed to put money into the development of carbon capture and sequestration [a way to catch emissions in the smokestack of a generation plant] for coal, which is very important because coal is so ubiquitous. That was one of the things that Rick Boucher [Democratic congressman from Virginia's coal country] was very concerned about. He thought there'd be a rush to natural gas unless we put in somewhere in the transition that coal would still be usable. And we wanted eventually to get to the point where we'd have coal that didn't pollute. That was a key point, and we finally reached an

25. Waxman, interview.
26. Podesta, interview.
27. Waxman, interview.
28. Markey, interview.

agreement with Boucher there. We finally got to the point where we had the votes on the Democratic side.

"I wanted Republican votes too. I went to Joe Barton, who was the former chairman and ranking Republican on the Committee. I said, 'Let's work together. I'm the new chairman. I want your help. We can do these things on a bipartisan basis.' And he said to me, 'I don't believe there's a problem with global warming. I just don't think it exists. Why would I want to work to find a solution to a problem that I don't think exists? It would be like me telling you, let's work on how we can eliminate the state of Israel.'

"I thought that was a little extravagant."

Waxman continued, "We were trying to frame it in terms of a win for national security by reducing our demand for foreign oil. A win for the economy because millions of new jobs would be produced with the new investment in trying to develop the technologies that reduce carbon and other greenhouse gas emissions. And a win for the environment because we would actually reduce the carbon, and if we got this bill through, it would help get other bills through. It would also help get a better international agreement because the U.S. alone can't deal with the climate problem. The whole philosophy was that there would be an economic gain if we got people to do the right thing by putting a price on carbon and rewarding them significantly in an economic way for accomplishing what was a worthwhile goal."[29]

Van Hollen said, "The energy bill was the Speaker of the House's signature issue. Climate change, energy, security, that whole issue. So, you started to try to move the energy bill through the system on the House side. We began to encounter some political issues. We had members from different parts of the country—some from coal states, some from other states—who were getting real heartburn with the idea of moving an energy bill, especially as it became clearer that we were also going to do healthcare. It was also a bandwidth issue. And for regional reasons in both chambers the energy bill in the form that the House was talking

29. Waxman, interview.

about was as big if not a bigger lift than the healthcare bill."[30]

Waxman counted on Carol Browner to be his strong ally for cap-and-trade in the administration, and she delivered Obama's help. Waxman said, "Ultimately the president actually helped a lot in the House on the cap-and-trade bill. There was one time when we were trying to get the votes for it in committee and he had all the Democrats on the committee come to the White House and he said, 'I wanted to be president to do big things. There are a lot of things we can do in life where our lives would be a lot easier than being in public office. We could have more time with our families. We could make more money. But all of us want to accomplish important things for the American people.' And he was helpful in calling members. We didn't know if we could get the votes in the House. The president was bringing members in, talking to them, calling them, meeting with them personally. A strong boost came from Nancy Pelosi. She wanted us to succeed. She felt this was a historic and most important area where we had to act. Nobody else was as enthusiastic."[31]

My local congressman, Chris Van Hollen, agreed to introduce as a bill the Green Bank concept that Larry Summers had politely but quickly rejected. Van Hollen persuaded Congressman Henry Waxman and Congressman Ed Markey to include the idea of a Green Bank into their cap-and-trade bill.

Congressmen Jay Inslee (later governor of Washington) and John Dingell offered the Van Hollen Green Bank Act, creating a bank under the new name of Clean Energy Deployment Administration, as an amendment to the cap-and-trade bill. Adopted in March by a vote of 51 to 6, it was one of the few, if not only, bipartisan measures passed in the Energy and Commerce Committee.[32] On May 21, 2009, the Waxman-Markey cap-and-trade bill, American Clean Energy and Security Act ("ACES"), passed the House Energy and Commerce Committee.

---

30. Van Hollen, interview.
31. Waxman, interview.
32. Ultimately, only a single Republican on the Energy and Commerce Committee voted for the cap-and-trade bill, Mary Bono, widow of the late Sonny Bono, elected from his district in climate-change-believing California.

On June 26, 2009, the bill squeaked through the House with 219 votes in favor and 217 against. Imported in the cap-and-trade bill, the idea of the green bank hoped to find its Senate doppelganger in a conference committee.

The House Versus the Senate

In the Senate, the cap-and-trade bill belonged in the jurisdiction of the Senate Environment and Public Works Committee. Senator Barbara Boxer of California chaired the committee. Senator James Inhofe of Oklahoma, a carbon-intense state, was the ranking Republican. He once threw a snowball in the Senate to disprove the existence of global warming. Inhofe would never negotiate a bipartisan bill with Boxer. Moreover, minority leader Mitch McConnell was from the old coal state of Kentucky. He would back up Inhofe's opposition to any cap-and-trade bill.

Democratic Senator Jeff Bingaman of New Mexico chaired the Senate Energy and Natural Resources Committee. He thought Boxer's committee would struggle to vote out a bill. He was sure he could craft a bipartisan bill with Senator Lisa Murkowski of Alaska, the ranking Republican. For jurisdictional reasons, his bill could not regulate all greenhouse gas emissions, but it could regulate the electricity and energy industries.

Over on the Senate side I did the bad thing—in terms of Senate protocol—of going directly to Senator Jeff Bingaman with the green bank idea. One is supposed to approach the staff first. They will be called in later anyhow. Must get them on one's side. But Jeff's wife, Anne, and I had collaborated on many a topic while I was FCC chair and she was the head of the antitrust division of the Department of Justice. I had been to their house for their annual Christmas party. Time was short. Anne arranged the meeting. I asked the senator if he would introduce the Van Hollen (by then Dingell-Inslee) measure in the bill he was drafting as a bipartisan measure in the Senate Energy and Natural Resources Committee. He agreed.

That committee traditionally operated on a bipartisan basis. Its bill required all electric utilities to buy a certain amount of clean power (renewable energy standard, or RES) or impose a utility-only cap system. Electricity generation accounted for a third of all emissions (with transportation and other activities each contributing thirds as well). Bingaman included in his bill a green bank inside the Department of Energy, which lay squarely in their jurisdiction.

If the White House and Senate Democratic leadership had chosen the Bingaman-Murkowski bill as a vehicle for legislation, that measure could have been bigger in scope. It might have federalized the national transmission system by subsidizing developers to build transmission lines that connected clean power generation to distribution utility grids. Similarly, the government could have paid for the extension of the natural gas distribution network to reach major urban areas relying on fuel oil for heating or needing natural gas for industrial processes. The dream reform law could have caused the Federal Energy Regulatory Commission to be patterned more after the Federal Communications Commission by giving it the authority to preempt state regulation that interfered with the creation of a clean power platform. Funding might have been provided for a decade's worth of innovation in batteries, carbon-capture from coal-fired boilers, and other breakthrough technologies. Even as it was drafted, the Bingaman-Murkowski bill was a viable bipartisan vehicle for significant change.

When Bingaman saw Waxman-Markey move in the House, he quickly persuaded Lisa Murkowski to pass their bill out of the Senate ENR committee on June 17, 2009. From June 2009 to January 2010, Bingaman pleaded with the Senate leadership to put his bill on the Senate floor. He pointed out that the Republicans who supported it in his committee would vote for it. Sixty votes were very likely. Democratic senators Barbara Boxer and John Kerry were not sympathetic. They wanted a cap-and-trade bill to go to the Senate floor. They and some White House staffers thought if they could pass anything like it, then in the conference committee the White House would have more control. No one in the environmental camp wanted to face the fact that even if a cap-and-trade bill miraculously got to the Senate floor, it would not garner all Democratic votes, much less a Republican vote. It could not pass.

Pete Rouse said, "The most important decision for President Obama was to sign off on the timeline and priorities for action. In retrospect, should we have pushed that cap-and-trade energy bill, and forced it through the House by that one-vote margin? The fact of the matter is, that bill was likely not going to pass the Senate."[33]

Tom Mann, a Brookings scholar expert on Congress, thought that to pass climate change legislation, "the only hope was bringing along John McCain, Lindsey Graham, and other Republicans who had shown some interest. There were serious efforts to do that. But the prospects for success were even lower than for healthcare. If Obama had selected climate change as the top priority and healthcare second, he would have gotten neither. I just have no doubt about that. I never believed that a serious cap-and-trade or carbon tax could clear Congress." By that, Mann meant a bill regulating all emissions generated from the entire economy. He added, "I'm less certain that a utility-only cap could not have passed," meaning that if the legislation had focused only on electricity generation by utilities, it might have passed, because as monopolies, utilities can always recover their costs from customers.[34]

Browner said, "I wonder if we might not have been better off—and you could only say this with hindsight—of taking smaller bits and getting them done so that you'd have six bills or eight bills rather than one large clean energy bill. Your votes might change. So you could get some people to be for a transportation bill. You could get some people to be for a utility bill. You could get some people to be for a renewable bill. You would just sort of keep moving through the pieces."[35]

If the Senate had passed the Bingaman-Murkowski bill in June 2009, or even later, then the House and Senate conferees would have crafted a compromise between it and Waxman-Markey. That would have been completed in the short window in which the Democrats had a 60-vote margin in the Senate. Perhaps a cap system limited to the utility sector would have survived. Very likely RES would have become law. In any event, Obama would have won a major legislative victory.

---

33. Rouse, interview.
34. Mann, interview.
35. Browner, interview.

The Senate had not acted on energy legislation when in April 2010 the BP oil spill took place. Senators Menendez and Nelson, with millions of constituents near beaches, had to oppose new drilling. That made the Bingaman bill more complicated. His bill raised revenue from auctioning drilling rights. In trying to stop the leaking and win approval for an effective response, the Obama White House barred drilling. That killed the Bingaman bill, which by then was the last chance for a major energy reform.

Gerry Waldron thought that for Obama, "Putting all his chips on healthcare versus promoting an energy bill was a tactical mistake. Financial services should have been a layup. I think he could have passed energy. For healthcare, I didn't see how it could be explained as job-creating. On the energy bill you could talk about construction jobs. Anyhow, whatever went second was going to be hurt on the Senate side. So the president privileging healthcare caused the chances of the second energy bill to go down dramatically."[36]

Should Democrats have even tried for cap-and-trade? Axelrod said, "No, I think that was a mistake. There was always a great deal of skepticism among some of us because it wasn't clear that we were going to get cap-and-trade through the Senate. I just didn't see how. Knowing what we know now, I certainly would have rethought that decision. I would have done something in energy but done it another way," Axelrod said.[37]

Ed Markey said, "As you look backward it is clear that the Senate was going to be paralyzed by healthcare. In retrospect, now that we know we didn't have the votes in the Senate, I wish we had passed a national renewable electricity standard. That could have passed the Senate. It was in the Waxman-Markey bill. We would have had more Republican support for that in the Senate and House. But we thought we could get 60 Senate votes for the more expansive version of cap-and-trade and we could meet the Senate in conference."[38]

36. Waldron, interview.
37. Axelrod, interview.
38. Markey, interview.

My Personal Alternative Then: Speed Switch to Clean Power, using Bingaman-Murkowski bill on vehicle in the Senate (Measures are purposely redundant).

1. Focus. Focus on electricity in the 15 states that account for almost two-thirds of GHG emissions; in those states auction subsidies to generation firms that promise to reduce GHG 60 percent over a decade. Pay for cheapest methods.
2. Faster, Better, Cheaper. Make clean power the lowest cost option for utilities by offering low interest 20-year loans to clean power generators through local green banks.
3. Finance. Capitalize national green bank for assembling public-private pool of funds distributed through state and local retail green banks. Loan to any clean power platform project. Be self-sustaining in five years.
4. Government purchase. All government users to buy only renewable power at any market-set price.
5. Nationalize coal. In 2009 almost all American coal resources could be bought for about $40 billion. Nationalize the bankrupt coal companies, phase out production, keep coal in ground, ban imports.
6. Sell TVA and Bonneville. Privatize government electricity firms by selling to buyers that promise to convert to renewables and nuclear.
7. Subsidize EVs by mile. Do not subsidize the purchase of an electric vehicle; subsidize each mile driven by EV. Cause fleets, taxis, Uber and Lyft drivers to convert to EVs, reduce gas miles driven.
8. Help low-income families. Provide vouchers to low-income families to buy a minimum amount of clean power for free.
9. Mandate National RES. Require all utilities to buy set amount of renewable power, increasing annually until reaches 80 percent.
10. Pay for transmission transformation. Just as Obama asked on December 16, use federal funds to pay for new transmission lines bringing exclusively clean power at zero cost to utility distribution firms.

15

A Tale of Two Inaugural Addresses

You have to ask yourself two questions:
Who am I? And how may I become myself?

— Paul Beatty, *The Sellout*

Immediately after being sworn in, the new president faces the most stylized, stultifying of tests: the inaugural address. The January wind kills the speaker's ardor, the distance from the people below Capitol Hill attenuates emotional connection with the crowd. The reverberations of loudspeakers, like memories of past addresses, garble the most careful articulation. The challenge would intimidate any actor. Nevertheless, on the grand stage, before a throng on the mall, and over the electromagnetic waves to millions in their homes, presidents on that day of personal fulfillment, like baseball players who have won the World Series or CEOs on the first day in the big office, want to explain the meaning of their triumph.

The two modern presidents sworn in during economic calamity—Franklin Roosevelt and Barack Obama—both needed to overcome the challenge of that first speech. They each had to convince their audiences that good times would come again.

In the opening addresses of their presidencies, they chose the image of leadership that marked their tenures.

They chose very different personas, with very different consequences.

Campaigning on the West Coast in September 1932, Franklin Roosevelt became convinced he would win the election. At the Palace Hotel in San Francisco the night of September 22–23, he pulled Raymond Moley into his room to outline his initial thoughts on the inaugural address. According to Moley, Roosevelt said he wanted to express a "mixture of warning and of assurance" in the inaugural speech. The speech should "provide an example of positive and expeditious action."[1]

In November, Roosevelt won in the landslide he had sensed coming, and as was true for Obama, his party controlled the House and the Senate. In that era the inauguration was in March instead of January, so Roosevelt did not turn to the topic of his address again until February 3. On a night train to Jacksonville, Florida, Roosevelt dictated notes to Moley and another aide, Ed Flynn. Moley turned them into a draft that he carried to Roosevelt's stately New York home, Hyde Park, on February 27.

Like Obama, Roosevelt loved the midnight hours. With Moley's draft and a scotch at hand, Roosevelt settled in. He unlocked the iron that caged his powerless legs, fueled himself with alcohol and nicotine, and from nine p.m. until the wee hours rewrote the speech in longhand. At one point Roosevelt looked up and asked Moley how to spell "foreclose." When the work was done, Moley threw his original text into the fireplace, and took Roosevelt's handiwork away for typing. When Louis Howe saw the new draft the next morning, he inserted the famous phrase "The only thing we have to fear is fear itself."

Moley had seen it printed on a poster in a New York haberdasher's window. The copywriter apparently knew the work of Henry David Thoreau, the Duke of Wellington, or Montaigne, each of whom had expressed the idea. Moley assumed Howe, who was not particularly well-read, had seen the placard.

On March 3, Roosevelt read the draft again, and made "very few changes." Moley kept the text under his pillow that night, then handed it to Roosevelt as the president-elect left for the ceremony.

---

1. Raymond Moley, *The First New Deal* (New York: Harcourt, Brace & World, 1966) 114–120.

On March 4, 1944, Roosevelt swore the oath of office on his family Bible, published in 1686 in Dutch. Arrayed in morning coat and striped trousers, he was in all respects aristocracy, and he spoke in ornate, orotund diction. Yet over the common medium of the time, radio, his arched, monied accent carried a soothing quality. Some would call him a traitor to his class, but his dramatic exercise of command inspired the great mass of the people.

Obama Picked a Leadership Style

Unlike Roosevelt, Obama decided on his economic recovery program and launched it in Congress before inauguration. Indeed by the time Obama was sworn in, both Houses had nearly agreed on the stimulus. That law spent an extra year's worth of the annual domestic discretionary spending in the federal budget, an amount equal to about 5 percent of the GDP. Indicating how much bigger the United States as an enterprise had become between the Roosevelt and Obama presidencies, the Obama stimulus equaled 100 percent of the GDP in 1933, in inflation-adjusted terms.

In certain demographic terms Obama's America was more vulnerable to economic woe in 2009 than was Roosevelt's country in 1933. Obama's people were much older than Roosevelt's. In 1930 almost half of rural America was 19 or younger; a third of urban America. In the whole country, only 17 percent were 45 to 64, and few, only 5 percent, were older than 65.[2] By contrast, in Obama's time, only 28 percent were 18 or younger; 26 percent were 45 to 64; and more than 12 percent were 65 or older. The aged lacked time to work patiently out of economic trouble.

In sheer quantitative size, the problem of unemployment required more governmental action in 2009 than in 1933. In Obama's first term, the jobless mustered 15 million by 2010. During his eight years in office, tens of millions more had trouble finding work, and work at good pay. In 1933 Roosevelt had to put 13 million to work, and in that poorer

2. "Statistical Abstract of the United States: 1930," United States Census Bureau, https://www.census.gov/library/publications/1930/compendia/statab/52ed.html.

country people felt more grateful for any wages and were more willing to share tough times together.

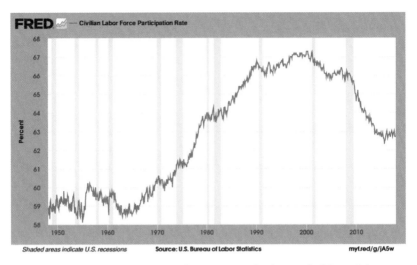

"FRED®" charts ©Federal Reserve Bank of St. Louis. 2015. All rights reserved. All "FRED®" charts appear courtesy of Federal Reserve Bank of St. Louis. http://research.stlouisfed.org/fred2/.

The housing problem too was quantitatively bigger for Obama than for Roosevelt. Almost two-thirds of families owned their homes in 2009; less than a half did in 1933. The evaporation of home equity affected the majority of Americans in Obama's time. In 1933, not nearly as many people depended on housing prices for savings, or even had savings. About a third of a million went into foreclosure in 1933, but nearly a million homes went into foreclosure in 2008; nearly a million more would be foreclosed in 2009.

Such was the situation when Obama prepared his inaugural address.

In November, Jon Favreau, age 27, met with Obama to begin their collaboration on it. According to press accounts, they exchanged drafts four or five times over the next two months.[3] The principal draft, it is said, Favreau typed on his laptop while at a Starbucks. The goal of

---

3. Ed Pilkington, "Barack Obama's Inauguration Speech...Crafted by 27-Year-Old in Starbucks," *Guardian*, January 20, 2009, https://www.theguardian.com/world/2009/jan/20/barack-obama-inauguration-us-speech.

the text was to emphasize "responsibility"—the theme of Bill Clinton's much-panned second inaugural. Unlike Roosevelt, Obama did not initially contemplate "warning and assurance." He and his speechwriter did not yet know the severity of the recession.

Also like Roosevelt, Obama would reach the country in visual more than verbal terms, because of cable, satellite, broadcast, and the Internet. His face would express far more than his words could do. For the first time in American history a person of color was assuming the most important job in the world. Nearly two million people went to the Mall to mark this act of reparation for the centuries on the cross. The moment far exceeded Jack Johnson becoming heavyweight champion or Hank Aaron beating Babe Ruth's home run record, although it resembled these accomplishments. This black hero had won the approval of white audiences and white money to a degree no minority had ever accomplished in America. In this historical context, Obama could not help but want to convey triumph in America's long battle against racism. That argued against the negative verbal depiction of the economic distress that Roosevelt used to bond with his audience.

The Inaugural Committee moved the podium to the front of the Capitol and erected big video screens at locations down the Mall all the way to the Washington Monument. The temperature did not rise above freezing. The wind, like a messenger with bad news, made everyone shudder. For warmth and hope, the country's political leaders gathered close around resplendent Obama as he prepared to take the oath of office.

When Abraham Lincoln made his circuitous train trip through rebellious Maryland to be sworn in, he became separated from his possessions, including his books. For his oath-taking, he required the clerk of the Supreme Court to fetch him a King James Bible of a widely distributed Oxford University edition. On that book the man from Illinois who would become the greatest president placed his hand to take the oath. On that same book another president from Illinois, Barack Obama, swore the same words—or would have, had Supreme Court Chief Justice John Roberts not so badly bungled the language that Obama repeated. The next day lawyers arranged for a do-over of the oath in the White House to be sure that the magic creation of authority had worked. The existing power structure would or could not smoothly accept Obama.

Roosevelt Took Command

Franklin Roosevelt began his speech by describing "common difficulties" in terms drawn from epic narrative.[4] Values of assets, stocks, goods had "shrunken to fantastic levels.…the means of exchange are frozen in the currents of trade…the withered leaves of industrial enterprise lie on every side.…the savings of many years in thousands of families are gone."

In this hideous landscape of ice and ruin, Roosevelt named the worst of the calamities: "A host of unemployed citizens face the grim problem of existence, and an equally great number toil with little return." However, the hero knew he could lead his followers to a better place because "our distress comes with no failure of substance…no plague of locusts." Indeed, "Plenty is at our doorstep." Therefore, only fear was to be feared.

The crisis called for explanation and invited blame. The new president provided both, saying, "The rulers of the exchange of mankind's goods have failed, through their stubbornness and their own incompetence, have admitted their failure, and abdicated.…The money changers have fled from their high seats in the temple of our civilization." There were enemies, monsters. They were the bankers.

However, because the banks were already closed, Roosevelt did not need to oust the bankers. Instead, he needed to get them back to work. The legislation his team was drafting with Hoover's Treasury staff enabled the government to recapitalize banking. As one congressman put it, "The president drove the money-changers out of the capital on March 4—and they were all back on the ninth."[5] In this respect, Obama and Roosevelt were on strikingly similar paths. Geithner was well into option two, his recapitalization plan, even as Obama delivered his inaugural address.

---

4. "Franklin D. Roosevelt: Inaugural Address, March 4, 1933," The American Presidency Project, https://www.presidency.ucsb.edu/node/208712.
5. North Dakota congressman William Lemke, quoted in David M. Kennedy, *Freedom from Fear: The American People in Depression and War* (New York: Oxford University Press, 2001).

Roosevelt named his top priority: "Our greatest primary task is to put people to work." The only fiscal "action" Roosevelt proposed to "put people to work" was what is now called "infrastructure" and then was called "public works." As explained by historian Elliot Rosen, most thought this was not likely to reduce unemployment quickly or deeply because "public projects were slow to get under way, their cost was high relative to the number employed"—meaning equipment and material, rather than labor, accounted for much of the spending—"and useful projects were limited."[6] Unfortunately, Obama's advisers successfully made the same arguments against infrastructure spending in the winter of 2008–2009.

Moreover, Roosevelt was unwilling to have government make up for the amount of investment that the Depression had made disappear. Private investment fell from $16 billion in 1929 to $344 million in 1933. Even if government substituted for only half the gap, Roosevelt would have to persuade Congress to spend between $7 and $8 billion. At the time, the total annual federal expenditure for goods and services was between $2 and $3 billion; close to another billion went for veteran's benefits (which Roosevelt soon cut by 50 percent). Doubling or tripling the size of the federal budget in a single year was beyond anyone's imagination.

Obama emphasized joblessness much less and had little to offer in terms of "public works." He too balked at spending enough to compensate for the evaporation of private investment. Obama must have understood that the housing slump had worried middle class Americans for years and now unemployment, like a bomb going off down the street, would bring fear into every home. Plenty of people told him to study Franklin Roosevelt's inaugural address. If he channeled Franklin Roosevelt's New Deal into his own speech, he could offer stimulus, legislative reforms and regulation as balm, as promise that the American Dream was no bygone fantasy. Obama did not want to give that speech. He had seen that Carter lost faith in the New Deal's solutions, Reagan attacked them, and Bill Clinton abandoned them. George W. Bush gave the

6. Elliot A. Rosen, *Roosevelt, the Great Depression, and the Economics of Recovery* (Charlottesville: University of Virginia Press, 2007), 73–74.

country instead a Global War on Terror, and government-funded pharmaceuticals for seniors. After these decades of decline in government's aspirations, Obama had reason to doubt that middle-class Americans would trust his capability as President to restore the savings lost in home equity's disappearance, to guarantee good jobs at rising wages.

Besides, Obama's own empathy lay more with the downtrodden than the middle class. He had committed the gaffe—defined as accidental honesty—of criticizing those in the geographic and economic middle of the country as people who "cling to guns or religion or antipathy to people who aren't like them." Dating back to the "war on poverty" in the Johnson administration, Democrats thought government should help people in reverse order of status, income, and wealth. The least should be first. If he were to advance government as the agent of the middle class victimized by Bush policies and Wall Street perfidy, Obama would have to find a tone that had sometimes escaped him and his party. Donald Trump would bottle this message and intoxicate his belligerent, faithful followers. Obama preferred to champion the poor, the unemployed, the about-to-be-foreclosed, and the chronically ill in seasoned discussion with the rest of the population.

A big difference between Roosevelt and Obama also lay in their visions of leadership. Roosevelt posited that "our people…realize…our interdependence" and therefore "move as a trained and loyal army." He said, "I assume unhesitatingly the leadership of this great army of our people dedicated to a disciplined attack upon our common problems." If Congress did not adopt either Roosevelt's programs or adequate alternatives, then he would ask Congress for "broad Executive power to wage a war against the emergency, as great as the power that would be given to me if we were in fact invaded by a foreign foe."

The people were an army; Roosevelt, their general. They "want direct, vigorous action." They "have made me the present instrument of their wishes." Congress had better pass the laws Roosevelt thought necessary to "put people to work" or concede that as commander in chief he could do what he thought best to win the war against unemployment.

Roosevelt described a new power relationship in the United States: the people would support their president, and Congress would follow the president's leadership. In the expression of leadership, Roosevelt's speech resembled Trump's inaugural address in 2017.

Unlike Roosevelt, Obama presented himself as a philosophical commentator. The new president said, "Cynics fail to understand…that the ground has shifted…that the stale political arguments that have consumed us for so long no longer apply." Apparently, he alluded to Reagan's famous statement in his 1981 inaugural that "government is not the solution to our problem; government is the problem," and Bill Clinton's statement in his 1996 State of the Union that "the era of big government is over." Obama did not reject this "stale" discussion about the place of government in the American economy or society as much as he sidestepped the issue: "The question we ask today is not whether our government is too big or too small, but whether it works—whether it helps families find jobs at a decent wage, care they can afford, a retirement that is dignified. Where the answer is yes, we intend to move forward. Where the answer is no, programs will end." Echoing Michael Dukakis's failed paean to "competence" in 1988, this fell far short of Roosevelt's commitment to action.

Obama said we do not ask "whether the market is a force for good or ill," because '[i]ts power to generate wealth and expand freedom is unmatched." At that very moment the "market" was shrinking wealth. In the next decade it would undermine democracy in the West. The French economist Thomas Piketty would argue that capitalism inevitably makes the rich vastly richer and the poor hopelessly unequal. Obama's recital of neoliberal dictum died on his tongue. Rather than beginning the transformation of political thinking toward progressivism, Obama tepidly spoke for limited regulation by noting that "without a watchful eye, the market can spin out of control."

Axelrod's poll results may have discouraged Obama from offering a new vision for government. He told the president-elect that the American people may have elected him by a handsome margin but they did not understand or agree that government should be shipping taxpayer dollars to banks and automobile companies. Axelrod said, "I was in the room when he made the decisions about the auto bailout. I had all the polling data. I told him that even people in Michigan, even Michigan, opposed."

Axelrod said that Obama replied, "If we can get the automobile companies to use our leverage [public funds to take them through bankruptcy, writing off debts and some obligations to unions] to get them to rationalize their businesses [pay labor less, write off some debt] and to create cars for the 21st century, they can become a source of renewal for the manufacturing sector, so I think it's worth the risk."[7] However, Obama avoided discussing the automobile bailout in the inaugural address and offered no plan for expanding manufacturing's share of the economy.

Obama Decided Against Boldness

For the inaugural address, said David Axelrod, "I thought there needed to be real sobriety. You think of Roosevelt in 1933. You have to be at once straightforward with the American people about the magnitude of the challenge and you also want to leave them with a sense that these problems are resolvable because you don't want to leave them hopeless."[8]

Axelrod explained, "What I came to realize was that for the American people, even while they felt pummeled by this emergency, there was something larger going on, and it had been going on not for just a few years but for many years. The problem is that the march of technology tends to marginalize labor. What's striking as I went back to look at Bill Clinton's campaign speeches in '92, talking about the viability of the middle class, I realized these forces have been going on for 35, 40 years: the flattening out of wages, the explosion of technology and its impact on productivity, shareholder pressures that created globalization. All these forces had been conspiring for a very long time."

Axelrod said later that in retrospect he wished that the speech were different in two respects.[9] "The first would be to address this longer-term crisis, challenge. The second was to be more emphatic about the fact that

---

7. Axelrod, interview.
8. Axelrod, interview.
9. Axelrod may have read a fellow Chicagoan: "I had the attention of the public for nearly a year, and I taught it nothing." Saul Bellow, *Humboldt's Gift* (New York: Viking Press, 1975), 15.

it took years to get into the mess and it was going to take a long time to get out of it.

"Our campaign was very much about reclaiming the American Dream, but then we became very focused on the immediate crisis. We started gauging success based on employment. So the two things I would do differently in retrospect: I would have talked more about the long-term challenge and the short-term crisis as distinct problems."

Axelrod continued, "In terms of the tone relative to Roosevelt's male-factors of great wealth, there was an ongoing debate within the White House about that. My view was on the aggressive side and not just for political reasons but because I really felt it. If you want to find one word to sort through all the forces that are at play, one value that drives people in their analysis, it's responsibility."

He concluded, "There is a sense on the part of a lot of Americans that they work hard every day, they meet their responsibilities, they pay their bills, they take care of their families. Above them they see people who acted recklessly or worse and they are not accountable. They get bailed out, they continue to make fortunes. The same group of people feel like below them there are people who get handouts, who aren't meeting their responsibilities. That's the most primal force in American politics today."[10]

Axelrod explained Favreau started with the "responsibility" theme. But this first step headed away from any call for collective action. It tempered audacity in devising government plans for restoring wealth and income to those who had been hurt by the Great Recession. As a theme, "responsibility" did anticipate that many would oppose government-led help for the unlucky, but did not attack that problem. Axelrod made his observations well before the emergence of Donald Trump, but he saw what was coming. The disappointment of 2016 was in the unimaginable future when Obama gave his address. Instead he looked back.[11]

---

10. Ibid.
11. Trump and his European "counterparts" are a "symptom" of the "crisis of democratic liberalism." Edward Luce, *The Retreat of Western Liberalism* (London: Little, Brown, 2017), 11. The "populist right…began to steal the left's clothes…Trump…was the first Republican presidential nominee to promise to increase spending" on the safety net, whereas neoliberals would only defend, or reduce entitlements. Ibid., 101–103.

Aspiring to an ethical statement, as Roosevelt did also, Obama enumerated that which was bad: recriminations and worn-out dogmas that for far too long have strangled our politics…childish things." What else was bad? "[S]hortcuts…settling for less…leisure…seek[ing] only the pleasures of riches and fame." What was good? "[R]isk-takers…doers… makers of things."

One should grant nearly unlimited license to an inaugural addresser's rhetoric. Any utterances launched into the freezing winds that crossed the Mall needed some quotient of hot air to reach the crowd. Yet, what were the "childish" things of which Obama said we were guilty? Issuing spurious collateralized debt obligations was the sort of fraud that only an adult could concoct. What were these worn-out dogmas? Neoliberalism was one, but surely not what he meant. What risk-taking was Obama going to support? Geithner wanted to build more prudent balance sheets in the finance sector. Summers wanted consumers to spend more, on whatever pleased them, including seeking the pleasure of riches. Innovation and competition were not part of the economic recovery plan. What did Obama mean?

Similar Measures, Different Methods

Roosevelt's programmatic agenda was in large part cockamamie. The government would not really ship people from New York, Chicago, and Philadelphia to work on farms in the Dust Bowl from which the current occupants were fleeing. Raymond Moley admitted, "There was no overall plan. There were only pieces of a program and ideas that still lacked formulation."[12] Five largely incompatible schools of thought contended: liquidationists, inflationists, progressive trust-busters, national planners, and socialistic advocates of government ownership of economic activities. No economic theory prevailed in Roosevelt's councils and, in any event, Moley admitted, "I doubt that either Roosevelt or I could have passed an examination such as is required of college students in elementary economics. Certainly Roosevelt learned nothing at Groton,

---

12. Moley, *The First New Deal*, 223.

Harvard or Columbia Law School that prepared him for decisions that he had to make."[13]

However, when no one seemed to understand what was happening, Roosevelt offered an explanation, and was willing to experiment. The speech transformed Roosevelt from a winning candidate into the hero who would vanquish the monster. What Roosevelt said he would do was less important than that he inspired confidence. In the play *Henry V*, Shakespeare has Ely say to Canterbury about the new king, "We are blessed in the change." So the vast majority of Americans felt blessed to see Roosevelt replace Hoover.

Roosevelt must lead, and hence needed a direction. Therefore, on Saturday, March 18, Roosevelt and Moley sketched out the greater part of what became the Hundred Days and the First New Deal. Moley said, "If Franklin Roosevelt and I on that March day in 1933 were deficient in economic knowledge, we projected into our calculations a very broad view of the national scene and…a large measure of common sense."[14] Moley used as a framework a memorandum written right after the election by prodigious, precocious Adolf Berle, a Harvard College and Law School graduate, recreated as economist Larry Summers by means of metempsychosis. Lawyers in those halcyon days played the principal theorizing role for government policy.[15, 16]

Most of Berle's ideas ended upon the "list of the major legislative measures" that "Roosevelt dictated" as deserving priority. "These were temporary relief for the jobless and the needy, agricultural adjustment, farm- and home-debt refunding, banking reform, a Muscle Shoals setup of some kind, simplified bankruptcy procedures, and regulation of corporations."[17]

---

13. Ibid., 224.

14. Ibid., 225.

15. Berle noted that back in those days "academic economists did not soil their hands with practical questions. Application of this science is almost entirely a post–New Deal phenomenon."

16. Even then, Eric Posner and Glen Weyl noted: "economics has played virtually no role in all the major political movements of the past half-century, including civil rights, feminism, anticolonialism, the rights of sexual minorities, gun rights, antiabortion politics, and 'family values' debates." http://www.anderson.ucla.edu/faculty/sebastian.edwards/Papers%20Files/ddhop_49_1_01Edwards_Fpp.pdf

17. Eric Posner and Glen Weyl, "How Economists Became So Timid," *The Chronicle of Higher Education*, May 6, 2018, https://www.chronicle.com/article/How-Economists-Became-So-Timid/243326.

The Obama transition discussed measures strikingly similar to the "Muscle Shoals setup," which became the Tennessee Valley Authority that mobilized public-private investment to produce affordable power to Tennessee and the adjoining states that was Obama's national grid for renewable power. "Home-debt refunding" was HAMP. "Banking reform" was Dodd-Frank. "Simplified bankruptcy" was cramdown. The economic goals for Obama and Roosevelt also ran in parallel. Moley wrote, "Roosevelt stressed the raising of prices and provision for reemployment"[18]—in other words, putting people back to work, battling deflation, and raising national income for all workers. Obama's stimulus aimed at increasing employment, while Bernanke expanded the Fed balance sheet to avoid deflation.

Roosevelt's program, like Obama's, had a disappointing impact on unemployment. Raising worker incomes, both presidents discovered to their chagrin, only followed full employment. If Obama did not spend enough, Roosevelt erred more by cutting federal spending. Yet if only modestly successful in achieving his economic goals, Roosevelt effectively invented activist executive government in America. That institutional innovation alarmed business, preserved democracy. By weaving a social safety net he mitigated even the Great Recession that occurred more than seven decades later. For Obama's America, Social Security and unemployment compensation were continuing stimulus programs in themselves. As the economy shrank, they generated increased spending without new congressional action. Of course, Roosevelt's failure to provide basic healthcare to everyone bequeathed to Obama the principal post-recovery goal of his administration, the Affordable Care Act.

Roosevelt's galvanizing speech gave his agenda huge momentum. By contrast, Obama drained drama from his speech by nearly finalizing the economic recovery plan with Congress before the inauguration. He aspired to win approval for the plan by hitting its high points, but the reality of ARRA fell short of the rhetoric.

18. Ibid.

"We will build the roads and bridges…"

— His team had limited spending on this topic to about three percent of the stimulus, and as state and local governments severely cut their spending, construction spending dropped precipitously.

"…the electric grids and digital lines…"

— His team had refused to create a national transmission line siting authority, and limited broadband to less than one percent of the stimulus package.

"We'll restore science to its rightful place, and…raise healthcare's quality and lower its cost."

— Obama's administration did take guidance from science, but research funding dropped at a steady pace during his tenure. The Affordable Care Act aimed at improving most people's healthcare, but did not lower cost for most consumers.

"We will harness the sun and the winds and the soil to fuel our cars and run our factories…"

— The solar and wind tax breaks in the stimulus increased investment in renewable power and electric vehicles, and each garnered some share in their relevant markers.

"And we will transform our schools and colleges and universities to meet the demands of a new age."

— The stimulus did not tackle the student debt problem. The rest of the education agenda, especially a national curriculum, proved dubious and disagreeable to many teachers, parents, and students.

Obama did not mention the transformational, pillar-building legislation he would ask Congress to pass. That he reserved for a speech to a joint session of the House and Senate a month later, on February 24, 2009, when he asked Congress to pass bills regulating the financial industry, energy emissions, and the healthcare industry. By choosing that forum, Obama planted himself firmly in the legislative process. He did not use the inaugural address to galvanize the country behind his leadership. He was a prime minister. As such, at least until he had 60 votes in the Senate, he wanted and needed bipartisan support. Senator Minority Leader Mitch McConnell already had decided to block everything Obama wanted. In his inaugural address, Roosevelt threatened Congress. Obama chose the opposite approach, empowering his opponents. Nothing good came of that.

The president closed by calling for "a new era of responsibility—a recognition of the part of every American that we have duties to ourselves, our nation, and the world." To dramatize "responsibility"—the theme Favreau started with long before the depths of the Great Recession were perceived—he invoked an image of rowers in the same boat. He recalled George Washington's crossing of the ice-clogged Delaware River the night of Christmas Day, 1776, in order to carry out a surprise attack on the Hessian mercenaries fighting on the British side during the Revolutionary War. Emanuel Leutze's 1851 oil painting of this scene was an icon of most school curricula. One of Leutze's three versions hung in the West Wing, and perhaps Obama or Jon Favreau had seen it there, if they did not recall it from a high school history textbook. Possibly they also enjoyed the barely visible fact that the rowers in the boat included a black man. He's third from the bow, facing east.

Lieutenant James Monroe is behind Washington. He's the one with the flag. When he was inaugurated president in 1817 he lived at 2017 I Street Northwest, Washington, D.C., in a building now known as the Arts Club, because the White House had not been rebuilt after its destruction in the War of 1812. The night of his swearing in he held a ball on the second floor. My wife and I married there in 1980. For that reason, I particularly liked this portion of Obama's speech.

Obama tried to make the story relevant to people who lacked a connection to Monroe: "In this winter of our hardship...let us brave once more the icy currents, and endure what storms may come....Let it be said that...with eyes fixed on the horizon"—like Washington and Monroe—"we carried forth that great gift of freedom and delivered it safely to future generations."

Emanuel Gottlieb Leutze, Washington Crossing the Delaware, 1851.
Photo by Google Cultural Institute.

Obama's word painting of a painting illuminated a contradiction in the soul of America. By referring to freedom, Obama nodded to individual responsibility. The boat was supposed to demonstrate collective action. For most of his two terms, this brave, inspiring man could not reconcile these antipodal aspects of the country's culture. Most of the time, on most issues, he had to cross his Delawares under his own power.

Epilogue

*If I had told you eight years ago that America would reverse a
great recession, reboot our auto industry, and unleash the lon-
gest stretch of job creation in our history...if I had told you that
we would win marriage equality, and secure the right to health
insurance for another 20 million of our fellow citizens—you
might have said our sights were set a little too high.*

*But that's what we did. That's what you did. You were the
change. You answered the people's hopes, and because of you, by
almost every measure, America is a better, stronger place than it
was when we started.*

— Barack Obama, farewell address, January 10, 2017

Less than two years after assembling, Obama's advisory team began
disbanding.

Peter Orszag was first to leave, departing in the summer of 2010. He
went to work at Citigroup and later moved to a private equity firm.

Larry Summers quite reasonably might have been disappointed that
Obama reappointed Republican Ben Bernanke to run the Fed in August
of 2009, and then selected Janet Yellen for that post in 2013. In his whole
life, that job most suited him. However, unlike Orszag, Summers made
no injudicious remarks when he left the White House in December 2010,
a month after the Republican takeover of the House in the November
2010 elections. He returned to Harvard, where he taught at the Kennedy School. He joined some boards and associated with the prominent
venture capital firm Andreessen Horowitz. More than any of the others

from the Obama team, he continued to address economic issues as a public intellectual. Writing in the *Financial Times*, speaking at conferences, blogging, writing academic papers, he explained what was happening in the economy and offered advice to policymakers. In November 2013 Summers began elucidating the theory of secular stagnation, picking up on the thinking of Depression-era economist Alvin Hansen.[1]

Christy Romer returned to Berkeley in September 2010, at the beginning of the school year for her youngest child.

Obama lived up to his promise to Austan Goolsbee and selected him to be the chair of the Council of Economic Advisers succeeding Romer. In that role, Goolsbee helped Obama craft the second stimulus with the Republicans in December 2010. He returned to the University of Chicago in 2011.

Tim Geithner stayed at Treasury until after Obama won reelection. In 2013 he wrote his memoir, *Stress Test*. He taught at Yale, a haven for neoliberals. In 2014 he became president of a private equity firm.

Rahm Emanuel left the White House in September 2010, weeks before the Democrats' very bad midterm election. Pete Rouse became the new chief of staff. Emanuel got his dream job the next year. By 2017 he had twice been elected as Chicago's mayor.

Phil Schiliro departed in 2011, but returned to the White House in 2013–2014 to help save the troubled launch of the Affordable Care Act. He now lives in New Mexico.

Carol Browner became a consultant in Washington, D.C.

Joe Aldy went to the Kennedy School at Harvard.

Jason Furman stayed in the White House the full eight years, ending as chairman of the Council of Economic Advisers, and then went to Harvard, where neoliberals and neoconservatives split a dime's worth of difference in their thinking.

Lee Sachs left Treasury in 2010, Matt Kabaker in 2011.

After losing the speakership in the wake of the November 2010 elections, Nancy Pelosi remained head of the House Democrats. Harry Reid

---

1. Larry Summers, Speech, International Monetary Fund, November 8, 2013. Larry Summers, "Why Stagnation May Prove To Be the New Normal," *Financial Times*, December 15, 2013, https://www.ft.com/content/87cb15ea-5d1a-11e3-a558-00144feabdc0.

lost his position as majority leader of the Senate when the Republicans took control of that chamber in the November 2014 election. He stayed as minority leader until he retired in January 2017. Henry Waxman did not seek reelection in 2014. Ed Markey was elected to the Senate from Massachusetts in 2014. Barney Frank did not seek reelection in 2012.

Barack Obama won reelection in 2012 by a popular vote margin of 51 percent to Romney's 47 percent. It was the first time since Franklin Roosevelt's reelection in 1944 that a Democrat was reelected with a majority of the popular vote. Critical to his victory was Obama's second stimulus—the deal he negotiated with the Republicans after they won the House in November 2010.[2] Romney was shocked that he had not been able to defeat Obama. The economy performed just well enough in the nick of political time, with unemployment dropping below eight percent late in 2012, and Democratic identity politics produced enough turnout to reelect Obama.

At the end of his two terms, the administration's economic recovery plan and the country's natural resilience began to provide a rising standard of living for many Americans. Obama's healthcare reform mattered to many. The climate change strategy was not optimal, but some progress in building the clean power platform occurred. Housing frustrated Obama, but in 2017 nominal values finally returned to pre-recession levels after a decade-long slump.

Whereas his successor feasted on division and displayed many character flaws, most people admired Obama and his family. During his presidency, Obama obtained popular support and led by dint of personality, as modern presidents must do. He was rational, honest, compassionate, a little aloof, and a bit guarded. Democrats liked him a lot. Democratic congressmen from districts won from Republicans in 2006 and 2008 supported him on the stimulus, healthcare, and climate change.[3] Democratic Senators sided with Obama on 95 percent of non-unanimous votes in 2009–2010.[4]

2. David M. Herszenhorn and Jackie Calmes, "Obama and G.O.P. Agree on Tax Cuts," *New York Times*, December 6, 2010, http://www.nytimes.com/2010/12/07/us/politics/07cong.html.

3. George C. Edwards, *Overreach: Leadership in the Obama Presidency* (Princeton: Princeton University Press, 2015), 173.

4. Ibid., 174.

During the Trump presidency, Obama could reasonably brood about what motivated the Republican decision not to cooperate on any part of his limited but still meaningful reform agenda: not immigration or infrastructure, not Obamacare or climate.[5] He might recall the mad, virulent reaction to what he said about Harvard's Skip Gates when the police accosted that African-American professor on his own doorstep. Obama accurately noted that police typically help white people get into their own homes when they have misplaced their keys. The media treated that sympathy with the homeowner as bias against cops. He had to serve the policeman and Gates beers on the White House lawn to settle the furor.

Obama suffered other insults, generally with remarkable grace. High on that list was Senate Majority Leader Mitch McConnell's refusal in 2016 to confirm Merrick Garland to the Supreme Court. Another was Trump's long questioning of Obama's place of birth. Certainly neither his race nor his honorable character enabled Obama to win bipartisan support for most of his agenda.

From the moment of the election victory in 2008, everyone on the transition team understood the problem of obtaining Republican support for Obama's agenda. In an interview on September 18, 2017, Larry Summers said that "at the first meeting with President Obama, when the question was asked how much fiscal stimulus we should have, I said… 'We need to get as much as we possibly can and so…I was frustrated when the political constraints held the number down….I was frustrated as one sometimes is in government by the political constraints, but they don't elect technocrats. They elect presidents, and they elect congressional officials."[6]

---

5. Ibid., 159–60. The Republicans in the House voted 171 to four to block the second half of TARP funds being released to Treasury. They voted 177 to zero against the stimulus. They voted 173 to three against the conference report on financial regulation, unanimously against healthcare reform and the 2010 FY budget, 167 to seven against mortgage modification, and 169 to eight against climate change mitigation.

6. David Beckworth, "Is Larry Summers a Fan of Nominal GDP Level Targeting?" Seeking Alpha, September 19, 2017, https://seekingalpha.com/article/4107857-larry-summers-fan-nominal-gdp-level-targeting.

Summers explained that the "constraints" came from "people who were worried about sticker shock around big budget deficits, people who were worried about what the impact on market psychology would be of large budget deficits, issues of how fast the government could mobilize to spend money in an efficient way."[7] Unfortunately, the December 15, 2008, memorandum that he gave Obama effectively articulated these concerns. None proved valid. Instead, the most serious issue proved to be the failure of the economy to approach potential output for many years. Obama's challenge was not only Congress, but also the limitations of the advice he acted upon.

The technocrats' advice did not suitably fit the situation. Obama's "technocrats" can reasonably contend that Congress would not have passed a bigger, better economic recovery plan. However, they did not tell him or anyone that the economic recovery plan they pushed him to adopt would produce such disappointing growth.

To the degree possible, advisers should keep decision makers informed. In the winter of 1963–64, Defense Secretary Robert McNamara should have told new President Lyndon Johnson that either the United States had to occupy South Vietnam with a million troops or negotiate a treaty with North Vietnam. After November 11, 2001, Defense Secretary Donald Rumsfeld should have told President George W. Bush that an invasion of Iraq would require an occupation by a million soldiers for at least a decade. In November, December, and January the economic "technocrats" needed to tell Obama quite specifically how shortchanging the stimulus would have dire consequences. Especially as a more dire picture emerged, they needed to update their predictions.

Corrections, however, can make advisers appear wrong. They have to admit their inability to guess accurately. That asks a lot of them. They can lose their positions that way, and Johnson, Bush, and Obama might still have taken the decisions that defined their legacy.

In 2018 Summers summed up his perspective on this history in a conversation with me: "The stimulus was as big as the political traffic would bear. There was tremendous Republican opposition and significant

7. Summers, interview.

Democratic fear of huge deficits. The Senate did not want the stimulus to go longer than two years in any case.

"Christy Romer and I thought there was no risk even from excessive stimulus, meaning more than the economy might have needed to start growing again, but Tim Geithner and Peter Orszag thought that if we appeared insufficiently focused on the deficit, damage might be done to business confidence in ways that would negatively affect the recovery. I did not share those views, but the disagreement was moot given the limits on what could be achieved politically.

"There has been much subsequent discussion of whether there should have been more infrastructure investment. If there had been a desire to do a longer fiscal stimulus—beyond two years, in order to accommodate infrastructure planning—that would have been desirable. But the Senate did not have that desire. And despite Joe Biden's herculean efforts, it was not administratively feasible to have spent more money than we did in the two years planned for the stimulus.

"Where the political judgment of the incoming administration went wrong, and I shared this error, was in believing that if there was a need for more economic stimulus it would not be difficult to legislate to that end. In fact deficit hysteria was so strong that this judgment proved incorrect.

"If we had known this judgment was incorrect I would have been more uncomfortable in the winter of 2008–2009 with the size and length of the stimulus. But I don't know that the outcome would have been different because I have not heard to this day a political tactic that would have obtained a bigger stimulus."[8]

In December 2017 Paul Krugman calculated that underutilization of capacity during Obama's two terms amounted to $8 trillion.[9] If the economy had rapidly recovered, and been stimulated to specific objectives, then in Obama's tenure new investment could have shifted the entire economy to five platforms: clean and cheap power, clean and

8. Summers, interview.
9. Paul Krugman, "Pessimism and Paralysis in the Aftermath of the Financial Crisis," *New York Times*, December 9, 2017, https://www.nytimes.com/2017/12/09/opinion/pessimism-and-paraly-sis-in-the-aftermath-of-the-financial-crisis.html.

cheap water, good sewage, ubiquitous broadband, and repaired highways, bridges, and dams. Eight trillion dollars buys a lot of infrastructure and services. If that investment-driven growth had occurred, the median household income in 2017 would be about $70,000 per year instead of a little below the $60,000 range. Not only would the economy have been absolutely bigger as Obama's successor took office, but also it would have had the potential to grow still bigger in the future.[10]

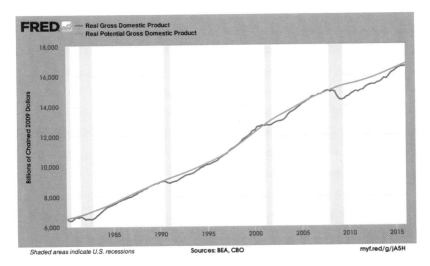

"FRED®" charts ©Federal Reserve Bank of St. Louis. 2015. All rights reserved. All "FRED®" charts appear courtesy of Federal Reserve Bank of St. Louis. http://research.stlouisfed.org/fred2/.

Bernanke thought the recession was "almost certainly the worst in human history."[11] However, in 2008 Paulson, Geithner, Bernanke, and other veterans of Wall Street alarmed Bush and Obama excessively about the risk of a financial system meltdown. The steps they took before the election, with Obama's help, ensured that nothing like one-third or one-fourth unemployed would occur. Still, they remained stunned,

10. "The country has rebounded in many ways, but is also more unequal, less vibrant, less productive, poorer, and sicker than it would have been had the crisis been less severe."
Annie Lowrey, "The Great Recession Is Still with Us," *The Atlantic*, December 01, 2017, https://www.theatlantic.com/business/archive/2017/12/great-recession-still-with-us/547268/.
11. Bernanke, *The Courage to Act*, 336.

fearful, intently focused on restoring profitability to the finance sector. They convinced Obama that a run on another bank or two might cause the entire system of financing capitalism to collapse. Wall Street might topple. If it did then all Western economies would crash together. The Chinese might be the only winners. The emergence of a global Chinese empire could follow. Americans could see unemployment rise about 20 percent. The country might lose its role as the global idea factory. The dollar might not be the global currency. Then the United States could only borrow as much as the Chinese would permit.

Out of fear, the Bush administration officials and the Clintonite advisers wanted Obama to take responsibility for the American and global economy. This was not what Axelrod meant by "responsibility" as the big theme in politics. In their view, the new young president had a duty to bolster the old order. Reform could wait. Contradicting their close-mouthed behavior before the Lehman bankruptcy, they scared Congress, the markets, and the Democrats.

Pressured by these experts, campaigning around the clock, Obama adopted the unpopular economic measure of TARP. He chose to maintain continuity with Bush administration decision-making during the inevitably hectic transition. His Clintonian advisers gave him no other alternative.

Daschle and others convinced him that his legacy lay in legislative reforms. Democratic think tanks had worked on these measures for years. Their neoliberal dogmas presented Obama no appealing choices. The healthcare and climate change reforms were unpopular and unhelpful to the middle class.

Obama thought that as a hero of his time he must complete healthcare reform efforts because others had failed in the past. He must pass cap-and-trade because environmentalists wanted a price on carbon to save the world. These intrusive, complex, and legislatively difficult bills ended up being monuments to what political scientist George Edwards called "overreach."[12] Democrats called them noble. The price for that self-regard ran high. Obama would have done better to pursue legislation and

12. Edwards, *Overreach*.

regulation that changed market structure, conduct, and performance with the goal of improving everyone's standard of living in the immediate present. He should have put more audacious measures in the stimulus and linked them to smaller, more manageable, more numerous, and more popular legislative measures.

In an eerie political version of the equations for time that run equally well backward or forward, after his two terms Obama seemed to be just as much responsible for the failures of George W. Bush (two unwinnable wars, economic catastrophe) as for the process that somehow made unspeakable Donald Trump the president. A kind of rough justice supported this illogical accusation. Obama did slide into the Bush administration's embrace of the Wall Street plutocracy. Eight years later he delivered, like an obstetrician handing a baby to a feckless parent, a spanking good economy that Trump fed with candy. In the long gestation of Obama's tenure, the middle class stewed, fumed, and then erupted at the ballot box in November 2016.

As the financial crisis receded, the economics profession turned to vigorous debate about itself. The Chicago School held that the efficient market hypothesis and rational expectations never aspired to predict stock prices and therefore could not be deemed inaccurate simply because they had not foreseen the crisis.[13] Another view took as self-evident the irrationality of market behavior in 2008 and from that concluded that behavioral economics should be ascendant.[14] This elite navel-gazing produced no new policy guidance for government.

Of course Hillary Clinton, the echt neoliberal, still won the popular vote in 2016. The "demos" should have prevailed. However, Clinton lost the Electoral College in significant part because of the disappointed expectations of the middle class, and, it seems, white backlash against the identity groups composing the Democratic party. Voters expected

13. See John Cassidy, "Interview with Richard Thaler," *New Yorker*, June 20, 2017, https://www.newyorker.com/news/john-cassidy/interview-with-richard-thaler.

14. See Robert Shiller generally, e.g. Robert J. Shiller, *Finance and the Good Society* (Princeton, NJ: Princeton University Press, 2012) and Robert J. Shiller, *Irrational Exuberance* (Princeton, NJ: Princeton University Press, 2001).

Middle-class areas were more likely to move away from Democrats in 2016

Change in Democratic share of the presidential vote, 2008-2016

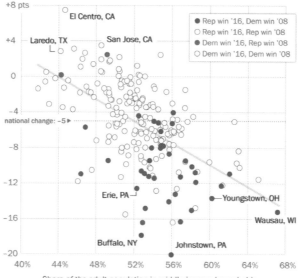

El Centro, CA

Laredo, TX   San Jose, CA

- ● Rep win '16, Dem win '08
- ○ Rep win '16, Rep win '08
- ● Dem win '16, Rep win '08
- ○ Dem win '16, Dem win '08

national change: −5 ▶

Erie, PA   Youngstown, OH

Wausau, WI

Buffalo, NY   Johnstown, PA

Share of the adult population in middle-income households

Note: Middle-income adults live in households with incomes two-thirds to double the national median size-adjusted household income, about $42,000 to $125,000 annually in 2014 for a three-person household. Incomes in each metropolitan area are adjusted for the cost of living in the area relative to the national average cost of living.

Source: Middle-class data from Pew Research Center analysis of 2014 American Community Survey (IPUMS). Election data from Pew Research Center analysis of 2008 and 2016 county-level election returns.

PEW RESEARCH CENTER

Graph 1 from "GOP Gained Ground in Middle-Class Communities in 2016," Pew Research Center, Washington, D.C., December 2016, http://www.pewresearch.org/fact-tank/2016/12/08/ gop-gained-ground-in-middle-class-communities-in-2016/. Used with permission.

more from the incumbent Democratic president, and they rejected his chosen successor.

In the event of the next crisis, again the government will have to choose between restoring the profitability of the financial industry or more directly helping the millions of families harmed by an economic downturn. Neoliberalism will argue again for the *ancien régime*. Neoconservatives will call for a *caudillo*.

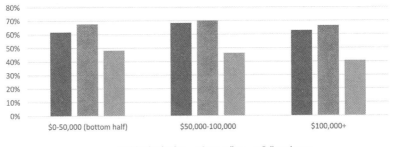

Percent of white voters who supported Donald Trump

$0-50,000 (bottom half) $50,000-100,000 $100,000+

■ High school or less   ■ Some college   ■ College degree

Data from American National Election Study. Figure created by Nicholas Carnes and Noam Lupu.

Nicholas Carnes and Noam Lupu, "It's Time to Bust the Myth: Most Trump Voters Were Not Working Class," The Washington Post, June 5, 2017, https://www.washingtonpost.com/news/ monkey-cage/wp/2017/06/05/its-time-to-bust-the-myth-most-trump-voters-were-not-working-class/?utm_term=. a81ff41f7760 (accessed 13 Feb. 2018). Used with permission.

What will progressives propose? They might learn this from 2008–2009: in a crisis, use public authority to increase the income and wealth of most Americans. Do what is mathematically certain to achieve reasonable, broad-based growth. In light of developments in the Trump years, this approach will call for dramatic shifts in spending and the creation of new institutions. The total federal debt load will be so high and government institutions so severely undermined that only sweeping structural reform will renew the peoples' trust in government as an agent of collective, honest action.

Berkeley professor Wendy Brown writes that neoconservatism longs for the state to set "the moral-religious compass for society, and indeed for the world."[15] Neoliberalism causes its opponents to argue for "an anachronistic welfare statism." Brown wonders whether under this pressure "the democratic dream—the rule of the demos for the demos—is finished." She asks, "How might the extraordinary powers that construct and organize collective life today be democratized?"

15. Wendy Brown, "American Nightmare: Neoliberalism, Neoconservatism, and De-Democratization," *Political Theory*, December 1, 2006, doi:10.7312/blau17412-078.

In pursuit of a democratic ideal, these pages plead for platforms that benefit the public at large. I argue for institutions that can uphold and extend collectively determined values and beliefs. This is, after all, what the Internet was supposed to be, before it became a tool, somehow at the same time, for both government control and complete disruption. The goal, which technology and politics can still advance toward, is a fully participant-driven and effectively functioning democracy. The purpose of government still is to guarantee both the freedom of everything and the wellbeing of all.

Platforms by definition encourage collective solutions, but do not compel everyone to participate. Nor do they spring from a donor-donee relationship, like old school welfare. The fundamental premise is that collective problems of huge scale—like caring simultaneously for the planet and billions of people—require agents of the common good to create and share widely, universally the benefits of a high and rising standard of living. Government, consortiums of nonprofits, and leagues of well-intended people, can cooperate to be such agents. Corporations that wish to abandon their unconditioned pursuit of profit for their shareholders might also contend for this role, or at least support such platform creation by others.

Nor are platforms merely technical aggregations of goods and services. Instead they include agreed-upon means for pursuing goals. A working republic, where every vote mattered equally and candidates sought a majority of the whole electorate, would be such a platform. A global trade treaty to exclude from global commerce carbon emissions–intense products would be another. So too would be a method to rid the world of nuclear weapons. As to any important problem, the "rule of the demos for the demos" will fashion a good plan for collective action.

A decade after the Lehman-catalyzed financial crisis, the academy swilled around a mixture of two contrary beliefs: people did not behave as predictive models dictated, and the models prized by neoliberalism were right enough in the long term. Neither led to useful advice for politicians. Instead, cut adrift in the current of events, established political leaders in many countries succumbed to challengers who used blame and growing hate to explain how and why western governments reacted to the Great Recession by helping the rich and hurting the middle class.

Using the many modes created by the saturating new media, the paradigmatic Donald Trump, heard and imitated around the world, blamed immigration, global economic competition, and elites (those who transmitted the ideological DNA of neoliberalism) for underemployment, low wages, lack of savings, anxiety, and envy. Although he appalled at least a slight majority of Americans, he offered more comprehensible causation than did neoliberals. In truth, the prescriptions of Democratic neoliberalism had proved disappointing as ways to address the Great Recession.

The advice given to Obama was regrettable in at least five important ways. (1) The economists spoke too soon, repeatedly. They did not accurately diagnose the problems they were bent on solving. (2) Frightened by the extent of the Lehman effect, they urged inadequately considered government help for financial firms. (3) Consumed by belief in the importance of urgency, they rejected programs that would have required possibly time-consuming political advocacy. (4) They aimed at a very modest economic recovery. (5) When all knew, early in January 2009, that the situation was worse than they thought and their remedies far less salutary than predicted, they chose to change the topic rather than explain reality to Congress, much less the country.

The Bush administration set up Obama and his team. Treasury Secretary Paulson must have underestimated the negative effect of Lehman's crash, but he knew the event would occur, knew it would be bad, knew the Democratic Congress would not stop him from stopping it, and quite consciously decided to let it happen. Fed Chair Bernanke and future Treasury Secretary Geithner collaborated in these decisions. All three counted on Obama and his advisers to fix what they broke. That is why they let it break: they wanted the fix, also known as the bailout but more properly understood as the prioritization of financial recovery over economic recovery, put in place by the Democratic faction that controlled Congress.

This course of conduct ran from the Bear bailout in March to September 2008. It was preceded by willful blindness in regard of the real, as opposed to financial, economy. For the better part of the two previous years, all the knowledgeable people in the Bush administration understood that the middle class was suffering a severely increasing number of economic afflictions, especially including the erasure of savings and the decline of good jobs. The chief evidence was the decision to obtain legislation authorizing government takeover, and infinite financing authority for the two principal underwriters of home mortgages, Fannie Mae and Freddie Mac. Secondary evidence consisted of the Bush stimulus package. But at no time did the Republican policy shapers contemplate effective, long-term measures that would help the middle class cope with the downturn in housing, the labor market, or long-term economic prospects, also known as hope itself. If Obama rode a wave of discontent into office, he and his advisers also failed to develop such proposals.

By the middle of Trump's first term, some Democratic leaders attributed his success to racism. They thought the 40 percent plus of Americans who fervently supported Trump either were out-and-out prejudiced against anyone with a tinge of color in their skin, whether of African, Hispanic, or Asian origin, or they suffered from false consciousness, believing incorrectly that members of other groups were prized by Democrats above those whose ancestors had come to America on the Mayflower or, more likely, some people-packed freighter from Genoa, Hamburg, Dublin, or Glasgow. This explanation risked suicide in political terms, given the level of whiteness in the swing states that the antiquated Electoral College system makes critical to the choice of president. It also probably mistook symptom for cause. Most Americans in the classes ranging from lower-middle to upper-middle in fact had suffered a decade that disproved the theory of progress loosely known as the American Dream. They had sound ground to believe that the Obama decisions had not ameliorated their troubles much, if at all. If middle-class white males and females who voted for Trump instead of Clinton in 2016 tended to believe that Democratic policies of the previous decade did not much benefit people like them, they were not wrong.

Admittedly, Trump, like all Republican presidents going back to Richard Nixon, explained the world to these voters in racial terms. He brought out the worst in his people. Democrats did an injustice to many, however, by ascribing racism to all Trump supporters, and even if that might be part of an explanation for Trump's Electoral College triumph, Democrats erred by believing that moral superciliousness would generate useful policies if and when they again obtained political power at the state or federal level.

In the event that the wheel of time spins Democrats out of defeat, thinking about what to do then should start with thinking about the purpose of political power. It is to do something, not to enable capitalism to work efficiently. Government need not be anti-capitalist, or insistent on control as in the case of China. However, it must deliver benefits to most everyone, with special emphasis on providing what capitalism does not. In the context of 2008–2009, the government needed to create a high and rising standard of living for all Americans. If the cost had been public spending at two or three times the level set by the stimulus, retrospectively everyone can see that neither inflation nor financial instability would have offset the gains.

This improvement should have been centered on the same pillars of reform Barack Obama had started to discuss from his spectacular 2004 convention speech. College education should have cost people next to nothing. Health care should have been extremely affordable for almost everyone, and especially for those with severe conditions, it should have been guaranteed. Corporations should have been practically forced to increase investment by tax code revisions (which should never have been left to Trump). Public money should have replaced coal with renewables, delivering electricity at the same or lower rates to everyone. Federal dollars, coupled with private investment, needed to rebuild the platforms of power, transportation, sewage, water, and communications in every city and town, regardless of the historic assignment of most of these public good problems to state and local government or exclusively the private sector. All Americans should have been given a jumpstart on long-term saving in stock market indices instead of housing, while those whose savings already were in housing should have received great deals for refinancing by a government that did not scruple to decide who had borrowed too much to buy their dream house.

Most importantly, the Obama team should have insisted that the entire economic recovery package not be blown through Congress in a few weeks at the beginning of 2009. Instead, the long duration of rebuilding America needed to be put on the mantelpiece. Obama's inaugural address should not have assigned responsibility to everyone in the country for the cavalcade of woes that were certain to unroll in the coming months. Instead, his government, like Franklin Roosevelt's in 1933, needed to seize responsibility for the fixes, and demonstrate that it had the will to find a way to make everyone better off in the short and long term.

Going forward, all the problems that needed solving in 2008–2009 are for the most part still begging for good governmental policies. Little that Trump has done or promises to do will give Americans better ways to get to work, cleaner water to drink, or less sewage in rivers. His administration will make climate change more severe and the urgency of battling rising waters even greater. His policies will leave healthcare less improved for most people than Obama's good bill had intended to do. His judiciary will deny most people redress for most social injuries.

Progress, then, beckons all Americans to think of new ways to deal with still-difficult circumstances. Would-be candidates especially need to be bolder than the restrictions of neoliberalism permitted Obama's advisers to be. They also have to be willing to experiment, to be flexible when the situation changes, to be open to new people and new ideas not previously sanctioned by neoliberalism.

As Americans never-endingly struggle to define the country's common culture, they will see with increasingly clarity that the bookends of his predecessor and successor put Obama in a most favorable light. He always stood for inclusion, tolerance, and unity. He worked hard, acted with integrity, stood for high-minded principles.

Barack Obama's election also redeemed in part the bondsmen whose history is the saddest part of the history of America. Race is still the tragedy of the American narrative, but thanks to Obama, and his family, a world beyond color differences can be more clearly seen. In contrast too with scandals that diminish our sense of honor, Obama lifted us all by running the most decent administration in modern American history.

Under terrible pressure, with limited knowledge, and boxed in by doctrines unsuited for this crisis, Barack Obama thoughtfully made more critical decisions prior to his inauguration than any president in American history, with the exception of Abraham Lincoln. He acted with courage, conviction, and compassion. Presidents for years to come will have difficulty measuring up to his rare combination of grace and acumen. His experience, however, should teach again the wisdom Abraham Lincoln shared with Congress on December 1, 1862: "The dogmas of the quiet past are inadequate to the stormy present. The occasion is piled high with difficulty, and we must rise—with the occasion. As our case is new, so we must think anew, and act anew. We must disenthrall ourselves, and then we shall save our country."

*The Federal Communications Commission staff awarded each commissioner
a sash. Miss Congeniality as applied to me has a touch of satire. 1996.*

*Former President Bill Clinton tells a joke to me (middle) and a
business colleague before giving a speech in Chicago. 2006.*

Vice President Al Gore asks me (foreground) and Greg
Simon to list all the vice presidents in order. We laugh.
Air Force Two, en route to Buenos Aires. 1994.

Senator Barack Obama with my wife Elizabeth
Katz and me at a D.C. fundraiser. 2008.

Acknowledgments

More than four dozen people made this book possible by graciously talking to me and my tape recorder about the critical decisions made by Barack Obama. I had their words transcribed, selected portions for insertion into the book, and asked each person to review their remarks. Upon reflection, some chose different words, others amplified their statements, and a few decided they had said what they wanted to say on their first try. Only one decided he did not want to be quoted, and he is not mentioned in the book. To my mind, all the quoted persons are honorable people who acted in the best interest of the American people, under unimaginable pressure and with terrible urgency. If the book contends that some regret is in order, the actors themselves may share the same feeling to some extent on some issues. Anyone who with the benefit of hindsight does not wish to have taken some hard decisions differently is probably not as reflective as a good life requires. In my judgment, the quoted persons and others involved in Barack Obama's defining decisions, including the president himself, should be very proud of their public service and their accomplishments. I am very grateful that so many allowed me to memorialize their thinking and decisions. Their names are revealed, of course, in the pages.

Among my many friends who encouraged me to write this book, I thank in particular Richard Tedlow, my dear friend since junior year in college. In innumerable hours of perambulation, this marvelous teacher, writer, and professional historian literally walked me through the book. Many words and thoughts came from him, as did constant support. I could not have discovered what I think is true without his help.

Other great friends who read the manuscript, often more than once, and without exception provided crucial insights and comments include Michael Buas, Paul de Sa, Tom Craft, Ira Fishman, Eddie Lazarus, Blair Levin, Ann Logan, Bill Young, and Mark Young. Son Nathaniel Hundt and sister Lindsey Hundt also were great sources of inspiration and editorial suggestions.

I am very grateful to my agents Jeff Posternak and Andrew Wylie. Their advice was invaluable, and I am the perfect example of how kindly they treat all their authors, regardless of sales or honors.

My assistant Grace Choi provided acute observations, diligent corrections, and a keen sense for how to get things done. When I say that my assistant Stephanie Herndon truly made this possible, I mean that managing the manuscript through dozens of iterations for two years with never a word of complaint was an act of personal and professional kindness for which I am deeply thankful. My publisher and long-ago friend from our college newspaper team, Arthur Klebanoff, was a fount of good advice and moral support. I thank the editorial team of Melissa Flamson, Megan Hustad, and Eva Talmadge for punctilious exactitude and useful comments.

Bibliography

ABSHIRE, David M. *Triumphs and Tragedies of the Modern Presidency: Seventy-Six Case Studies in Presidential Leadership*. Westport, CT: Praeger, 2001.

AKERLOF, George A., and Rachel E. Kranton. *Identity Economics: How Our Identities Shape Our Work, Wages, and Well-Being*. Princeton, NJ: Princeton University Press, 2011.

ALTER, Jonathan. *The Center Holds: Obama and His Enemies*. New York: Simon & Schuster, 2014.

ALTER, Jonathan. *The Promise: President Obama, Year One*. New York: Simon & Schuster, 2011.

ASHBERY, John. "Two Scenes." In *Some Trees*. New Haven, CT: Yale University Press, 1956.

AUDEN, W. H. "The Fall of Rome." In *Another Time*. New York: Random House, 1940.

AUDEN, W. H. "September 1, 1939." In *Another Time*. New York: Random House, 1940.

AXELROD, David. *Believer: My Forty Years in Politics*. New York: Penguin Putnam Inc, 2016.

BAIR, Sheila. *Bull by the Horns: Fighting to Save Main Street from Wall Street and Wall Street from Itself*. New York: Simon & Schuster Paperbacks, 2013.

BALL, Laurence. "The Fed and Lehman Brothers." NBER Working Paper. No. 22410. July 2016. http://www.econ2.jhu.edu/People/Ball/Lehman.pdf.

BAROFSKY, Neil M. *Bailout: An Inside Account of How Washington Abandoned Main Street While Rescuing Wall Street*. New York: Free Press, 2013.

BEATTY, Paul. *The Sellout*. New York: Farrar, Straus & Giroux, 2015.

BECKWORTH, David. "Larry Summers on Secular Stagnation, Fiscal Stimulus, and Fed Policy." Podcast. *Macro Musings*. September 18, 2017, March 21, 2018. https://seekingalpha.com/article/4107857-larry-summers-fan-nominal-gdp-level-targeting.

BERNANKE, Ben S. *Courage to Act: a Memoir of a Crisis and Its Aftermath*. New York: Norton, 2017.

BLINDER, Alan S. *After the Music Stopped: the Financial Crisis, the Response, and the Work Ahead*. New York: Penguin Books, 2014.

BLINDER, Alan S., and Janet Louise Yellen. *The Fabulous Decade: Macroeconomic Lessons from the 1990s*. New York: Century Foundation Press, 2001.

BLINDER, Alan S. *Hard Heads, Soft Hearts: Tough-Minded Economics for a Just Society*. Boston: Addison-Wesley, 1995.

BOHAN, Caren. "Obama Seeks to Counter Anti-Business Image." Reuters. June 27, 2008. https://www.reuters.com/article/us-usa-politics-obama-economy/obama-seeks-to-counter-anti-business-image-idUSN2732916620080627.

BOOKSTABER, Richard. *The End of Theory: Financial Crises, the Failure of Economics, and the Sweep of Human Interaction*. Princeton, NJ: Princeton University Press, 2017.

BURKE, Maureen. "People in Economics: The $787 Billion Question: Maureen Burke Profiles Christina Romer, Former Chair of the U.S. Council of Economic Advisers." *Finance & Development* 50, no.1 (March 2013).

CANNON, Lou. *President Reagan: The Role of a Lifetime*. New York: PublicAffairs, 2003.

CARO, Robert A. *The Passage of Power: The Years of Lyndon Johnson*. New York: Knopf, 2012.

CASE, Anne, and Angus Deaton. "Mortality and Morbidity in the 21st Century." Brookings Papers on Economic Activity (BPEA) Conference drafts. March 23–24, 2017.

CASSIDY, John. *How Markets Fail the Logic of Economic Calamities.* New York: Penguin Books, 2010.

CECCHETTI, Stephen G., and Kermit L. Schoenholtz. "Looking Back: The Financial Crisis Began 10 Years Ago This Week." Money and Banking. August 7, 2017. https://www.moneyandbanking.com/commentary/2017/8/6/looking-back-the-financial-crisis-began-10-years-ago-this-week.

CHAIT, Jonathan. *Audacity: How Barack Obama Defied His Critics and Created a Legacy That Will Prevail.* New York: Custom House, 2017.

CHINN, Menzie David., and Jeffry A. Frieden. *Lost Decades: The Making of America's Debt Crisis and the Long Recovery.* New York: Norton, 2012.

CLARK, Christopher M. *The Sleepwalkers: How Europe Went to War in 1914.* New York: Harper Perennial, 2014.

CLINTON, Hillary. "Hillary's First Joint Interview– next to Bill Clinton in 1992." *60 Minutes.* CBS. January 26, 1992. Television.

CLINTON, Hillary. "Making Hillary an Issue." *Nightline.* ABC. March 26, 1992. Television.

COHEN, Stephen S., and J. Bradford. DeLong. *Concrete Economics: The Hamilton Approach to Economic Growth and Policy.* Boston: Harvard Business Review Press, 2016.

CONARD, Edward. *Unintended Consequences: Why Everything You've Been Told about the Economy Is Wrong.* New York: Portfolio/Penguin, 2013.

CONTI-BROWN, Peter. *The Power and Independence of the Federal Reserve.* Princeton, NJ: Princeton University Press, 2017.

CORN, David. *Showdown: The Inside Story of How Obama Fought Back against Boehner, Cantor, and the Tea Party.* New York: William Morrow, 2012.

COWEN, Tyler. *Complacent Class: The Self-Defeating Quest for the American Dream.* New York: Picador, 2018.

COWEN, Tyler. "Is There a Rawlsian Argument for Redistribution as a Form of Social Insurance?," MarginalRevolution. September 23, 2017, 12:18 am. http://marginalrevolution.com/marginalrevolution/2017/09/rawlsian-argument-redistribution-form-social-insurance.html.

COYLE, Diane. *GDP: A Brief but Affectionate History*. Princeton, NJ: Princeton University Press, 2015.

DALY, Peter H., Michael Watkins, and Cate Reavis. *The First 90 Days in Government: Critical Success Strategies for New Public Managers at All Levels*. Boston: Harvard Business School Press, 2006.

DEATON, Angus. *The Great Escape: Health, Wealth, and the Origins of Inequality*. Princeton, NJ: Princeton University Press, 2015.

DONALDSON, Gordon, and Jay W. Lorsch. *Decision Making at the Top: The Shaping of Strategic Direction*. New York: Basic Books, 1985.

DOSTOYEVSKY, Fyodor. *Crime and Punishment*. Translated by Jessie Coulson. Oxford: Oxford University Press, 2008.

DREZNER, Daniel W. *The System Worked: How the World Stopped Another Great Depression*. Oxford: Oxford University Press, 2016.

DRUCKER, Peter F. *The Effective Executive: The Definitive Guide to Getting the Right Things Done*. New York: HarperBusiness, 2017.

DUNBAR, Nicholas. *The Devil's Derivatives: The Untold Story of the Slick Traders and Hapless Regulators Who Almost Blew Up Wall Street*. Boston: Harvard Business Press, 2011.

EDELMAN, Murray J. *The Symbolic Uses of Politics*. Champaign, IL: University of Illinois Press, 1985.

EDWARDS, George C. *On Deaf Ears: The Limits of the Bully Pulpit*. New Haven, CT: Yale University Press, 2008.

EDWARDS, George C. *Overreach: Leadership in the Obama Presidency*. Princeton, NJ: Princeton University Press, 2015.

EDWARDS, George C. *The Strategic President: Persuasion and Opportunity in Presidential Leadership*. Princeton, NJ: Princeton University Press, 2012.

EICHENGREEN, Barry J. *Hall of Mirrors: The Great Depression, the Great Recession, and the Uses—and Misuses—of History*. Oxford: Oxford University Press, 2016.

EINSTEIN, Albert. "To Max Born. 3 March 1947." In *The Born-Einstein Letters 1916–1955: Friendship, Politics and Physics in Uncertain Times*. New York: Macmillan, 2005.

EMANUEL, Ezekiel J. *Reinventing American Healthcare: How the Affordable Care Act Will Improve Our Terribly Complex, Blatantly Unjust,*

Outrageously Expensive, Grossly Inefficient, Error Prone System. New York: PublicAffairs, 2015.

THE FINANCIAL CRISIS INQUIRY REPORT: Final Report of the National Commission on the Causes of the Financial and Economic Crisis in the United States. Washington, DC: Government Printing Office, 2011.

FLORIDA, Richard. *The Great Reset: How the Post-Crash Economy Will Change the Way We Live and Work.* New York: HarperCollins, 2011.

FRANK, Barney. *Frank: A Life in Politics from the Great Society to Same-Sex Marriage.* New York: Picador, 2016.

FREEDMAN, David H. *Wrong: Why Experts* Keep Failing Us—and How to Know When Not to Trust Them.* New York: Little Brown and Company, 2010.

FREIDEL, Frank. *Franklin D. Roosevelt: Launching the New Deal.* New York: Little, Brown, 1952.

FROHMAN, Dov. *Leadership the Hard Way: Why Leadership Can't Be Taught and How You Can Learn It Anyway.* Hoboken, NJ: John Wiley & Sons, 2015.

GALBRAITH, James K. *The End of Normal: The Great Crisis and the Future of Growth.* New York: Simon & Schuster Paperbacks, 2015.

GARNAUT, Ross, and David Llewellyn-Smith. *The Great Crash of 2008.* Melbourne: Melbourne University Publishing, 2009.

GARROW, David. *Rising Star: The Making of Barack Obama.* New York: William Morrow, 2018.

GEITHNER, Timothy. *Stress Test: Reflections on Financial Crises.* London: Random House UK, 2015.

GHOSH, Amitav. *The Great Derangement: Climate Change and the Unthinkable.* Chicago: The University of Chicago Press, 2017.

GOODWIN, Doris Kearns. *Team of Rivals: The Political Genius of Abraham Lincoln.* New York: Penguin, 2013.

GORTON, Gary. *Misunderstanding Financial Crises: Why We Don't See Them Coming.* New York: Oxford University Press, 2012.

GORTON, Gary. *Slapped by the Invisible Hand: The Panic of 2007.* New York: Oxford University Press, 2010.

GRABELL, Michael. *Money Well Spent?: The Truth behind the Trillion Dollar Stimulus, the Biggest Economic Recovery Plan in History.* New York: PublicAffairs, 2012.

GRAEBER, David. *Debt: The First 5,000 Years.* New York: Melville House, 2014.

GREENE, Robert, and Joost Elffers. *The 48 Laws of Power.* London: Profile Books Ltd., 2010.

GROVE, Andrew S. *Only the Paranoid Survive: How to Exploit the Crisis Points That Challenge Every Company.* New York: Crown Publishing Group, 2010.

GRUNWALD, Michael. *The New New Deal: The Hidden Story of Change in the Obama Era.* New York: Simon & Schuster Paperbacks, 2013.

HARRISON, Lawrence E. *The Central Liberal Truth: How Politics Can Change a Culture and Save It from Itself.* Oxford: Oxford University Press, 2008.

HETZEL, Robert L. *The Great Recession: Market Failure or Policy Failure?* Cambridge: Cambridge University Press, 2014.

HIRSH, Michael. *Capital Offense: How Washington's Wise Men Turned America's Future Over to Wall Street.* Hoboken, NJ: John Wiley & Sons, 2010.

HOBSBAWM, Eric. *How to Change the World: Reflections on Marx and Marxism.* New Haven, CT: Yale University Press, 2014.

HOWELL, William G. *Power without Persuasion: The Politics of Direct Presidential Action.* Princeton, NJ: Princeton University Press, 2003.

HUDAK, John. *Presidential Pork: White House Influence over the Distribution of Federal Grants.* Washington, DC: Brookings Institution, 2014.

IRWIN, Neil. *The Alchemists: Three Central Bankers and a World on Fire.* New York: Penguin Books, 2014.

JEFFREY, Richard Carl. *The Logic of Decision.* Chicago: University of Chicago Press, 1999.

JOHNSON, Simon. *Thirteen Bankers: the Wall Street Takeover and the next Financial Meltdown.* New York: Vintage Books, 2013.

KANTOR, Jodi. *The Obamas.* New York: Back Bay Books, 2012.

KATZNELSON, Ira. *Fear Itself: The New Deal and the Origins of Our Time.* New York: Liveright, 2014.

KAY, John. *Other People's Money: The Real Business of Finance.* New York: PublicAffairs, 2016.

KAY, John. *Truth about Markets: Why Some Countries Are Rich and Others Remain Poor.* London: Penguin UK, 2004.

KENNEDY, David M. *Freedom from Fear: The American People in Depression and War, 1929–1945.* Oxford: Oxford University Press, 1999.

KLOPPENBERG, James T. *Reading Obama: Dreams, Hope, and the American Political Tradition.* Princeton, NJ: Princeton University Press, 2012.

KRUGMAN, Paul R. *End This Depression Now!* New York: Norton, 2012.

KRUGMAN, Paul. "Romer and Bernstein on Stimulus." Blog post. *New York Times*, January 10, 2009. https://krugman.blogs.nytimes.com/2009/01/10/romer-and-bernstein-on-stimulus/.

KUTTNER, Robert. *A Presidency in Peril: The Inside Story of Obama's Promise, Wall Street's Power, and the Struggle to Control Our Economic Future.* White River Junction, VT: Chelsea Green Pub., 2010.

KUTTNER, Robert. *Obama's Challenge: America's Economic Crisis and the Power of a Transformative Presidency.* White River Junction, VT: Chelsea Green Pub., 2008.

LILLA, Mark. *The Once and Future Liberal: After Identity Politics.* New York: Harper, 2017.

MANN, Geoff. *In the Long Run We Are All Dead: Keynesianism, Political Economy, and Revolution.* New York: Verso, 2017.

MANN, Thomas E., and Norman J. Ornstein. *It's Even Worse than It Looks: How the American Constitutional System Collided with the New Politics of Extremism.* New York: Basic Books, 2016.

MANSKI, Charles F. *Public Policy in an Uncertain World: Analysis and Decisions.* Boston: Harvard University Press, 2013.

MARX, Karl. *Das Kapital.* Hamburg: Verlag von Otto Meisner, 1876.

MAXWELL, John C. *The 21 Irrefutable Laws of Leadership: Follow Them and People Will Follow You.* Nashville, TN: Thomas Nelson, 1998.

MCARDLE, Megan. *The Up Side of Down: Why Failing Well Is the Key to Success.* New York: Penguin Books, 2015.

MCBRIDE, Bill. "Mortgage Debt and the 'Recovery.'" Blog post. Calculated Risk, February 24, 2005. http://www.calculatedriskblog.com/2005/02/mortgage-debt-and-recovery.html.

MCDONOUGH, John E. *Inside National Health Reform.* Oakland, CA: University of California Press, 2012.

MCLEAN, Bethany, and Joseph Nocera. *All the Devils Are Here: The Hidden History of the Financial Crisis.* New York: Portfolio/Penguin, 2011.

MIAN, Atif, and Amir Sufi. *House of Debt: How They (and You) Caused the Great Recession, and How We Can Prevent It from Happening Again.* Chicago: University of Chicago Press, 2015.

MIROWSKI, Philip, and Edward Nik-Khah. *The Knowledge We Have Lost in Information: The History of Information in Modern Economics.* Oxford: Oxford University Press, 2017.

MOLEY, Raymond. *After Seven Years.* Cambridge, MA: Da Capo Press, 1972.

MOLEY, Raymond. *The First New Deal.* San Diego: Harcourt, Brace & World, 1966.

MORGENSON, Gretchen, and Joshua Rosner. *Reckless Endangerment: How Outsized Ambition, Greed, and Corruption Led to Economic Armageddon.* New York: St. Martin's Griffin, 2012.

NEUSTADT, Richard E., and Charles O. Jones. *Preparing to Be President: The Memos of Richard E. Neustadt.* Washington, DC: AEI Press, 2000.

OBAMA, Barack. *The Audacity of Hope: Thoughts on Reclaiming the American Dream.* New York: Crown Publishers, 2009.

OBAMA, Barack. *Dreams from My Father: A Story of Race and Inheritance.* Edinburgh, UK: Canongate, 2016.

PAULSON, Henry M. *On the Brink: Inside the Race to Stop the Collapse of the Global Financial System.* New York: Business Plus, 2011.

PLATH, Sylvia. "Wellesley." In *The Journals of Sylvia Plath.* Edited by Ted Hughes and Frances McCullough. New York: Anchor Books, 2013.

POSNER, Richard A. *A Failure of Capitalism: The Crisis of '08 and the Descent into Depression.* Boston: Harvard University Press, 2011.

POWELL, Jerome H. "The Case for Housing Finance Reform." Speech delivered at the American Enterprise Institute. July 6, 2017.

"The Sense That the System Is Rigged Relates to Governments' Failure to Address Inequality and Concentration." ProMarket. April 15, 2017. https://promarket.org/sense-system-rigged-relates-directly-governments-failure-address-inequality-concentration-power/.

PULIZZI, Henry J., and John D. McKinnon. "Lazear Sees No Recession for U.S. Economy." *Wall Street Journal*, May 8, 2008.

QUIGGIN, John. *Zombie Economics: How Dead Ideas Still Walk among Us.* Princeton, NJ: Princeton University Press, 2012.

RAJAN, Raghuram G. *Fault Lines: How Hidden Fractures Still Threaten the World Economy.* Noida, UP, India: Harpercollins India, 2012.

REINHART, Carmen M., and Kenneth S. Rogoff. *This Time Is Different: Eight Centuries of Financial Folly.* Princeton, NJ: Princeton University Press, 2011.

REMNICK, David. *The Bridge: The Life and Rise of Barack Obama.* New York: Vintage Books, 2011.

RIDLEY, Matt. *The Rational Optimist: How Prosperity Evolves.* New York: Harper Perennial, 2011.

RODRIK, Dani. "Rescuing Economics from Neoliberalism." *Boston Review,* November 6, 2017. http://www.bostonreview.net/class-inequality/dani-rodrik-rescuing-economics-neoliberalism.

RORTY, Richard. *Consequences of Pragmatism: Essays: 1972–1980.* Minneapolis, MN: University of Minnesota Press, 2008.

ROSEN, Elliot A. *Roosevelt, the Great Depression, and the Economics of Recovery.* Charlottesville, VA: University of Virginia Press, 2007.

RUBIN, Robert Edward, and Jacob Weisberg. *In an Uncertain World: Tough Choices from Wall Street to Washington.* New York: Random House, 2004.

RUMELT, Richard P. *Good Strategy, Bad Strategy: The Difference and Why It Matters.* London: Profile Books, 2017.

RUSSELL, Bertrand. "On History." *The Independent Review*, 3 (1904): 207–15.

SANTELLI, Rick, and Wilbur Ross. *Squawk Box.* CNBC. February 19, 2009. Television.

SCHEIBER, Noam. *The Escape Artists: How Obama's Team Fumbled the Recovery.* New York: Simon & Schuster, 2012.

The Wolf of Wall Street. Directed by Martin Scorsese. Red Granite Pictures (presents) / Appian Way / Sikelia Productions (as Sikelia) / EMJAG Productions, 2013.

SHILLER, Robert J. *The Subprime Solution: How Today's Global Financial Crisis Happened and What to Do about It.* Princeton, NJ: Princeton University Press, 2012.

SORKIN, Andrew Ross. *Too Big to Fail: The Inside Story of How Wall Street and Washington Fought to Save the Financial System and Themselves.* New York: Penguin Group, 2011.

STARR, Paul. *Remedy and Reaction: The Peculiar American Struggle over Healthcare Reform.* New Haven, CT: Yale University Press, 2013.

STIGLITZ, Joseph E. *Freefall: America, Free Markets, and the Sinking of the World Economy.* New York: W. W. Norton & Company, 2010.

SUMMERS, Larry. "The Economy Is on a Sugar High, and Tax Cuts Won't Help." *Washington Post.* December 10, 2017.

SUMMERS, Larry. "Wake Up to the Dangers of a Deepening Crisis." *Financial Times.* November 25, 2007. https://www.ft.com/content/b56079a8-9b71-11dc-8aad-0000779fd2ac.

SUSKIND, Ron. *Confidence Men: Wall Street, Washington, and the Education of a President.* New York: Harper Perennial, 2012.

TETLOCK, Philip E. *Expert Political Judgment: How Good Is It? How Can We Know?* Princeton, NJ: Princeton University Press, 2017.

THOMPSON, Derek. "Conservative Economist: 'Find the Unemployed and Hire Them.'" *Atlantic.* August 26, 2010.

THURBER, James. "The Glass in the Field." *New Yorker.* October 31, 1939.

TUGWELL, Rexford G. *The Brains Trust.* New York: ACLS History E-Book Project, 2005.

TURNER, Adair. *Economics after the Crisis: Objectives and Means.* Cambridge, MA: The MIT Press, 2012.

Unforgiven. Directed by Clint Eastwood. Burbank, CA: Warner Bros./Malpaso Productions, 1992.

VROEY, Michel de. *A History of Macroeconomics from Keynes to Lucas and Beyond.* Cambridge, UK: Cambridge University Press, 2016.

WESSEL, David. *In Fed We Trust: Ben Bernanke's War on the Great Panic.* New York: Three Rivers Press, 2010.

WESSEL, David. *Red Ink: Inside the High-Stakes Politics of the Federal Budget.* New York: Crown Business, 2012.

WHITE, Richard. *Republic for Which It Stands: The United States During Reconstruction and the Gilded Age, 1865–1896.* Oxford: Oxford University Press, 2017.

WINGFIELD, Brian, and Josh Zumbrun. "Bad News for the Bailout." *Forbes.* September 23, 2008. https://www.forbes.com/2008/09/23/bailout-paulson-congress-biz-beltway-cx_jz_bw_0923bailout.html#2a8ab895fb37.

WOLF, Martin. *The Shifts and the Shocks: What We've Learned—and Have Still to Learn—from the Financial Crisis.* New York: Penguin Press, 2015.

WOLFFE, Richard. *Renegade: The Making of a President.* New York: Three Rivers Press, 2010.

WOLFFE, Richard. *Revival: The Struggle for Survival Inside the Obama White House.* New York: Broadway Paperbacks, 2011.

WOODWARD, Bob. *The Price of Politics.* New York: Simon & Schuster, 2013.

ZANDI, Mark. *Financial Shock: A 360° Look at the Subprime Mortgage Implosion, and How to Avoid the Next Financial Crisis.* Upper Saddle River, NJ: FT Press, 2009.

ZELIZER, Julian E. *The Fierce Urgency of Now: Lyndon Johnson, Congress, and the Battle for the Great Society.* New York; Penguin Press, 2015.

Index

Page numbers followed by *f* indicate figures.